ALL THE LAWS
BUT ONE

ALL THE LAWS BUT ONE

CIVIL LIBERTIES IN WARTIME

William H. Rehnquist

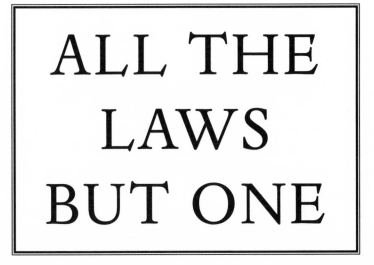

ALFRED A. KNOPF   NEW YORK   1998

THIS IS A BORZOI BOOK
PUBLISHED BY ALFRED A. KNOPF, INC.

www.randomhouse.com

Grateful acknowledgment is made to the following for
permission to reprint previously published material:
Doubleday: Excerpts from *In Brief Authority* by Francis Biddle,
copyright © 1962 by Francis Biddle. Reprinted by permission
of Doubleday, a division of Bantam Doubleday Dell
Publishing Group, Inc.
Macmillan Library Reference USA: Excerpts from *The Oliver
Wendell Holmes Devise History of the Supreme Court of The United
States*, Vol. 5: *The Taney Period, 1836–1864* by Carl B. Swisher,
copyright © 1974 by Macmillan Publishing Company.
Reprinted by permission of Macmillan Library Reference
USA, a Simon & Schuster Macmillan Company.

Library of Congress Cataloging-in-Publication Data
Rehnquist, William H.
All the laws but one: civil liberties in wartime / William H.
Rehnquist. — 1st ed.
p.   cm.
Includes bibliographical references.
ISBN 0-679-44661-3
1. Civil rights—United States—History—19th century.
2. United States—History—Civil War, 1861–1865—Law and
legislation.   3. Habeas corpus—United States—History.
I. Title.
KF4750.R44   1998
342.73'085—dc21   98-12641
CIP

Manufactured in the United States of America

First Edition

To Nancy

Are all the laws, but one, to go unexecuted, and the government itself to go to pieces, lest that one be violated?

—President Lincoln, in a message
to a special session of Congress,
July 4, 1861

CONTENTS

Contents

ILLUSTRATIONS

Following page 112

President Abraham Lincoln, 1863
Photograph by Alexander Gardner, National Portrait Gallery, Smithsonian Institution, Gift of the James Smithson Society, CBS Television Network, and James Macatee

Chief Justice Roger B. Taney
Photograph by Mathew Brady, Collection of the Supreme Court of the United States

Secretary of State William Henry Seward
Photographer unknown, National Portrait Gallery, Smithsonian Institution

Secretary of War Edwin M. Stanton
Engraving by Bobbett & Hooper after Henry Louis Stephens, National Portrait Gallery, Smithsonian Institution

General Ambrose Burnside
Photograph by Mathew Brady, National Portrait Gallery, Smithsonian Institution

Justice David Davis
Artist unknown, Collection of the Supreme Court of the United States

John Wilkes Booth
Photograph by Charles DeForest Fredricks, National Portrait Gallery, Smithsonian Institution

Mary Surratt
Photographer unknown, Collection of the Library of Congress; LC-B816-1347

President Woodrow Wilson
Painting by John Christen Johansen, National Portrait Gallery, Smithsonian Institution; transfer from the National Museum of American Art; gift of an anonymous donor through Mrs. Elizabeth C. Rogerson, 1926

Illustrations

Justice Oliver Wendell Holmes
Drawing by Samuel Johnson Woolf, National Portrait Gallery, Smithsonian Institution; Gift of Thomas S. Corcoran and Gallery purchase

Judge Learned Hand
Photograph by Philippe Halsman, National Portrait Gallery, Smithsonian Institution

President Franklin Delano Roosevelt
Painting by Henry Salem Hubbell, National Portrait Gallery, Smithsonian Institution; transfer from the National Museum of American Art, gift of Willard Hubbell, 1964

Secretary of War Henry Stimson
Drawing by Samuel Johnson Woolf, National Portrait Gallery, Smithsonian Institution; Gift of Muriel Woolf Hobson and Dorothy Woolf Ahern

Chief Justice Harlan F. Stone
Drawing by Samuel Johnson Woolf, National Portrait Gallery, Smithsonian Institution; Gift of Muriel Woolf Hobson and Dorothy Woolf Ahern

Justice Hugo Black
Photograph by Harris & Ewing, Collection of the Supreme Court of the United States

Lieutenant General Robert Richardson
Photographer unknown, Courtesy of the U.S. Army Museum of Hawaii

Judge Delbert Metzger
Photographer unknown, Courtesy of the Honolulu Star-Bulletin

ACKNOWLEDGMENTS

My "EDITOR OF FIRST RESORT" has been my daughter, Nancy Spears. She has told me that she felt one of her principal tasks was to make me sound less like a lawyer, and I hope she has succeeded. I know that the manuscript profited from her carefully considered and finely tuned suggestions. My editor at Alfred Knopf, Patricia Hass, has also done an admirable job, and made me sound even less like a lawyer.

In gathering research materials for the book, I have been greatly assisted by Shelley Dowling, the Librarian of the Supreme Court, and Patricia McCabe, Linda Maslow, Catherine Romano, and Sara Sonet of the Library staff. In gathering photographs for the book, I received valuable help from Alan Fern, Director of the National Portrait Gallery, and Ann Shumard and Anthony Segaria of his staff. Similar assistance was furnished by Gail Galloway, the Curator of the Supreme Court, and Catherine Fitts of her staff. Special thanks are due to Franz Jantzen for his efforts in obtaining hard-to-get photographs, and Judy Bowman of the Army Museum of Hawaii and Jane Halsman Bellow of the Philippe Halsman Estate have also lent their assistance.

My secretaries, Janet Barnes and Laverne Frayer, have faithfully and cheerfully transcribed drafts and more drafts of the manuscript.

Finally, former law clerks Craig Bradley, Ted Cruz, Rick Garnett, and David Hoffman, and former aide Greg Michael, helped me out with various portions of the manuscript.

ALL THE LAWS
BUT ONE

CHAPTER I

Mr. Lincoln Goes to Washington

"**A** COLD DRIZZLE of rain was falling February 11 when Lincoln and his party of fifteen were to leave Springfield on the eight o'clock at the Great Western Railway Station. Chilly gray mist hung on the circle of the prairie horizon. A short locomotive with a flat-topped smokestack stood puffing with the baggage car and special passenger car coupled on; a railroad president and superintendent were on board. A thousand people crowded in and around the brick station, inside of which Lincoln was standing. One by one came hundreds of old friends, shaking hands, wishing him luck and Godspeed, all faces solemn. Even huge Judge Davis, wearing a new white silk hat, was a somber figure."[1]

On that dreary Illinois winter day in 1861, President-elect Abraham Lincoln began his journey to Washington, D.C., where he hoped to be inaugurated as President on March 4. "Hoped to" because there were already rumors afloat that secessionist sympathizers would somehow prevent his inauguration from taking place. In the November presidential election, Lincoln had prevailed over three opponents, receiving 180 electoral votes. The incumbent Vice President, John Breckenridge, the candidate of the South, received 72; John Bell, the candidate of the Constitutional Union Party, 39; and Lincoln's longtime Democratic opponent Stephen Douglas, only 12. But the electoral vote did not tell the whole story of this bitterly contested election. Lincoln received a minority of the popular vote, slightly less than 1.9 million votes out of a total of some 4.7 million. In ten states of the South, he did not get a single popular vote. Indeed, he was not even on the ballot in some states. He was elected by the nearly solid electoral votes of the North, together with those of California and Oregon. In an election dominated by the issue of the extension of slavery, Lincoln received no electoral votes from any state south of the Ohio River.

Unquestionably, then, he was a sectionally chosen President, and soon after his election the states of the Deep South began to carry out their threat to secede from the Union. Within days of the election, the two Senators from South Carolina resigned their seats, and the state legislature enacted a bill calling a convention to determine whether it should secede from the Union. Delegates were duly elected, and on December 20, 1860, the convention voted to take South Carolina out of the Union. By the time Lincoln was boarding the train to Washington, South Carolina, Georgia, Florida, Alabama, Mississippi, and Louisiana had passed ordinances of secession, and delegates from these states were meeting in Montgomery, Alabama, to launch the Confederate States of America.

From the rear platform of the car that would bear him and his party on their slow and circuitous journey to Washington, Abraham Lincoln said goodbye to his Springfield friends:

> My friends–No one, not in my situation, can appreciate my feeling of sadness at this parting. To this place, and the kindness of these people, I owe everything. Here I have lived a quarter of a century, and have passed from a young to an old man. Here my children have been born, and one is buried. I now leave, not knowing when, or whether ever, I may return, with a task before me greater than that which rested upon Washington. Without the assistance of that Divine Being, who ever attended him, I cannot succeed. With that assistance I cannot fail. Trusting in Him, who can go with me, and remain with you and everywhere for good let us confidently hope that all will yet be well. To His care commending you, as I hope you and your prayers will commend me, I bid you an affectionate farewell.[2]

Lincoln's train moved eastward over the flatlands of Illinois and Indiana, reaching Indianapolis in the late afternoon. There he was greeted by Governor Oliver P. Morton, and spoke in the evening from the balcony of his hotel. The next day, February 12—Lincoln's fifty-second birthday—the special train took him and his party from Indianapolis to Cincinnati, where he could look across the Ohio River to the state of Kentucky, where he had been born.

When little Abe was seven, he moved with his parents and brother north across the Ohio River, to Indiana. His mother, Nancy Hanks Lincoln, died when he was nine, and at the age of twenty-one he moved with his father and family to a farm near Decatur, Illinois. He worked in a store in New Salem, was elected to the Illinois legislature, and then moved to Springfield, where he began the practice of law in 1836. Six years later, he married Mary Todd, ten years his junior and the daughter of an aristocratic Kentucky family. Four sons were born to them during their twenty-five years in Springfield.

On February 13, the Lincoln train arrived in Columbus, Ohio, and was greeted by friendly crowds. In Washington, D.C., on this same day, the Joint Session of Congress provided for by law met to count the electoral votes. There had been threats, and excitement ran high. All of the doors to the Capitol were patrolled by armed guards, and during the day there was much street fighting between secessionist and Union sympathizers. Ironically, it was Vice President Breckenridge who declared Abraham Lincoln to have been elected President by the Electoral College.

The next day the special train went from Columbus to Pittsburgh, and then on to Cleveland and Buffalo. In Buffalo, Lincoln was met by Grace Bedell, a little girl who had written him that she thought he ought to grow a beard, advice which he had followed. The train proceeded from Buffalo across upstate New York, and on February 18, when it neared Albany, Jefferson Davis was sworn in as President of the Confederate States of America in Montgomery. At that moment there were six states in the Confederacy, but a few days later, on February 23, Texas would vote to secede. All seven states of the Deep South would then regard themselves as being out of the Union. Jefferson Davis, in his inaugural address, had said that the Confederate

5

States of America were taking their place among the independent nations of the earth. "If denied that place, they would seek 'the final arbitrament of the sword'; they would with firm resolve 'appeal to arms and invoke the blessings of Providence on a just cause.' "[3]

Two days later, Lincoln arrived in New York City, already the financial center of the country and one of the world's great ports—and considerably more sympathetic to the South than other parts of the North. Indeed, Mayor Fernando Wood had expressed a wish to declare New York a "free city," independent of both the United States of America and the Confederate States of America. Wood closed the exchange of remarks between himself and the President-elect with a firm insistence on conciliation with the South: "To you, we look for a restoration of friendly relations between the States, only to be accomplished by peaceful and conciliatory means, aided by the wisdom of Almighty God."[4] When the ceremonies were finished, Lincoln was ferried across the Hudson River to New Jersey, and made his way across the state to Trenton, where he addressed the state legislature. New Jersey was the first state on his journey that he had not carried in the election; Douglas had narrowly beaten him there.

Lincoln then proceeded by train to Philadelphia, where he was scheduled to raise the American flag over Independence Hall the next day. That evening, his longtime friend Norman Judd asked him to come to his hotel room to meet with Allan Pinkerton, the founder of the Pinkerton Detective Agency. Pinkerton told Lincoln he had evidence of a plot to assassinate him as he went through the city of Baltimore the day after the flag-raising at Independence Hall. Lincoln questioned Pinkerton at length, and heard the details of a plot by a group of fanatics led by a barber named Fernandina. Pinkerton urged the President-elect to depart directly for Washington that evening, but Lincoln refused. He intended to keep his commitment to raise the flag over Independence Hall the next day, and to visit Harrisburg and speak to the Pennsylvania legislature.

Later that evening Frederick Seward, son of Lincoln's Secretary of State-designate William H. Seward, arrived in Philadelphia bearing a message from his father. The message transmitted a warning from Colonel Stone, chief of the militia for the District of Columbia—much the same warning that Pinkerton had conveyed: a New

York detective who had been on duty in Baltimore for several weeks had found evidence of a plot to assassinate Lincoln while his party was passing through Baltimore.

There was reason to credit these rumors. Out of about ninety thousand votes cast in Maryland, Lincoln had received some twenty-two hundred, and Douglas, the other candidate to do well in the North, slightly less than six thousand. The great majority had gone either to Breckenridge or to Bell. Not surprisingly, in view of the sentiments expressed by this vote, Lincoln had received no invitations to speak or to be welcomed in Baltimore. And the logistics of train travel through that city seemed made to order for some sort of disturbance or riot. Passengers coming in from the North bound for Washington had to change stations, and each railroad car was separately drawn by horses between the two depots.

Lincoln pondered the matter for a day, completed his activities in Philadelphia and Harrisburg, and then agreed to go surreptitiously from Harrisburg to Philadelphia, and thence to Washington. On February 22—Washington's Birthday—he was called from a dinner in Harrisburg, changed into a traveling suit, and quietly boarded a carriage to the railroad depot. He was accompanied only by Ward Lamon, an Illinois lawyer who had come with him from Springfield. When the special train—consisting of one locomotive and one passenger car—got to Philadelphia, they met Pinkerton, and the three of them boarded the last car of the New York–Washington train. Lincoln went to his berth and closed the curtains. The train reached Baltimore in the middle of the night, unnoticed by anyone, and at six o'clock on the morning of February 23, Lincoln arrived at the railroad station in Washington. He was wearing a soft, slouched hat, a muffler, and a short bob-tailed overcoat. He was met by Illinois Congressman Elihu Washburne and escorted to Willard's Hotel, the city's premier hostelry.

As Lincoln and William Seward sat at breakfast at Willard's that morning, they presented, in more ways than one, a marked contrast. Lincoln was remarkably tall—six feet four inches—and gangly: physical features that cartoonists were quick to note. Seward, while slender, was shorter than average and somewhat stooped. His hair was white, and his most prominent feature was a large nose, compared by some to the beak of a parrot. He was eight years older than Lincoln.

Until the 1860 Republican Convention unexpectedly nominated Lincoln for President, Seward had been the acknowledged leader of the party. He had begun his long career in elected public office in New York as a member of the Anti-Masonic Party, then, in 1838, was elected the first Whig governor of that state. He served two terms as the state's chief magistrate, returned for a few years to a successful private practice of law in Auburn, and was then elected to the Senate as a Whig in 1849, and reelected in 1855. The Republican Party had only come into existence in 1854, when it was founded by groups in Wisconsin and Michigan as an expression of outrage against Congress's enactment of the Kansas-Nebraska Act. That law repealed the Missouri Compromise of 1820, which forbade slavery in certain parts of United States territories. During his second term in the Senate, Seward allied himself with the Republican Party.

Lincoln's offer of the State Department to Seward had been made through Seward's longtime political ally Thurlow Weed, a well-known Albany newspaper editor, lobbyist, and political fixer of sorts. Seward had accepted, but he was not happy. He had still not gotten over his disappointment at losing the nomination in Chicago, and was further disappointed that Lincoln was seeking to make his Cabinet a "ministry of all the talents." He was including almost as many former Democrats as former Whigs. Seward would have much preferred to have only men of his own stripe chosen, and on the eve of Lincoln's inauguration he would threaten to withdraw his acceptance of the post of Secretary of State. Lincoln responded with a curt note insisting that he remain, saying to his personal secretary, John Hay, "I cannot let Seward take the first trick."

Seward was a warm, companionable person, devoted to drinking brandy after dinner and swapping stories. He was so fond of smoking cigars—which he did constantly—that his speaking voice had become husky. Lincoln would enjoy a camaraderie with him during the war years that he achieved with no other member of his Cabinet. For all his craftiness and occasional deviousness, Seward had none of the pomposity that infected Salmon P. Chase, another prominent Republican, whom Lincoln would appoint Secretary of the Treasury. He had none of the aura of corruption that surrounded Simon Cameron, whom Lincoln would designate Secretary of War. Seward had allowed Thurlow Weed to work with him in managing his political career, but he did not profit materially from the activities of his crony.

Throughout his life, Seward had manifested a sympathy for the underdog. In private practice in Auburn, he had defended a black man charged with murder on the grounds that the defendant was insane, attracting much opprobrium in the community for this position. He had been of counsel in the famous *Van Zandt* case, in which an Ohio farmer had been charged with violating the Fugitive Slave Act by helping slaves on their way to Canada. As Governor of New York, he had signed a law abolishing imprisonment for debt.

Seward had carried his opposition to slavery onto the floor of the United States Senate. He had opposed the Compromise of 1850, declaring in a speech that there was a "higher law than the Constitution," though he later unsuccessfully attempted to "clarify" what he meant by this phrase. At another time he had spoken of an "irrepressible conflict" between the slave states and the free states. As the election of 1860 grew near, however, he had trimmed his sails, referring to the northern states as "labor" states and to the southern as "capital" states. Between the time of Lincoln's election and his arrival in Washington. Seward had taken both public and private steps to conciliate the newly seceded states, often without any express approval from the President-elect.

"Governor" Seward, as he was usually called, was a complex personality. He was gentlemanly, subtle, and smiling, but not quite elegant or effete; there was too much of western New York in him for that. He was brilliant and cynical, but not quite a polished trifler; he was too much a man of the party machine, the intimate of the astute political manager Thurlow Weed. In spite of his sixty years, he attracted young men with his warmth and kindness, and by the unassuming simplicity of his manner. Although his doctrine of " 'the irrepressible conflict' between free labor and slavery had made him hated throughout the South, he was considered a man without convictions, a Jesuit and an opportunist. . . ."[5]

Sitting at breakfast at the Willard Hotel on the morning of Lincoln's arrival, Seward must have had mixed feelings about the President-elect and about the incoming administration. Only a year earlier, the overwhelming view of political pundits had been that he, not Lincoln, would be the Republican nominee for President. Now he would be Secretary of State in the Cabinet of a man whom he barely knew, and whom he regarded as his inferior in virtually every way. And the new administration would confront the greatest crisis in the history of the nation.

CHAPTER 2

Lincoln Suspends Habeas Corpus

T EN DAYS AFTER his arrival in Washington, Lincoln was inaugurated as sixteenth President of the United States. At noon on March 4, the outgoing President, James Buchanan, rode in an open carriage from the White House to Willard's Hotel, from which he shortly emerged arm-in-arm with his successor. The two then rode down Pennsylvania Avenue in a procession to the still-unfinished Capitol, its dome not yet in place. There, on a platform erected on the east portico of the building, Lincoln delivered his inaugural address before a crowd of ten thousand people.

Parts of the address were conciliatory; he repeated earlier assurances that the new administration would make no effort to interfere with slavery in those states where it already existed, or to defy the constitutional provision for the recapture of fugitive slaves. But in other parts of the address he was firm: No state could legally secede from the Union created by the Constitution. He went on to say: "I shall take care as the Constitution itself expressly enjoins upon me, that the laws of the Union be faithfully executed in all the States. . . . The power confided to me will be used to hold, occupy and possess the property and places belonging to the Government, and to collect the duties and imposts." Even so, he tempered his firmness by adding: "but beyond what may be necessary for these objects, there will be no invasion—no use of force against or among the people anywhere."

He concluded with these well-known words:

I am loth [*sic*] to close. We are not enemies, but friends. We must not be enemies. Though passion may have strained, it must not break our bonds of affection. The mystic chords of memory, stretching from every battlefield, and patriot grave, to every living heart and hearthstone, all over this broad land, will yet swell the chorus of the Union, when again touched, as surely they will be, by the better angels of our nature.

Chief Justice Roger B. Taney, shrunken and showing his eighty-four years, then stepped forward and administered the constitutional oath to the new President. Taney was a relic of an earlier era; Andrew Jackson had appointed him Chief Justice in 1836.

Lincoln received nothing like the "honeymoon" that is supposed to be accorded newly elected Presidents. On the day after his inauguration, bad news came from Major Robert Anderson, commanding the federal garrison at Fort Sumter, in the harbor of Charleston, South Carolina. The provisions for his troops were sufficient to last for only four more weeks or, if stretched, forty days at the most. Thus there began for Lincoln and his Cabinet several weeks of intense and agonized deliberation about what policy to adopt with respect to this fort and other federal forts in the seceded states.

Fort Sumter was located on an island in the harbor. In any military engagement, its small garrison would be completely at the mercy of the shore batteries lined up around the harbor's perimeter. Anderson estimated that twenty thousand troops would be required to hold the fort against an attack, a number confirmed by the commanding general of the Army, Winfield Scott. There were simply not twenty thousand soldiers available for this purpose; and if there had been, there were not enough ships available to transport them. Confederate troops in Charleston no longer permitted supplies to be delivered to the fort. In January the Confederates had fired upon and driven off a ship, *Star of the West*, carrying reinforcements to Sumter.

James Buchanan had been criticized for his weakness and indecisiveness in the period between the secession of South Carolina in December and his departure from office in March 1861. His position had been that the Southern states had no right in principle to secede, but there was nothing the government could do about it if they chose to separate themselves from the Union. Would the peaceful surrender of Fort Sumter make the Lincoln administration look like simply a Republican copy of the Buchanan administration? What of Lincoln's inaugural pledge to "hold, occupy and possess the property and places belonging to the Government"? What would be the next demand of the Confederate states if the government meekly surrendered Fort Sumter?

But if the government did not give up Sumter, it would very likely be eventually reduced by hostile fire and taken by the South. What then? If the fort could not be peaceably surrendered without irreparable damage to the Union cause, its capture by force of arms must surely provoke Union reprisal, and that reprisal would very likely mean civil war. This was the message brought back to Lincoln by several personal emissaries whom he had sent to South Carolina to ascertain the state of public opinion there.

The President convened his Cabinet on March 9 and submitted this question to them in writing: "Assuming it to be possible to now provision Fort Sumter, under all the circumstances, is it wise to attempt it?" The Cabinet members were requested to submit written answers the following week. When they convened again, five answered the question in the negative. Montgomery Blair, Postmaster General, answered in the affirmative. Salmon P. Chase answered, "yes, if it meant peace, but no, if it meant war." Chase's answer, unhelpful as it was, caught the larger geopolitical implications of sending supplies to Fort Sumter. In addition to the seven states that had already seceded, there were seven more "slave" states which remained in the Union: Virginia, North Carolina, Tennessee, Arkansas, Maryland, Kentucky, and Missouri. The first four were thought of as the states of the "Upper South"; the last three were re-garded as "border states." The states of the Upper South were playing what was essentially a waiting game, choosing not to join the Deep South so long as the national government did not seek to use force against the latter. But if the North did attempt to "coerce" those seven states, it seemed quite probable that the Upper South would join the Confederacy. Such action would have enormous consequences militarily; if North Carolina and Virginia became part of the Confederacy, the frontier between the two governments would move from the North Carolina–South Carolina border north to the Potomac River. Washington, instead of being deep within Union territory, would be on that frontier. The national capital, with all its symbolic significance, would be vulnerable to Confederate raids and perhaps to a full-scale attack.

In the three border states, sentiment on secession was sharply divided. Each of them recognized the institution of slavery, but each had a substantial body of public opinion that favored the Union cause. Would coercion by the North risk the secession of these states too? If not only Virginia but Maryland as well should secede, Washington would be surrounded by the Confederacy. And from the point of view of ability to wage a long war, the addition of even the four states of the Upper South to the Confederacy would significantly enlarge its area and its productive capacities.

It is not entirely clear what Lincoln's position was during this debate within his Cabinet. There is some reason to think that in the beginning he was willing to give up Sumter, but at any rate he eventually swung around to the view that the fort must be held. Following a state dinner on March 25, Lincoln again convened the Cabinet, and by this time the members were equally divided as to whether or not Sumter should be provisioned. Lincoln thereupon ordered a naval expedition to be assembled to bring provisions to the beleaguered garrison, but because of a misunderstanding, and meddling by Seward, the expedition was late in starting and had fewer ships than were originally planned for. Even as the fleet was about to sail, Lincoln met with a delegate from the convention sitting in Richmond, which had been debating secession since the middle of February. Rumors swirled in Washington and elsewhere in the nation.

During this hectic period, Seward was dealing on his own with three Confederate emissaries, the principal one of whom was John Campbell, a former Justice of the United States Supreme Court who had resigned his office when Alabama seceded. On March 15, Seward assured Campbell that Fort Sumter would be evacuated within "a few days"; nearly a week later, he repeated this assurance. Yet at the same time he gave hints of a sterner policy to a correspondent for the London *Times*. In each of these instances, he acted without any consultation with Lincoln.

Seward not only dealt on his own with these matters, but on

April 1 he wrote Lincoln an extraordinary letter in which he sought to establish himself in the role of "prime minister" to a President lacking his own experience on the national scene. He told Lincoln that after a month the administration was "yet without a policy, domestic or foreign," and suggested that hostilities with foreign powers be provoked in order to once more unite the northern and southern states of the Union. He concluded by offering to execute himself whatever policy was adopted. Lincoln penned a reply which apparently was never sent, but which may have served as talking points for a discussion with Seward. The letter said that if there must be oversight of administration policy, he, Lincoln, must be the one to do it.

On April 11, 1861, General P. G. T. Beauregard, commander of the Confederate forces in Charleston, sent a note to Major Anderson demanding the surrender of Fort Sumter and offering to remove all personnel and property at the post to any other fort in the United States that they might select. Anderson refused, saying that it was "a demand with which I regret that my sense of honor, and of my obligations to my Government, prevent my compliance." In the early morning of April 12, even as the relief expedition was sailing down the Atlantic coast, the Confederate batteries opened fire on Sumter, and the fort was pounded day and night through the 12th and 13th. On Sunday, April 14, Anderson surrendered.

By their firing on Fort Sumter, Beauregard and the Confederacy had greatly simplified Lincoln's decision-making. In his inaugural address, he had said:

> In *your* hands, my dissatisfied fellow countrymen, and not in *mine*, is the momentous issue of civil war. The government will not assail *you*. You can have no conflict, without being yourselves the aggressors. *You* have no oath registered in Heaven to destroy the government, while *I* shall have the most solemn one to "preserve, protect and defend" it.

Now the South had become the aggressor. Until the firing on Sumter, public opinion in the North was divided as to what policy the government should adopt toward the seceding states. Quite apart from the legal and philosophical issue of the right of a state to secede, a substantial body of opinion in the North agreed with Horace Greeley that the North should "let the erring sisters depart in peace." Such a policy, of course, would have left completely unresolved the numerous questions that would then arise. What, for example, would be done with federal military installations and other government property in the seceded states? But if the alternative was civil war, these difficulties seemed to many the lesser evil. The North should not, by its own initiative, precipitate such a war.

Most Northerners holding this view, however, reacted dramatically in favor of military action when it was the South that fired the first shot. The day after the surrender of Sumter, Lincoln issued a proclamation summoning to active duty the militia of the various states up to the number of seventy-five thousand, in order to suppress the rebellion. By the same proclamation, he called Congress into special session on July 4.

The night before, Lincoln's old Democratic rival Stephen A. Douglas had called at the White House. Douglas wholeheartedly endorsed Lincoln's call for troops, but told the President he should ask for two hundred thousand rather than seventy-five thousand. When Douglas left, he issued a statement declaring that although he continued to oppose the President politically, he would sustain him in his efforts to preserve the Union, maintain the government, and defend the federal capital.[1]

Now came the day of April 15, 1861, for years afterwards spoken of by millions of people as "the day Lincoln made his first call for troops." What happened on that day was referred to as the Uprising of the People. Mass action ruled. The people swarmed onto the streets, into public squares, into meeting-halls and churches. The shooting of the Stars and Stripes off the Sumter flagstaff—and the Lincoln proclamation—acted as a vast magnet on a national multitude. . . .

Then came mass meetings, speeches by prominent citizens, lawyers, ministers, priests, military officers, veterans of the War of 1812 and of the Mexican War, singing of "The Star-Spangled Banner" and "America," fife-and-drum corps playing "Yankee Doodle." Funds were subscribed to raise and equip troops, resolutions were passed, committees appointed to collect funds, to care for soldier families, to educate or ostracize the unpatriotic.[2]

The reaction of the Upper South and border states was quite different. Six of the seven governors responded to Lincoln's call for troops with defiant refusals, characterizing his request as unconstitutional and, indeed, wicked. Two days after Lincoln's call, the Virginia convention, which had been in continuous session since February but without a majority for secession, voted eighty-five to fifty-five to secede. The fifty-five opposing votes came almost entirely from the counties west of the Blue Ridge, which soon gave Virginia a taste of its own medicine by seceding from it and forming the new state of West Virginia.

Fear was rampant in the nation's capital:

In the eyes of the North, Washington was a cherished symbol of the nation's power, to be held and defended at all costs. To the South, the capital was a great prize whose capture would enhance the prestige of the rebellious government, and surely bring its recognition by foreign powers. The Confederate Secretary of War publicly boasted that before the first of May the Stars and Bars would float over the dome of the Federal capital. Richmond secessionists were panting for the attack, and the Enquirer called on Virginia volunteers to be ready to join the march of a southern army on Washington. The confidence of the disloyal residents of the capital increased the impression that the danger was imminent and acute.[3]

North Carolina formally seceded from the Union on May 21, but even before then state troops had seized three small federal installations on its coast. As soon as Virginia seceded, the North Carolina legislature authorized Governor John Ellis to give it military help. In Tennessee, the legislature convened shortly after Lincoln's call for troops, declared Tennessee's independence, and ordered a popular referendum on the question of secession. The secessionists carried this vote on June 8. In Arkansas, a state convention had rejected secession by a narrow margin, thirty-nine to thirty-five, in March, but it reassembled on May 6 and voted to secede by a margin of sixty-nine to one.

On the evening of April 18, the first dribbling of troops responding to Lincoln's call reached Washington: one company of regulars from Minnesota, and some four hundred volunteers from Pennsylvania. They had been stoned and harassed as they passed through Baltimore. The following day, there was news of a full-scale riot there, in which citizens had stoned Northern troops and the troops had fired back.

Baltimore was an absolutely critical rail junction for the purpose of bringing troops from the north or west into Washington, because the railroad coming down the coast from New York and Philadelphia, as well as the line from Harrisburg, ran through that city. The Baltimore & Ohio Railroad from the west joined the Baltimore–Washington line a few miles southwest of Baltimore at Relay House. This strategic location, plus the substantial degree of secessionist sympathy in Baltimore, made the city the Achilles' heel of the early efforts to bring federal troops to defend Washington. And the status of Maryland as a border state, whose adherence to the Union was problematic, exacerbated this difficulty. Maryland teetered both geographically and ideologically between North and South. If the secessionists were to gain the upper hand, the Union war effort could be seriously compromised.

Though small in area, Maryland comprises a remarkable diversity of geography, stretching from the Atlantic Ocean on the east to the summit of the Appalachians on the west. The first Europeans to set foot in the future colony of Maryland were a small group of men led by Captain John Smith in the summer of 1607. In the spring of that year, he had led the party of settlers that founded Jamestown, Virginia. In June, he set out in a barge that used both sails and oars to journey across to the eastern shore of the Chesapeake Bay, and thence back to the western shore to explore the Patapsco River, at whose mouth Baltimore would eventually be located.

George Calvert, who had become a favorite of King James I while serving as a clerk to the Privy Council, was knighted by the King, and in 1625 elevated to the Irish peerage as Baron of Baltimore in County Longford. He visited North America, and after viewing the fertile country surrounding Chesapeake Bay, returned to England and sought a grant of this territory from James's son and successor Charles I. But he died before the grant became final, and his rights were inherited by his son Caecilius Calvert. The King "requested" that the new colony be called Maryland, after his queen.

Two hundred colonists landed in southern Maryland in 1634 and began a settlement at St. Mary's, the first capital. In 1649, the colonial assembly passed the Act of Religious Toleration, which guaranteed freedom of religion to all sects of Christianity—a freedom that did not then exist in many of the other English colonies. The early English settlers along Chesapeake Bay developed a plantation system of agriculture whose primary crop was tobacco, supplemented by corn and wheat. Slaves were extensively used in the tobacco economy. But the part of the state west of Baltimore—with its small cities such as Frederick, Hagerstown, and Cumberland—was settled by Scotch-Irish and then Germans who had landed primarily in Philadelphia and spread out along the Cumberland Valley in Pennsylvania and the Shenandoah Valley in Virginia.

Baltimore lay between these two groups of very diverse settlers. In 1729, the provincial legislature authorized creation of "Baltimore Town," and the city that was founded as a result was made the seat of Baltimore County in 1768. In 1752, Baltimore consisted of twenty-five houses and about two hundred inhabitants. This was at a time when future rival port cities on the east coast—New York, Boston, and Philadelphia—were already populous and thriving. By 1796, Baltimore's population had increased to about twenty thousand, and its advantage over other east coast ports for shipment of produce was beginning to tell. Because land transportation generally cost more than water carriage, the longer the sea portion of a combined voyage, the cheaper. And Baltimore was the farthest west of any of the great east coast port cities. Grain being shipped from the interior of the United States to the east had, by and large, a shorter distance to go by land to Baltimore than it did to the other east coast ports. This also made it attractive economically to producers and shippers.

During the War of 1812, British ships under Admiral Ross had sailed up Chesapeake Bay and bombarded Fort McHenry in Baltimore harbor. Francis Scott Key, an American who was temporarily aboard an English warship during the action, had written the words to the "Star-Spangled Banner" at that time.

Work had begun on the Baltimore & Ohio Railroad, linking Baltimore with the west, in 1830, and by 1853 that line had reached the Ohio River. The Baltimore & Susquehanna Railroad, leading to Harrisburg and beyond, was begun in 1829, and the rail link between Baltimore and Washington was completed in 1834.

Riots such as those that took place with the passage of Union troops on April 19 were not new to Baltimore. Indeed, it was known colloquially by then as "Mob City." In 1853, there had been a melee among city firemen; in 1856, a riot between Democrats and Know-nothings after the election of that year; and in 1857, a pitched battle between the city militia and strikers against the Baltimore & Ohio Railroad.

The Governor of Maryland in 1861 was Thomas Hicks, a cautious Union sympathizer very much aware of the delicate balance of opinion in his state. Responding to Lincoln's call for troops, he requested from Secretary Cameron a guarantee that Maryland's militia would be used only in that state or in the District of Columbia. Having received it, he issued a proclamation counseling restraint to the citizens of the state, and agreed to furnish troops on the conditions stated.

But the citizens of Baltimore did not heed the Governor's counsel. Four days after Lincoln issued his call for volunteers, a Massachusetts regiment arrived from Philadelphia at Baltimore's President Street Station. Instead of having the troops march the mile-and-a-half route from there to the Camden Station, where they would board the train for Washington, it was decided that the railroad cars themselves, with the troops aboard, would be drawn through the city by horses. Ten cars carried the first contingent, and eight of them successfully passed a gathering mob on Gay Street. But the ninth car stopped momentarily, and in a trice all of its windows were broken by flying rocks and stones. Other cars were now assailed, and the troops sought shelter on the floors of their cars. Nine cars finally made it to Camden Station, but the tenth didn't. The mob placed rocks and sand on the horse-car tracks, and the soldiers alighted and fell back to the station whence they had come.

Five hundred men of the Massachusetts regiment were now at Camden Station, ready to depart for Washington; 350 were at President Street Station. Between them was a mob of twenty thousand

Confederate sympathizers. The troops decided to fight their way through on foot, and the mob closed in behind as they marched. The Baltimore police tried to form an escort, but the mob got between them and the soldiers. Mayor George Brown attempted to quiet the crowd by marching with the troops for a short way.

Soon the crowd loosed a volley of paving stones at the soldiers, who finally turned and fired their rifles into the crowd. People in the mob fired back. Two soldiers and four civilians were killed. The troops eventually made it to Camden Station, where the train immediately headed for Washington. Just as it did so, members of the crowd gave a cheer for Jefferson Davis; a soldier fired from the train and killed a prominent Baltimore merchant. In the final tally, sixteen people were killed, four soldiers and twelve civilians.

A mass meeting was called for 5 p.m. in Baltimore's Monument Square. Mayor Brown and Governor Hicks were among the speakers who urged the citizens of Baltimore to rise up and fight the "invasion." The next day's edition of the *New York Times*—Saturday, April 20, 1861—carried this headline on its front page:

STARTING FROM BALTIMORE

The Northern Troops Mobbed and Fired Upon—The Troops
Return the Fire—Four Massachusetts Volunteers Killed
and Several Wounded—Several of the Rioters Killed.

That night, Hicks, who was spending the night at Brown's home, was awakened by the Mayor and Marshal Thomas Kane, Chief of the Baltimore police, who urged him to order that railroad bridges north of Baltimore be burned in order to prevent more federal troops from entering the city. Hicks reluctantly agreed, and several spans on both the Harrisburg and Philadelphia lines were burned that night.

Several times in the next week, delegations of Baltimore officials either met with or wrote to Lincoln and Seward. First, they urged that no more federal troops be sent through the city; the administration agreed to this because General Winfield Scott thought that another route would do: The troops could detrain at Perryville, north of Baltimore on Chesapeake Bay, and go by ship from there to Annapolis, and from Annapolis by land to Washington. But a few days later, the Baltimore delegations were demanding that no troops go through Maryland at all, and that Lord Lyons, the British Minister, be asked to mediate the conflict between the North and the South. To this Lincoln replied that "our men are not moles, who can tunnel under the ground."

During the week following the Baltimore riots, the city of Washington seemed virtually cut off from the rest of the North. Not only were no troops arriving, but the telegraph lines had been cut and mail deliveries from the north were irregular. It was feared that ships would be unable to come up the Potomac because of a Confederate blockade on the lower part of the river.

Lincoln, by nature and habit so calm, so equable, so undemonstrative, nevertheless passed this period of interrupted communication and isolation from the North in the state of nervous tension which put all his great powers of mental and physical endurance to their severest trial. General Scott's reports, though invariably expressing his confidence and successful defense, frankly admitted the evident danger; and the President, with his acuteness of observation and his rapidity and correctness of inference, lost no single one of the external indications of doubt and apprehension. Day after day prediction failed and hope was deferred; troops did not come, ships did not arrive, railroads remained broken, messengers failed to reach their destination. . . .

In others' society [Lincoln] gave no sign of these inner emotions. But once, on the afternoon of the twenty-third, the business of the day being over, the Executive Office deserted, after walking the floor alone in silent thought for nearly an hour, he stopped and gazed long and wistfully out of the window down the Potomac in the direction of the expected ships; and unconscious of other presence in the room, at length broke out with irrepressible anguish in the repeated exclamation, "Why don't they come! Why don't they come!"[4]

It was during this period of deep uneasiness in the capital following the Baltimore riots and bridge-burnings that Lincoln began to consider the possibility of suspending the writ of *habeas corpus* along the rail routes from the north. *Habeas corpus*, an important safeguard of personal liberty derived from English common law, was a right available to anyone arrested or detained by the government. The writ was directed to the official who had custody of the prisoner, and required that official to explain to the court issuing the writ the basis for holding the prisoner. The court would then determine whether the prisoner should be released or remanded to official custody.

Seward, reminiscing many years later, said to F. B. Carpenter, who was then in Auburn to paint his portrait:

> There were two points in the administration . . . upon which all subsequent events hinged. One was the suspension of the Habeas Corpus Act. . . . The Habeas Corpus Act had not been suspended because of Mr. Lincoln's extreme reluctance at that period to assume such a responsibility. Those to whom he looked for advice, almost to a man, opposed this action.
>
> On Sunday morning* I went to the White House alone, and told the President that this step could no longer be delayed. He still argued against it. I told him emphatically that perdition was the sure penalty of further hesitation. He sat for some time in silence, then took up his pen and said: 'It shall be so!' The next day the proclamation suspending the Habeas Corpus Act was issued.[5]

Among those whom Lincoln consulted about the suspension of the writ was Attorney General Edward Bates, a cautious Missourian who had been born and raised in Virginia. Bates compiled what there was of legal precedent on the question. Governor Hicks decided to call the Maryland legislature into session on April 26—not in

---

*There is an inconsistency in the date here. April 19, the day of the riot in Baltimore, was a Friday, and Lincoln's order allowing the suspension of the writ of *habeas corpus* is dated April 27, which was a Saturday. It seems more likely that Seward's recollection of a visit to the White House on Sunday would be accurate nine years after it occurred than would be his memory of the lapse of time between his conversation with Lincoln and the date Lincoln's proclamation was issued. His visit to Lincoln probably, then, occurred on April 21.

Annapolis, which had been occupied by federal troops, but in Frederick, in western Maryland. The selection of the site was not inadvertent; most of the people in western Maryland were Unionists, and there would be no gangs of rowdies in the streets or in the galleries. The Governor urged the legislature to preserve its "neutral position" between the North and the South, and after some debate the legislature agreed. It refused to call a state convention to adopt an ordinance of secession but named committees to visit both Lincoln and Davis with a view to making peace.

When Lincoln first learned of Hicks's plan to convene the legislature, he considered arresting the legislators in order to prevent them from meeting. The matter was discussed in the Cabinet. But cooler heads prevailed, and Lincoln outlined his position in a formal directive to General Scott:

Washington, April 25, 1861

Lieutenant-General Scott.

My Dear Sir: The Maryland legislature assembles tomorrow at Annapolis, and not improbably will take action to arm the people of that State against the United States. The question has been submitted to and considered by me whether it would not be justifiable, upon the ground of necessary defense, for you, as General in Chief of the United States Army, to arrest or disperse the members of that body. I think it would not be justifiable nor efficient for the desired object.

First. They have clearly legal right to assemble, and we can not know in advance that their action will not be lawful and peaceful, and if we wait until they shall have acted their arrest or dispersion will not lessen the effect of their action.

Secondly. We can not permanently prevent their action. If we arrest them, we can not long hold them as prisoners, and when liberated they will immediately reassemble and take their action; and precisely the same if we simply disperse them—they will immediately reassemble in some other place.

I therefore conclude that it is only left to the Commanding General to watch and await their action, which, if it shall be to arm their people against the United States, he is to adopt the most prompt and efficient means to counteract, even, if necessary, to the bombardment of their cities and, in the extremest necessity, the suspension of the writ of *habeas corpus*.

Your obedient servant,
ABRAHAM LINCOLN

But Lincoln decided that more than watchful waiting was required with respect to the rioting and bridge-burning in Baltimore. Finally convinced of the wisdom of Seward's advice, he sent the following order to General Scott on April 27:

The Commanding General of the Army of the United States:

You are engaged in suppressing an insurrection against the laws of the United States. If at any point on or in the vicinity of any military line which is now or which shall be used between the city of Philadelphia and the city of Washington you find resistance which renders it necessary to suspend the writ of *habeas corpus* for the public safety, you personally, or through the officer in command at the point where resistance occurs, are authorized to suspend the writ.

Given under my hand and the seal of the United States, at the city of Washington, this 27th day of April, 1861, and of the Independence of the United States the eighty-fifth.

ABRAHAM LINCOLN

By the President of the United States:

William H. Seward
Secretary of State

CHAPTER 3

Taney Rebukes Lincoln

A T T W O O ' C L O C K in the morning of May 25, 1861, nearly a month after Lincoln's proclamation, a detachment of troops under Captain Samuel Yohe entered the home of John Merryman in Cockeysville, Maryland, and arrested him for participation in the destruction of the railroad bridges after the Baltimore riot of April 19. Cockeysville lay north of Baltimore, along the rail line between that city and Harrisburg. Merryman was taken from his home and imprisoned at Fort McHenry.

Merryman was a farmer, a state legislator, and a member of a militia cavalry company. He was arrested on Saturday, and he immediately obtained counsel, who drew up a petition for a writ of *habeas corpus* on his behalf. The petition was presented to Chief Justice Taney on Sunday. The writ was issued on that day and was made returnable the following morning at the federal courthouse in Baltimore.

Taney had now been Chief Justice for twenty-five years. Born in March 1777, in the midst of the Revolutionary War, to a family of the southern Maryland tobacco-planting aristocracy, he was raised as a Roman Catholic and was a communicant of that faith throughout his life. Under Maryland land law, his older brother would inherit the estate, and as a younger son he was left to his own devices as far as inheritance was concerned. He attended Dickinson College in Carlisle, Pennsylvania, graduating in 1795, and then read law in the office of a judge in Annapolis. Taney was admitted to the bar in 1799 and moved to Frederick, Maryland, where he remained for twenty-four years. It was there that he met and married Anne Key, the sister of Francis Scott Key, author of "The Star-Spangled Banner." She was a Protestant, and their six daughters were raised in her faith. In 1823, Taney moved to Baltimore to be better able to handle his successful law practice.

Taney had nothing of the imposing presence or the magnificent organ tones of Webster. Chronically ill throughout most of his life, so that a few days spent in arguing cases or later as a judge would send him to bed exhausted, he imparted no such sense of physical well-being and camaraderie as came from his frequent competitor, William Wirt. He was tall and flat-chested with broad, stooping shoulders. His features were irregular, his teeth discolored with tobacco, his gums visible when he smiled. His black clothes seemed never quite to fit him, and his prominently veined hands rendered no service in revealing gesture. His voice was flat and hollow.

And yet, it was said, when he spoke, his audience never thought of his appearance. Avoiding all the devices of conventional oratory, he talked simply and directly to judge or jury as the situation might require. . . . An observer remarked that "There was an air of so much sincerity in all he said that it was next to impossible to believe he could be wrong." Taney's capacity for capitalizing on lack of adornment in delivery in an era of great orators and his ability to give a sense of deep conviction was a sharp challenge to his opponents. Both to William Pinckney and to William Wirt is attributed the comment that it was possible to answer his arguments and to cope with his logic, but nothing was so much to be dreaded as his "apostolic simplicity." This trait, it is true, could be regarded by an enemy as it came to be by Daniel Webster as "cunning and jesuitical."[1]

Taney supported Andrew Jackson in his successful bid for the Presidency in 1828, and in 1831, after a Cabinet shake-up, Jackson named him Attorney General. At that time Attorneys General were allowed to maintain a private law practice, and Taney did so. He was a loyal ally of Jackson throughout the bitter fight over the rechartering of the Bank of the United States, and as Acting Secretary of the Treasury ultimately withdrew the government's funds from the bank at Jackson's direction. His actions so angered the Whigs, who controlled the Senate, that his nomination as Secretary of the Treasury was defeated by a narrow vote. The following year, 1835, Jackson nominated him as an Associate Justice of the Supreme Court, but the Whigs prevented the nomination from ever coming to a vote before the lame-duck session of the Senate adjourned. Jackson succeeded in his third attempt, when, in December 1835, he nominated Taney to be Chief Justice to succeed John Marshall, who had died the preceding summer. A newly elected Senate confirmed Taney by a wide margin.

Taney was fifty-nine when he took his seat in the center chair of the Supreme Court, and for the next twenty years the Court over which he presided gave general satisfaction to the country. Under Marshall, who had occupied that position from 1801 until 1835, the Court had been a staunch expounder of federal powers as opposed to those of the states. The Taney Court, in a series of decisions dealing with interstate commerce and the Contract Clause, retreated from this doctrinal position and found ways to give the states more authority without repudiating any of the decisions of the Marshall Court. Taney, like Marshall, was an able expositor of legal principles and wrote with a clarity that was the more remarkable for its rarity in nineteenth-century legal circles.

Then, in 1857, came the ill-starred decision in the *Dred Scott* case. That case involved the question of whether a slave who is taken by his owner from a slave state first to a free state, and then to a free territory, but then returned to the slave state whence he had come, was emancipated by virtue of his stay in the free state or the free territory. The lower federal court in which the action was brought decided that a slave could not be a "citizen" of any state for purposes of federal jurisdiction. His lawsuit seeking his freedom, therefore, could not be maintained in federal court on the ground that he was a citizen of one state and his master a citizen of another state.

Attorneys for the slave, Dred Scott, appealed this decision to the Supreme Court of the United States.

But now a new wrinkle appeared. Part of Scott's claim to freedom was based on his residence, with his master, who was an army surgeon, in Wisconsin territory, where slavery had been forever prohibited by the Missouri Compromise enacted by Congress in 1820. If the Supreme Court were to tackle the question of whether Congress had constitutional authority to prohibit slavery in the territories, a question of truly national significance and volatility would be involved. In 1854, under the leadership of Illinois Democrat Stephen A. Douglas, Congress had enacted the Kansas-Nebraska Act, which expressly repealed the Missouri Compromise limitation on slavery in the territories. Antislavery voters in the North had been outraged by this enactment, and as a result of it the Republican party was formed, partly devoted to prevention of any extension of slavery into the territories.

The case was argued to the Court in the spring of 1856, but no decision was reached and it was set down for reargument in December 1856, a month after the presidential election. The case was reached at the Court's conference early in 1857, and originally a majority apparently agreed that there was no need to decide on the validity of the Missouri Compromise; it was enough to decide only that Missouri law governed the question of whether Dred Scott remained a slave. Since Missouri law held that he did, and all Justices agreed that a slave could not be a "citizen" entitled to sue in federal court, the case could have been disposed of on relatively noncontroversial grounds.

But two of the Justices, John McLean of Ohio and Benjamin Curtis of Massachusetts, planned to dissent on the question of whether or not Scott was still a slave. They would therefore necessarily reach the question of the validity of the Missouri Compromise, and would vote to uphold it. The members of the original majority had second thoughts and decided that they too should decide the issue of the constitutionality of the Missouri Compromise and invalidate it. During the course of these discussions, the majority sought to persuade Justice Robert Grier of Pennsylvania that he too should join this view of the majority. Justice John Catron, who had continued to dabble in politics after his appointment by Jackson two decades earlier, requested President-elect James Buchanan to intercede with his fellow Pennsylvanian and bring him around to the view that the Missouri Compromise was unconstitutional. Buchanan did so, and Grier joined the majority view.

These machinations, of course, were grossly inappropriate; communication between the Supreme Court and the President on any pending case, to say nothing of a member of the Court urging the President to importune another Justice, violated even the relatively lax standards of that day. Buchanan briefly alluded to the case in his inaugural address on March 4, 1857, sanctimoniously declaring that the authority of Congress over slavery in the territories was "a judicial question, which legitimately belongs to the Supreme Court of the United States, before whom it is now pending, and will, it is understood, be speedily and finally settled. To their decision, in common with all good citizens, I shall cheerfully submit, whatever this may be."[2]

Two days later, on March 6, the Court assembled for the reading of the opinions in the *Dred Scott* case. Taney's opinion, which required two hours to deliver orally, said not merely that *slaves* could not be citizens, but that *Negroes* could not be citizens. In this respect it was joined only by two of his colleagues. The rest of his opinion, which was joined by a majority of the Court, went on to say that the Missouri Compromise exceeded the authority of Congress, because Congress was obligated to let citizens of all states of the Union take their property with them when they migrated to a territory—including Southerners who wished to bring with them slaves who were regarded as "property" under the laws of the southern states.

Northern opinion was outraged. Horace Greeley's *New York Tribune* said:

> The long trumpeted decision . . . having been held over from last year in order not too flagrantly to alarm and exasperate the Free States on the eve of an important presidential election . . . is entitled to just so much moral weight as would be the judgment of a majority of those congregated in any Washington bar-room.

William Cullen Bryant, editor of the *New York Evening Post*, wrote:

> Are we to accept, without question, these new readings of the Constitution—to sit down contentedly under this dis-

grace—to admit that the Constitution was never before rightly understood, even by those who framed it—to consent that hereafter it shall be the slaveholders' instead of the free men's Constitution? Never! Never!

Abraham Lincoln had also been a critic of the *Dred Scott* decision. At first his comment was mild; in June 1857 he said:

> We think the *Dred Scott* decision is erroneous. We know the Court that made it, has often overruled its own decisions, and we shall do what we can to have it overrule this. We offer no resistance to it.[3]

But when he addressed the Illinois Republican state convention in Springfield in June 1858, his criticism was a good deal more stinging. He asserted that there was a conspiracy to "nationalize" slavery involving Stephen A. Douglas, Franklin Pierce, President of the United States from 1853 to 1857, incumbent President James Buchanan, and Chief Justice Taney. Lincoln acknowledged that there was no direct evidence of such a conspiracy. "But," he went on,

> when we see a lot of framed timbers, different portions of which we know have been gotten out at different times and places and by different workmen—Stephen, Franklin, Roger, and James, for instance—and when we see these timbers joined together, and see they exactly make the frame of a house or a mill, all these tenons and mortises exactly fitting, and . . . not a piece too many or too few . . . we find it impossible to not believe that Stephen and Franklin and Roger and James all understood one another from the beginning, and all worked upon a common plan or draft drawn up before the first lick was struck.[4]

Seward, speaking in the Senate in March 1858, had made a much harsher attack on the machinations between Buchanan and Taney, adopting the same theme that Lincoln would pursue a few months later. Referring to the decision itself, Seward said:

... in this ill-omened act, the Supreme Court forgot its own dignity which had always been maintained with just judicial jealousy. . . . And they and the President alike forgot that judicial usurpation is more odious and intolerable than any other among the manifold practices of tyranny.[5]

Seward's attack so outraged Taney as to lead him to say privately that if Seward were ever elected President, he would refuse to administer the oath of office to him.

Taney did give the oath of office to Lincoln. But during his inaugural address, which immediately preceded the taking of the oath, the new President made a thinly veiled criticism of the *Dred Scott* decision:

> The candid citizen must confess that if the policy of the government, upon vital questions affecting the whole people, is to be irrevocably fixed by decisions of the Supreme Court, the instant they are made, in ordinary litigation between parties and personal actions, the people will have ceased to be their own rulers, having to that extent practically resigned their government into the hands of that eminent tribunal.[6]

The *Dred Scott* decision, which a later Chief Justice, Charles Evans Hughes, would describe as a "self-inflicted wound," seriously damaged the prestige of the Supreme Court throughout the North. As noted above, both Lincoln and Seward, aspirants for the 1860 Republican presidential nomination, were openly critical of it. And so, on the morning of May 27, 1861, when Taney arrived to hear the case of *Ex Parte Merryman* (at the Masonic building in which the federal court in Baltimore customarily sat), he had at least one strike against him in the eyes of the North. Four years earlier, he had authored the principal opinion in the *Dred Scott* case, which in the eyes of its many northern detractors had been a political decision to advance the cause of slavery in the southern states. Now he was to sit and decide the fate of a fellow Marylander who had been arrested by the administration of a newly installed Republican President.

The writ was addressed to General George Cadwalader, commander of the military district in which Fort McHenry lay, but at the appointed time Cadwalader himself did not appear. A few minutes later, one of the General's aides, a Colonel Lee, in full-dress uniform complete with red sash and sword, appeared to apologize for his superior's absence. Lee went on to describe some of the charges against Merryman, and on behalf of the General stated that he was duly authorized by the President of the United States to suspend the writ of *habeas corpus* for the public safety. He requested postponement of any action by the Court until he could receive instructions from the President. Counsel for Merryman inquired whether the Colonel had produced Merryman, and Lee replied that he had not. Taney then stated that the General had been commanded to produce the body of Merryman that morning, that he had failed to do so, and that he therefore directed that an attachment be issued against him returnable in the same courtroom at twelve o'clock noon the following day.

> In great excitement the people of Baltimore waited to see the outcome of this contest between the Chief Justice and the General, who in this affair represented the military authority of the President. On May 28th, well before the appointed hour, the courtroom was tightly packed and a crowd of some two thousand people were assembled in the street outside. . . . Leaving for the court from the home of his son-in-law, J. Mason Campbell, in the company of his grandson, Taney remarked that he himself might be imprisoned in Fort McHenry before nightfall. But he was determined to do his duty.[7]

When the Court convened on May 28, the Chief Justice inquired of the marshal whether he had made a return of service of the attachment. The marshal replied in writing that he had gone to the fort pursuant to the writ and sent his name in from the gate, but had been told there was no answer, and that he had been unable to serve the writ.

Taney then read the following statement from the bench:

I ordered the attachment yesterday, because upon the face of the return the detention of the prisoner was unlawful upon two grounds.

1. The President under the Constitution and laws of the United States, cannot suspend the privilege of the writ of *habeas corpus*, nor authorize any military officer to do so.

2. A military officer has no right to arrest a person, not subject to the rules and articles of war, for an offense against the laws of the United States, except in and of the judicial authority and subject to its control—and if the parties arrested by the military—it is the duty of the officer to deliver him over immediately to the civil authority, to be dealt with according to law.[8]

Taney went on to say that the marshal had the legal authority to summon a posse and bring the General into Court, but since the marshal would undoubtedly be met by superior force, such action could not be taken. Under the circumstances, Taney said, he would write out the conclusions on which the opinion was based and would "report them with these proceedings to the President of the United States, and call upon him to perform his constitutional duty to enforce the laws. In other words, to enforce the process of this Court."[9]

As soon as the Court had adjourned, Mayor Brown went up to congratulate Taney on his decision. Taney said, "Mr. Brown, I am an old man, a very old man, but perhaps I was preserved for this occasion."

"Sir, I thank God that you were," replied the Mayor.[10]

Northern opinion, as might have been expected, was critical of Taney's decision. The *Washington Evening Star* opined in its issue of May 29:

The action of Chief Justice Taney in this case is probably in accordance with the strict letter of the law. . . . Nevertheless, it exhibits a determination on his part palpably to ignore the existing state of the country, which signally justified the action of General Cadwalader with respect to Merriman [sic]—an individual whose conduct has proved him to be eminently dangerous to the cause of the maintenance of the Union. . . . Under these circumstances, there can be no doubt that public opinion will justify the refusal of General Cadwalader, in times like these, to deny to a man notoriously striving to overthrow the Constitution, Union and Government of the United States, the advantage of the writ of habeas corpus.

The *New York Times* in its issue of the same day said:

> In the case of John Merriman [sic], the interposition of Chief Justice Taney can only be regarded as at once officious and improper. . . . Judge Taney presents the ungracious spectacle of a judicial and the military authority of the United States at variance, the soldier eager to punish, and the jurist to exculpate a traitor. The antithesis might have been very easily avoided; and an impression that the zeal of the Justice might have been less fervent, had not the prisoner been a citizen of his own State, a neighbor, and a personal friend, would not have countenanced.

The *Baltimore Daily Republican* was more sympathetic, in its May 28 issue, giving this report of the proceedings which had taken place that morning:

> Shortly before the hour named, the doors of the courtroom were thrown open, when the crowd, which by this time had increased to several hundred, rushed in pell mell, until the room had become densely packed to such an extent as to render it exceedingly uncomfortable. Every nook and corner was occupied, and a general scrambling for positions progressed for some time, large numbers being unable to effect an entrance into the room. . . .
>
> The decision of the venerable Chief Justice was received by those assembled, many of whom were members of the bar, with heartfelt exclamations of approbation, such as "Thank God for such a man," "God grant that he may live many years to protect us," and many similar remarks.

Taney's written opinion, handed down several days after the announcement of his ruling from the bench, espoused two distinct propositions. The first was that only Congress, and not the President, may suspend the privilege of the writ of *habeas corpus*. The second was that only a party subject to the Articles of War (someone in the military) could be detained in prison or brought to trial before a military commission. Each was an extremely important proposition, but the first was a good deal narrower than the second.

The origins of the writ of *habeas corpus* in the common law of England are murky. It may have been used originally as a device to put someone in prison rather than to get him out. But by the time of the Stuart monarchy in the seventeenth century, it was recognized as a safeguard of personal liberty. A person arrested was entitled to have a court issue this writ to his custodian, directing the custodian to produce the prisoner in court and explain the reason for his detention. The Petition of Right in 1628 asserted that the King's courts had refused to issue the writ where a prisoner was detained by special command of the King or of the Privy Council, and this was remarked as an abuse. The great Habeas Corpus Act of 1671 secured the right by statute in England.

Article I of the United States Constitution deals with the "legislative power of the United States," which it vests in Congress. Section 8 of the Article grants to Congress several kinds of legislative authority—to regulate commerce among the several states, to raise and support armies, for example. Section 9, Clause 2 then prohibits Congress from doing certain things. The first of these prohibitions states:

> The Privilege of Writ of Habeas Corpus shall not be suspended, unless when in Cases of Rebellion or Invasion the public Safety may require it.

Taney reasoned that because the Suspension Clause was placed in Article I, which deals with the powers of Congress, it must have been intended that only Congress should have the power to suspend the privilege of the writ. Article II of the Constitution, dealing with the powers of the President, Taney read narrowly, thereby ruling out any express or implied authority the President might have in this area under his "war powers." He also pointed out that in England, Parliament had reserved to itself the authority to suspend the writ.

The Constitution as originally adopted contained no Bill of Rights as such, though it did prohibit Congress from enacting such measures as ex post facto laws or bills of attainder. But dissatisfaction expressed in several of the state debates on ratification, with the absence of any provisions guaranteeing individual rights, led to the adoption of the first Ten Amendments, familiarly known as the Bill of Rights, in 1791.

Those amendments guarantee, as against the federal government, the right to be free from unreasonable searches and seizures, the privilege against compulsory self-incrimination, the right to jury trial in criminal cases, among others. Nowhere in the Bill of Rights is there a mention of the writ of *habeas corpus*. The assumption has been that the limitation on suspension of the writ contained in Article I implies a guarantee of its existence. The assumption has never been tested, because the very first Congress provided for the writ by statute.

The second proposition that Taney endorsed was a good deal more far-reaching than the question of whether the President, as opposed to Congress, might suspend *habeas corpus*. Taney at least conceded that the power to suspend the writ lay somewhere in the federal government; the only dispute was whether the President could do it by himself or, instead, required the approval of Congress. Later on in the Lincoln administration, Congress solved this problem by authorizing the President to suspend the writ under given circumstances. But Taney also said that so long as the federal courts were open and functioning, one such as John Merryman, who was not a member of the Armed Forces, could be detained, charged, or tried only pursuant to the order of such a court. The writ of *habeas corpus*, which Taney dealt with in the first part of his opinion, simply gave to an individual the right to have his custodian justify his detention to a court. But *habeas corpus* does not speak at all to the sort of justifications that a court will deem sufficient to remand the prisoner to custody, rather than to order him discharged. Taney's second proposition dealt with the latter kind of question.

He based his reasoning on provisions of the Bill of Rights: the Fifth Amendment, providing that no one shall be deprived of life, liberty, or property without due process of law (and, in Taney's view, only the process of a court could afford "due process of law") and the Sixth Amendment, providing that "in all criminal prosecutions, the accused shall enjoy the right to a speedy and public trial, by an impartial jury of the state and district wherein the crime shall have been committed." He went on to again construe the authority of the President very narrowly, saying that his principal obligation in this area was to come to the aid of judicial authority, if it were resisted by force.

Taney concluded his opinion with these words:

> In such a case, my duty was too plain to be mistaken. I have exercised all the power which the Constitution and laws confer upon me, but that power has been resisted by a force too strong for me to overcome. . . . I shall, therefore, order all the proceedings in this case, with my opinion, to be filed and recorded in the Circuit Court of the United States for the District of Maryland, and direct the clerk to transmit a copy, under seal, to the President of the United States. It will then remain for that high officer, in fulfillment of his constitutional obligation to take care that the laws be faithfully executed to determine what measures he will take to cause the civil process of the United States to be respected and enforced.

Lincoln, not surprisingly, made no direct response to Taney's missive. But in his July 4 message to the special session of Congress, the President pointed out that the Constitution was silent as to which branch of the government might exercise the authority to suspend the writ and asserted that in an emergency when Congress was not in session the President had the authority to do so. He went on to say that the writ, which had been fashioned "with such extreme tenderness of the citizens' liberty," could, as interpreted by Taney, allow "all the laws, but one, to go unexecuted, and the government itself go to pieces, lest that one be violated." Here was Lincoln the advocate at his very best. There was no reference to the difficult constitutional issue but only the posing of a starkly simple question that seemed to admit of but one answer.

The administration continued to confine Merryman at Fort

McHenry, though he was permitted to see members of his family and numerous friends. They continued to agitate for his release, and the report of a legislative committee portrayed him as "the victim of military lawlessness and arbitrary power." In July, he was indicted for conspiracy to commit treason, for having conspired with numerous others in armed resistance to the government and for participating in the destruction of the bridges to prevent the passage of troops.

After indictment he was admitted to bail, and his prosecution was postponed time and again because of Taney's peculiar view of the function of the civil courts. One of the keystones of his opinion in *Merryman* had been the fact that the civil courts were open and functioning, and that anyone who violated the law could be indicted and tried in these courts. But not, alas, in the federal court in Baltimore. Taney had taken pains to see to it that cases such as Merryman's would *not* be tried in the Baltimore court:

> Taney was largely responsible for the fact that Merryman and some sixty others similarly indicted for treason were never prosecuted. He doubted whether they would receive a fair trial under the conditions of military rule obtaining in Baltimore, and he insisted that they not be tried in his absence. He instructed District Judge Giles not to try capital punishment cases by himself, and, as Taney was the only other judge designated to sit in the Circuit Court in Baltimore, this made the treason cases dependent on his presence. For over a year he was too ill to do circuit duty.[11]

But even when Taney regained his health, he refused to participate in the trials, nor would he allow District Judge Giles to preside by himself.

The Lincoln administration had ignored the rebuff, although John Merryman was freed on bail in the summer of 1861 and was never actually brought to trial on the charges on which he was indicted. But the administration would soon test its authority under the President's war powers in other parts of the nation.

CHAPTER 4

Seward and Stanton

S EVERAL ASPECTS OF the *Merryman* case are worth noting.
The first is that Taney's decision was quite precipitate, without
benefit of hearing argument from counsel. The second is the
disorganized state of federal law officers at this time. The third is the
administration's disregard of the decision, and the lack of any widespread public outcry against that disregard.

Merryman's counsel applied for the writ of *habeas corpus* on Sunday, May 26. The writ was issued by Taney on the same day—surely
not a normal business day for the judiciary—and was made returnable the next morning at the federal courthouse in Baltimore. General Cadwalader's aide Colonel Lee appeared in court at that time,
announced the existence of the presidential proclamation, and
requested time to receive instructions from the President. Taney
simply ignored this request and with no argument from counsel—
indeed, there was no counsel for the government—issued an *attachment* (an order to appear in court) against Cadwalader. The next day,
the marshal was unable to gain entrance to Fort McHenry in order to
serve the attachment, and Taney rendered his oral opinion to the
effect that the President had no authority to suspend the writ of
habeas corpus by himself.

The judicial process is quintessentially a deliberative one; indeed,
this is the key element that distinguishes it from the executive and
legislative process. Part of it is the requisite time for the judge to consider and decide, but part is also the opportunity for each side to persuade the court of the correctness of its position. The judge's mind

need not be, and often is not, unbiased at the beginning of the argument. A judge may have instinctive or preliminary reactions against the position of one side in a case, before ever hearing argument from counsel. But one of the purposes of argument is to allow counsel for such a side to try to persuade the judge that his preliminary or instinctive reaction is mistaken.

In the present day of congested court calendars, time limits have been placed on oral arguments, by rule in the appellate courts and on an ad hoc basis in trial courts. There is more reliance on written briefs or memoranda filed by counsel for each side. But in 1861, the oral tradition inherited from the English common law played a prominent part in the business of judging. The *Prize Cases*, which the Supreme Court would hear only two years after the *Merryman* decision, saw each side allowed six days to present its case. This is not to say that similarly extensive arguments would be expected in a trial court (such as the circuit court on which Taney was sitting as Circuit Justice). But the issue of the President's authority under the Constitution to suspend the privilege of the writ of *habeas corpus* was a tremendously important question of public law. Before that question was decided against the President, government counsel surely should have been heard from. Taney's hasty decision is all the more remarkable because he had only learned at the Monday session of the Court of the existence of the presidential proclamation. Obviously Colonel Lee, present not as legal counsel for the government but as a representative of Merryman's custodian (General Cadwalader), was incapable of arguing the government's legal case. Taney's refusal to countenance any delay at all for the purpose of allowing the government to present its case does not speak well for either his judgment or his impartiality. The fact that he may have reached the correct result on the merits of the case cannot excuse this want of process.

What would the government have done if the *Merryman* case had been briefly postponed to allow counsel to appear on its behalf? Alas, the government's legal officers were so seriously disorganized at this time—less than three months into the new administration—that it is difficult to say. Whatever Lincoln's many other virtues and talents, efficient administration was not one of them. Because the federal government was so much smaller than it is today, the duties of Cabinet members were not onerous. The result was that the more forceful and ambitious of them had time to meddle in the affairs of their colleagues. Perhaps that is the way Lincoln wanted it. Below the Cabinet level, there were United States Attorneys for each of the federal judicial districts, of which Maryland was one. There is no indication that General Cadwalader ever consulted the U.S. Attorney in Baltimore, or that he would have been expected to do so. Unlike the present day, when the Department of Justice in Washington, headed by the Attorney General, and employing hundreds of lawyers, maintains tight control over the work of the U.S. Attorneys in the field, the situation in 1861 was quite different. There was then, of course, an Attorney General who sat in the President's Cabinet, but he did not head a government department; the Department of Justice would not be created until 1870. And until Congress acted in August 1861, the Attorney General had no authority to control the actions of the United States Attorneys in the various judicial districts. He could and did advise them on points of law or on government policy. But he gave advice, not direction.

Attorney General Edward Bates, a rival of Lincoln's for the Republican presidential nomination, had a career similar to Lincoln's—mixing public office with the private practice of law. Born in 1793 in Virginia, he was educated by private tutors and served briefly with a unit of the Virginia militia in the War of 1812. In 1814, he journeyed nearly a thousand miles westward to join his brother in the frontier town of St. Louis, Missouri. He studied law in the office of a prominent St. Louis attorney and was admitted to the bar in 1816. He then began what would become nearly a half century of legal practice, interrupted along the way by numerous forays into public affairs. In 1823, he married Julia Coalter, the daughter of a prominent St. Louis family, and during the course of their marriage they had seventeen children, ten of whom were still living in 1860.

Bates was elected to Congress in 1826, but was defeated after one term by a Jacksonian Democrat. He returned to Missouri and the practice of law, but stayed active in politics and became a leader of what would ultimately become the Whig party in Missouri. In 1847, he was elected president by the two thousand attending delegates of a "Rivers and Harbors Convention" held in Chicago. The convention brought together those interested in federal support for internal improvements to roads, rivers, and harbors. Bates's role in that gathering won him national attention. He received a substantial number of votes at the 1852 Whig Convention, although he was unable to secure second place on the party's national ticket.

The passage of the Kansas-Nebraska Act in 1854 led to the formation of the Republican party, but Bates never became a member. As the 1860 election drew near, he was touted by some politicians and newspaper editors as a presidential candidate to oppose the Buchanan-Douglas Democrats. His appeal lay in his innate conservatism; he thought slavery wrong, but was content to wait and let it die a natural death. He believed that Congress had the power to control the extension of slavery into the territories. But he had no sympathy with abolitionists, and little more for relatively radical Republicans such as Seward and Chase.

In March 1860, the "opposition" convention in Missouri—made up of Republicans, Whigs, and "Know-Nothings"—endorsed Bates for President. The other principal candidates for the Republican nomination—Seward, Chase, and Lincoln—regarded him as a serious rival, and on the first ballot in Chicago, he received forty-five out of a total of more than five hundred votes. But his strength faded rapidly on the two succeeding ballots, which resulted in the nomination of Lincoln. Bates publicly endorsed Lincoln, but did not actively campaign for him. In the November election, Missouri was one of the few states carried by Democrat Stephen Douglas. Lincoln, however, thought it essential to include in his Cabinet members from the "border states," and invited Bates to come to Springfield in December. Shortly afterwards his selection as Attorney General was announced.

Bates is described by his biographer as having a "massive forehead, large Roman nose, and firm mouth and chin," presenting a "facial solemnity enlivened by piercing black eyes."[1] In Carpenter's painting of the first reading of the Emancipation Proclamation, Bates is one of the four bearded members of the gathering, along with the President, Edwin Stanton, and Gideon Welles. Bates sits at the far right of the group, a position that accurately suggests both his political outlook and his quite insignificant role in the Lincoln administration. The Chicago publisher Joseph Medill described Bates as "a fossil of the Silurian era—red sandstone at least—who should never have been quarried out of the rocks in which he was embedded."

There was considerable truth in this unflattering description. Bates had been born in the eighteenth century and was sixty-eight years old at the beginning of the Lincoln administration. He offered a conservatism anchored in the past. Compared with the brightly plumaged Seward, Chase, and Stanton, he was a sparrow. He had neither the desire nor the ability to compete with them in attempting to influence the policy of the administration.

Bates kept a somewhat sporadic diary, and its entries during April 1861 give no indication that he was consulted about or participated in Lincoln's decision to suspend the writ of *habeas corpus* by the proclamation of April 27. Following Lincoln's justification, in his July 4 speech to Congress, for disregarding Taney's *Merryman* decision, Bates issued an opinion justifying the President's action. It was not a very good opinion. It essentially argued that each of the three branches of the federal government established by the Constitution was coequal with and independent of the other two. The President was thus not subordinate to the judicial branch, and so the latter could not order him, or his subordinates, to free Merryman. This proposition had been refuted by Chief Justice Marshall's opinion in *Marbury* v. *Madison* more than half a century earlier. Bates also described the suspension of *habeas corpus* as a "political" rather than a "judicial" matter and on that ground as well not subject to judicial intervention. The opinion would persuade only those who were already true believers.

Why did not the government appeal Taney's ruling in *Merryman?* After all, he was speaking only as a member of a circuit court, and circuit court judgments were ordinarily reviewable by the Supreme Court. But there were significant procedural obstacles to such an appeal as the law then stood. And even if the route to the Supreme Court were open, the administration would surely have pondered whether it wished to follow it and run the possibility of converting a decision of a circuit court into a decision of the Supreme Court. There were only six active Justices at that time, and for several of these, enfeebled with age or otherwise infirm, "active" may be an overstatement. Four of the six—Taney, Wayne, Grier, and Catron— had joined in the principal portion of Taney's *Dred Scott* opinion. Both of the dissenters in that case—McLean and Curtis—were gone: Curtis resigned in 1857 because of his distress over the decision, and

McLean had died earlier in 1861. Peter Daniel, an extreme states'-rights Virginian, had died the preceding year. John Campbell from Alabama had resigned his office when his state seceded from the Union. Curtis had been replaced by Nathan Clifford, nominated in 1857 by James Buchanan and narrowly confirmed by a Senate vote of 26–23. Abolitionists and Free-Soilers opposed Clifford because he had defended the institution of slavery, even though he hailed from Maine. Given this makeup of the Court, an appeal of the *Merryman* decision must have appeared to the administration as a risky course of action, to be avoided if possible.

Although there was considerable support among northern legal scholars for the correctness of that part of Taney's *Merryman* opinion dealing with the President's authority to suspend the writ of *habeas corpus*, including an article by former Justice Curtis, there was no extended public criticism of the administration's disregard of the decision. This attitude stemmed at least in part from Taney's authorship of the principal opinion in the *Dred Scott* case, the outcome of which inflamed the North and would cast a cloud over the High Court for at least a generation. Although members of the federal judiciary have what is in effect life tenure, and need not fear the loss of their office or any diminution in their salary, neither they nor the courts upon which they sit are totally immune from currents of public opinion.

Another reason for this lack of widespread criticism of the administration was that at this time courts simply did not play as large a role in determining how the country should be governed as they do now. There was much less government at the national level than there is today, and people expected what there was to come from Congress and the President, not from the judiciary.

As noted above, Merryman was eventually released on bail from Fort McHenry, and, though indicted for treason, never stood trial. But the administration proceeded to move on other fronts, not only against persons such as Merryman, who was scarcely an innocent bystander to the disruptive activities in Baltimore, but against others whose only offense was expressing sympathy for the South. In the late summer of 1861, more than a dozen Maryland legislators suspected of secessionist sympathies were arrested to prevent them from moving to enact an ordinance of secession for their state.

Newspaper publishers did not escape the government net either. The State Department kept a record book entitled "Arrests for Disloyalty," in which the following is one of many examples:

Daniel Deckart was arrested by U.S. Marshal Lamon of the District of Columbia, in September, 1861, and committed to the Thirteenth Street prison Washington. He was the publisher of the paper in Hagerstown, MD., called The Hagerstown Mail, and it is presumed that he made it a disloyal sheet, though there are no charges on file in the Department of State against him. Having made application for his release and expressed a willingness to take the oath of allegiance an order was issued from the Department of State directing General Porter, Provost Marshal of Washington, to release Deckart on his taking the oath of allegiance and stipulating not to enter or correspond with any of the insurrectionary states. He was accordingly released October 9, 1861.[2]

The Administration was especially concerned about the New York press, which had a disproportionate impact on the rest of the country. In that era before wire services, newspapers in smaller cities frequently simply reprinted stories that had been run earlier in metropolitan journals. In New York, the *Tribune*, the *Herald*, and the *Times* generally supported the Northern war effort, but several other papers did not. In August 1861, a grand jury sitting in New York was outraged by an article in the antiwar New York *Journal of Commerce* which listed over one hundred newspapers published in the North that opposed "the present unholy war." The *Journal of Commerce* frequently editorialized in no uncertain terms about what it called the "malfeasance" of the Lincoln administration.

The grand jurors inquired of the presiding judge whether such vituperative criticism was subject to indictment. Because the grand jury was about to be discharged, the judge did not oblige, and the jurors simply requested that a list of several New York papers, including the *Journal of Commerce*, be called to the attention of the next grand jury. They had heard no evidence and received no legal instructions from the judge; they had simply made a "presentment"—a written notice taken by a grand jury of what it believes to be an indictable offense.

Relying on this thin reed, the administration proceeded to act. Postmaster General Montgomery Blair ordered that the postmaster in New York exclude from the mails the five newspapers named by the grand jury. The papers of that day were almost entirely dependent upon the mails for their circulation. Gerald Hallock, the part-owner and editor of the *Journal of Commerce*, was obliged to negotiate with the Post Office Department to see what would be required to allow the paper to resume its use of the mails. He was told that he must sell his ownership in the newspaper, which, since he was the principal editorialist, would deprive it of its voice against the war. Hallock reluctantly agreed, and retired.

The *New York News*, owned by Benjamin Wood, brother of New York Mayor Fernando Wood, decided to fight the ban. Benjamin Wood sought to send the paper south and west by private express, and hired newsboys to deliver it locally. The government then ordered U.S. marshals to seize all copies of the *News*, and one newsboy in Connecticut was arrested for having hawked it. Eventually, Wood gave up.

Remarkably, other New York papers did not rally round the sheets that were being suppressed. Instead of crying out about an abridgment of First Amendment rights—as they would surely do today—their rivals simply gloated. James Gordon Bennett's *Herald* was "gratified" to report the death of the *News*, and the *Times* observed that Ben Wood should be thankful he could still "walk the streets."

An equally extreme example of infringement of rights protected by the First Amendment is revealed by the following letter:

Alexandria, February 9, 1862

Honorable W. H. Seward, Secretary of State:

Today the Reverend J. R. Stewart was arrested in the pulpit of St. Paul's Church in Alexandria for omitting the prayer for the President of the United States by your detective here, Mr. Morton. The omission of that prayer occurred in the same church in my presence weeks since. I reported the fact to the headquarters of the [Army of the] Potomac for the information of the government, but did not deem it an act that authorized or called for my interference. . . . May I ask to be put in possession of the government's views in such cases. My own views and object in the performance of duty here has been to win rather than force back the affections and adherence of Southern people to the Constitution and its blessings. This I have and still believe the policy to reinstate the Constitution in all its integrity.

> W. R. Montgomery
> Brigadier General

On October 14, 1861, Lincoln again wrote General Scott, authorizing him to suspend the writ of *habeas corpus* "anywhere between Bangor, Maine, and Washington." There was no record of any serious disturbances in New England which would seem to have justified the considerably longer line of suspension than had been provided for in the proclamation of April 27. Interestingly enough, the original draft of this proclamation has been found in William H. Seward's papers and is written entirely in his hand.[3]

A week after Lincoln's proclamation, Seward ordered the Provost Marshal of Washington, Andrew Porter, to establish a strict military guard over the residence of William J. Merrick, Judge of the Circuit Court of the United States for the District of Columbia.[4] On the same day, Seward advised the Comptroller of the Treasury that until further orders no further salary was to be paid to Judge Merrick. These rather extraordinary measures were based on one of a number of allegations contained in an unsigned letter to General Scott from someone in Cook County, Illinois, to the effect that a letter had been received in Chicago from Merrick stating that Washington would be in the hands of the secessionists by March 4. (This, of course, was October 1861, seven months later.)

The event that precipitated Seward's orders seems to have been Merrick's issuance of a writ of *habeas corpus* at the behest of the father of a seventeen-year-old enlistee in the Union army who later had a change of heart. According to an affidavit filed in his court by Merrick, the father's attorney undertook to serve the writ himself, because there were no deputies available to perform this duty on Saturday afternoon, October 19. When he gave the writ to the marshal to whom it was directed, the Provost Marshal placed him under arrest. When Merrick reached his home that evening, he discovered an armed guard in front of his house; the guard remained there for several days. The judge did not appear at his place on the bench on Monday, October 21, but the two remaining members of the three-judge court ordered an attachment for contempt to issue against the Provost Marshal, returnable the following Saturday.

By that day, the Provost Marshal had made no answer to the writ, but District Attorney C. C. Carrington appeared, representing the deputy marshal who had been entrusted with the serving of the attachment. The deputy marshal stated that he had not served the writ because he had been ordered not to by the President, and that the President had suspended the writ of *habeas corpus* in cases of soldiers in the army. The court took the matter under advisement, and four days later rendered its decision. The judges said that they had had no previous notice of the President's suspension of the writ; therefore, they said, whatever the authority of the President to suspend the writ, it was properly issued in this particular case. But, they continued, they had no physical power to enforce the writ against the President's military subordinates, and therefore nothing could be done by them.

Seward was never a shrinking violet, and in the *Merrick* case he not only assumed control of internal security measures but also encroached on the territory of Secretary of the Treasury Salmon P. Chase. Seward's performance of these functions would last only until February 1862, when they would be transferred to the new Secretary of War, Edwin M. Stanton.

Seward is said to have boasted to the British minister, Lord Lyons: "My Lord, I can touch a bell on my right hand and order the imprisonment of a citizen of Ohio; I can touch a bell again and order the imprisonment of a citizen of New York; and no power on earth, except that of the President, can release them. Can the Queen of England do so much?" But when his performance of this function is compared with the way in which it was conducted after its transfer to Stanton, Seward's role seems less oppressive. Less than nine hundred civilians were arrested during his ten months of responsibility, whereas under Stanton the wartime total would soar to around thirteen thousand. Many arrests during Seward's tenure, moreover, were not made at his personal behest but were ordered by military officers or law-enforcement people in the field. The State Department kept records of these arrests but often did not initiate them. More important, none of the civilians apprehended during Seward's tenure were tried for any offense before a military commission; this procedure came only under Stanton. In a sense, to be sure, detention of an individual without charges is more arbitrary than detention on charges to be tried before a tribunal. But a large majority of those detained without charges, though they were confined in thoroughly unpleasant prisons, were eventually released after a few months' time. Those convicted by a military tribunal often served sentences considerably longer than that.

Those arrested in the border states during the year 1861 generally were incarcerated in Fort Lafayette, a grim, gray bastion located on a small island in the Narrows of New York Harbor. Prisoners were assigned to a casemate (a chamber in which a cannon could be emplaced) with anywhere from ten to forty other unfortunates. They slept on straw mattresses placed on iron beds; the food was bad, and the water contained various small living creatures.

Prisoners with the patrician background characteristic of many secessionists in those states combated this regimen in several ways. They reorganized the groupings within the casemates so that they ended up pretty much together—the better not to sully themselves by too much contact with prisoners from a less fortunate background. They organized their own mess, and for a fee had their food catered from outside the prison.

In later October, some inmates were transferred en masse to Fort Warren, in Boston Harbor. There they found a much less rigorous environment. At Christmas there were roast fowl, oysters, and even eggnog. On Christmas evening there was a mock trial of Seward on charges of having abolished the Constitution and the laws:

> About fifty of the prisoners were present and participated in it; a stuffed figure had been made, representing the culprit, who was seated in the criminal box; a judge was selected, twelve jurymen drawn, the prisoner was assigned counsel, the prosecuting attorney opened the case, and the examination of witnesses went on in due form; speeches were made by counsel

on both sides, and the case given to the jury, who after some deliberation (I fear they were biased) found the prisoner at the bar guilty; the judge, after making the usual preliminary speech on the enormity of his crime and the justness of his condemnation, pronounced the sentence and he was immediately executed. One of the garrison officers was present, and between the trial and a bucket of eggnog on the table in the corner of the room where he stood, seemed to enjoy it very much.[5]

A great stir was created at Fort Warren by the arrival of James Mason and John Slidell as prisoners. Mason and Slidell had been named ministers plenipotentiary to represent the Confederacy in Great Britain and France. They had escaped through the northern naval blockade to Cuba, and there boarded the British mail packet *Trent.* Shortly afterwards, the American naval vessel *San Jacinto* stopped and searched the *Trent* and removed the Confederate envoys. The *Trent* affair loomed for several weeks as a possible casus belli between the United States and Great Britain. Lincoln and Seward finally realized that they must surrender the envoys, and they did so in late December 1861.

While in Fort Warren, Mason and Slidell were treated as virtual celebrities. Accommodations believed to be suitable to their rank were made for them, including enlarged living space and carpeting on the floors. No other prisoners, not even the border state aristocrats, rated this treatment, though they clearly found conditions at Fort Warren preferable to those at Fort Lafayette.

Why did Seward, whose assigned task was the conduct of foreign relations, take on these internal-security responsibilities? One answer is that in Lincoln's Cabinet (as noted earlier) the various Secretaries did not necessarily stick to their formally assigned tasks. Seward, it was thought by many at the beginning of the administration, would effectively become its Prime Minister, with Lincoln pretty much of a figurehead. Seward's memorandum to Lincoln in April 1861 shows that he held precisely that view, even if Lincoln did not. Seward was willing to move into any power vacuum, and internal security after the outbreak of the Civil War was a classic power vacuum. One might have thought these responsibilities more properly belonged to the Secretary of War. But the Secretary, Simon Cameron, was not up to handling even the core functions of his department, newly burdened as it was by the demands of a major war. He had obtained his post as a result of a bargain that Lincoln's managers had struck with the Pennsylvania delegation to the Republican Convention at Chicago, and the President soon had cause to regret the arrangement.

Cameron was born in 1799 in a small village in the Susquehanna Valley of Pennsylvania. After the death of their father he and his five brothers and sisters were left with other townsfolk in Sunbury to be raised. At the age of seventeen he was apprenticed to the publisher of the *Northumberland Gazette*, and from that day he was on his own. He moved to the state capital, Harrisburg, where he rose to the position of assistant editor of the *Harrisburg Republican*. In his early twenties, he bought a part interest in the paper with money borrowed from an uncle. This transaction was the first of many by which he amassed a considerable personal fortune. At about this time he married Margaret Brua, the daughter of a director of a Harrisburg bank. Of the ten children born of this marriage, six grew to maturity.

Cameron entered politics and became a champion of the protective tariff, a measure much sought after by Pennsylvania manufacturers. He was a backer of Andrew Jackson and remained a Democrat until 1856, when he switched to the newly formed Republican party. He became the "boss," first of the Democratic party in Pennsylvania and then of the Republican party. He thus set a precedent in that boss-ridden state that endured well into the twentieth century.

He was twice elected to the United States Senate by the Pennsylvania legislature—once in 1843 as a Democrat, and again in 1857 as a Republican. In each election, another candidate was the odds-on favorite; but in both, Cameron was narrowly elected after a last-minute shift of votes. It was as if he and his opponent were running a footrace; his opponent led him by a long distance, but just before the finish line they entered a dark tunnel. When the two runners emerged, Cameron had miraculously forged ahead of his rival. What had happened in the "tunnel"? His opponents cried fraud, of course.

Cameron was in a sense Pennsylvania's favorite-son candidate at the Republican convention in 1860. But because of the byzantine nature of Pennsylvania politics, the state's delegation was not solidly behind him. Though Cameron had pledged his support to Seward after the first ballot, his managers made a deal with Lincoln's associates to move Pennsylvania into the Lincoln column on the second ballot. Leonard Swett and David Davis, two of Lincoln's managers, promised in turn that Pennsylvania would have a seat in the Cabinet, although Lincoln had told them not to make any binding pledges on his behalf.

After he won the nomination, Lincoln sought desperately to avoid the pledge to Cameron. The Pennsylvanian wanted to be Secretary of the Treasury but ultimately settled for Secretary of War. Lincoln did not finally offer Cameron the position until a few days before the inauguration.

In 1860 the regular army of the United States numbered less than seventeen thousand, of whom a good portion were Southerners. The War Department had eight bureaus and employed a total of about ninety people. Even a very gifted Secretary would have had difficulty making the transition to a war footing. But while Cameron had demonstrated great acumen in private business, somehow it did not translate into the public sector. He was not a good organizer, and kept virtually no records of the various transactions he authorized. He did not profit personally from the many contracts which he let, but a number of his friends did.

On December 1, 1861, the annual report of the Secretary of War was due at the White House, where Lincoln would use it in making his annual report to Congress on the state of the Union. Cameron, departing from the usual monotony of such reports, included in it a recommendation that the government arm former slaves to help quell the rebellion. He had submitted that part of the draft to a fellow Pennsylvanian, Edwin M. Stanton, who read it and suggested alterations that made it even stronger. Then Cameron, kicking over the usual procedural traces, sent copies of his report to strategically selected post offices, with instructions to release them at the same time that Lincoln's address to the Congress was released. Lincoln, however, got word of this devious trick through the printer, and ordered that the report be altered to remove the objectionable sections. If this step was to be taken, he said, it would be taken by him, not by a subordinate.

Thereafter Cameron's days in the Cabinet were clearly numbered. In early January 1862, Lincoln curtly advised him by note that the U.S. ministry in Russia was now open and he would appoint Cameron to it. A face-saving exchange of letters was arranged, and Cameron resigned his War Department post after little more than ten months of service.

On the following day, Lincoln nominated Edwin M. Stanton as Secretary of War.

Stanton was born in Steubenville, Ohio, in 1814. His father died when Stanton was twelve years old, and he then withdrew from school and worked in a local bookstore. He studied in his spare time and in 1831 entered Kenyon College, in Gambier, Ohio. That institution, founded by Salmon P. Chase's uncle, Philander Chase, was but a few years old at the time. After two years at Kenyon, Stanton again ran short of money and dropped out of school. He worked for a short time in Columbus, where he studied law and was admitted to the bar in 1836. In 1839, he returned to Steubenville and formed a partnership with Senator Benjamin Tappan.

In 1836, he had married Mary Lamson, and two children were born of this marriage. Her death in 1844 was a terrible blow to him.

Stanton was successful in his chosen profession from the beginning, and in 1847 he moved to Pittsburgh in search of greater opportunity. He represented the state of Pennsylvania in the *Wheeling Bridge* case, heard twice by the Supreme Court of the United States in the 1850s. The Wheeling and Belmont Bridge Company was building what was then the longest suspension bridge in the world across the Ohio River at Wheeling, in what is now West Virginia, ninety miles downriver from Pittsburgh. The bridge's central span was ninety feet above the low-water mark, not sufficiently high to allow clearance by the tall smokestacks on the large river steamers. The result could have been to cut off the city of Pittsburgh from downriver traffic on the Ohio, traffic essential to that city's commercial prosperity.

The Supreme Court appointed a Special Master to take evidence, and the Master concluded that the bridge obstructed navigation and should be either raised higher above the channel or torn down. The Master was no doubt influenced by Stanton's dramatic gesture in chartering a river steamer and having it run full tilt under the bridge, only to have its eighty-five-foot-high smokestack sheared off by the span. The Supreme Court accepted the Master's findings and ordered that the bridge be raised to a level of 110 feet or torn down.

Pennsylvania's victory was short-lived, however. At the behest of the bridge faction, Congress passed a statute declaring the bridge to be a lawful structure, and the Supreme Court later upheld its authority to do so. Still, this development in no way detracted from the national stature that Stanton achieved as a result of his efforts in this case. He became an attorney for the Erie Railroad Company and represented Senator David Yulee of Florida when the latter's seat in the Senate was challenged.

Stanton first met Lincoln, if that is the proper term for their encounter, in Cincinnati in 1855. He had been retained as cocounsel with two widely known patent lawyers to defend a suit for patent infringement brought by Cyrus McCormick, inventor of the McCormick reaper, against the John H. Manny Company of Rockford, Illinois. The McCormick reaper was a major breakthrough in the field of mechanizing agricultural implements, and the monetary stakes were high. It was originally thought that the case would be tried in Chicago, and since none of Manny's counsel was from Illinois, they decided to retain a local attorney. The lawyer they selected was Abraham Lincoln, who had experience trying cases in the federal court in Chicago. He was paid a retainer of $100.

Ultimately, however, the case was tried in Cincinnati, where Lincoln's familiarity with the Illinois court would be of no use. No further thought was given to him by Manny's counsel. As Stanton and his cocounsel were leaving their hotel in Cincinnati to go to court to try the case, they were accosted by Lincoln, who had come for the trial. Lincoln's effort to join them was rebuffed, and he was not invited to sit at counsel's table during the trial. Stanton regarded the gangling Illinois lawyer as something of a bumpkin, and did not hesitate to show it.

In 1856, Stanton married Ellen Hutchinson of Pittsburgh, and four children were born of this marriage. In the same year, the family moved from Pittsburgh to Washington, D.C. It was from the nation's capital that Stanton witnessed the growing controversy over slavery. He had been a Democrat all his life and did not depart from his allegiance. When even Stephen Douglas broke with the Buchanan administration over the adoption of a constitution for Kansas Territory, Stanton sided with Buchanan, not Douglas.

In 1857, Buchanan named Jeremiah S. Black Attorney General. Stanton had known Black when the latter was Chief Justice of the Supreme Court of Pennsylvania, and Black now offered Stanton the position of Special Counsel to the government in the California land cases. By the Treaty of Guadalupe Hidalgo, which had ended the Mexican War in 1848, the United States had agreed to recognize titles in the territory ceded by Mexico (which included California) if there had been a valid grant from the Mexican government. Claims based on those titles had to be first presented to a commission, but the commission's decision could be appealed to the courts. Soon after his appointment as Attorney General, Black became convinced that the commission had granted recognition to claims based upon fraudulent or forged documents. Stanton's job would be to spearhead the court challenges to these grants.

Ellen Stanton understandably opposed her husband's taking on this assignment because it would mean a long separation. There was no transcontinental railroad at this time, and either of the two ways to get from the east coast to California was long and arduous. One was by steamer all the way south around Cape Horn, and then all the way back north to San Francisco; the second was by steamer to Panama, then by rail across the fever-infested isthmus, and then by steamer north to San Francisco. The amount of work Stanton had to do once he reached California could not be ascertained in advance; but it would undoubtedly take months, if not a year or two.

Stanton eventually accepted Black's offer and sailed for San Francisco by way of the isthmus in February 1858. A month later, his ship passed through the Golden Gate and into the city harbor. He immediately plunged into his work. He found that it would be necessary to reconstruct the land archives during the time of Mexican rule, and set about that daunting task with the help of several assistants. He was nothing if not diligent; he wrote to Black that the California climate was so wonderful that he could "work from 14 to 18 hours a day the month round without flagging."[6] His legal work was successfully concluded in the fall of 1858, but the illness of his son, who had accompanied him, prevented him from returning immediately to the east. He finally got home in February 1859, just a year after he left, and resumed his private practice of law.

Stanton watched the upcoming election of 1860 from the sidelines. He supported Breckenridge, the candidate of the pro-slavery southern wing of the Democratic party, though he himself disapproved of slavery. After Lincoln's election in November, the southern states began to secede, and Buchanan was unable to decide what, if anything, he could or should do about it. Black asked Stanton to review a memorandum on the subject that he had prepared for the President. Stanton, a staunch Unionist, thought secession to be illegal and believed that the government had the authority to suppress it. Buchanan's cabinet was divided between southern and northern sympathizers, and when Black was made Secretary of State, Stanton succeeded him as Attorney General. From this position he labored mightily to keep the President from making major concessions to the seceding states. He was so concerned about Buchanan's course in the last days of his administration that he secretly reported the confidential deliberations of the Cabinet to William Seward, soon to be Lincoln's Secretary of State. These reports, made through an intermediary, exhibited a duplicitous side of Stanton which would surface again when he served in the Cabinet of Andrew Johnson.

With Lincoln's inauguration on March 4, Stanton returned to private life. He had no more confidence in Lincoln than he had had in Buchanan. Seward and Chase pressed Lincoln to appoint Stanton to federal office in recognition of his work in the last days of the Buchanan administration, but no suitable post was available. But this all changed in January 1862, with Cameron's resignation as Secretary of War—a resignation precipitated by the report that Stanton had helped Cameron draft.

Lincoln was anxious to bring a "war" Democrat into his Cabinet—someone identified with the Democratic party who was still in favor of prosecuting the war against the Confederacy. He also wanted someone with sufficient ability and determination to bring order and efficiency to the vastly expanded functions of the War Department.

Stanton proved to be an inspired choice. He brought a high degree of executive ability to his new post, including the internal-security duties that Lincoln would shortly assign to the War Department. The process of apprehending suspect civilians would be made more regular and orderly, although it would also become thereby, in effect, a system of martial law, considerably more dangerous to civil liberties than had been Seward's rather haphazard efforts. In the process of carrying out his duties, Stanton would come first to respect, then to admire, and finally to worship Lincoln.

CHAPTER 5

Burnside and Vallandigham

W ITHIN A MONTH after Stanton took over the War
Department, Lincoln issued his "Executive Order,
No. 1, Relating to Political Prisoners." It recited the
unprecedented nature of the Civil War, the near-paralysis of the government by treason in the first stages of the conflict, the apprehension of the public, and early military reverses suffered by the armed
forces of the North. These factors, Lincoln said, had justified his
resorting to "the extraordinary powers which the Constitution con-
fides to him in cases of insurrection." He explicitly chided the judiciary, stating that it "seemed as if it had been designed not to sustain
the Government but to embarrass and betray it."

But, Lincoln continued, it was clear that the government could
withstand these trials and tribulations, and it could therefore now
proceed on a more normal basis. He directed that all political prisoners still in military custody be released upon taking an oath not to
give aid and comfort to the enemy. The Secretary of War, however,
was given authority to except from the order anyone detained as a spy
or anyone whose release would be "incompatible with the public
safety." This was the first such order signed by Stanton.[1]

Most political prisoners were now released, and for the next six
months "political" arrests declined in number. But in July 1862, Congress enacted the innocuously entitled Militia Act, which authorized
the Secretary of War to draft for nine months members of state mili-

59

tias that had not been upgraded. The following month, Stanton issued an order "by direction of the President," suspending the writ of *habeas corpus* both for draft resisters and for "persons arrested for disloyal practices."[2] For the first time the suspension of the writ was nationwide. Another order, issued the same day, provided that U.S. marshals and local police chiefs were authorized and directed to arrest and imprison "any person or persons who may be engaged, by act, speech, or writing, in discouraging volunteer enlistments, or in any way giving aid and comfort to the enemy, or in any other disloyal practice against the United States." Such persons, the order states, would be tried by a military commission.

In September 1862—ironically, two days after the publication of the Emancipation Proclamation—Lincoln himself issued a proclamation covering much the same ground as Stanton's order of the previous month. The President's proclamation provided that persons "discouraging volunteer enlistments, resisting militia drafts, or guilty of any disloyal practice affording aid and comfort to rebels" should be subject to "martial law and liable to trial and punishment by courts-martial or military commissions. . . ."

Both Stanton's order in August and Lincoln's proclamation in September did far more than merely suspend the writ of *habeas corpus*. The suspension merely prevented judicial inquiry into the cause of a prisoner's detention; the amnesty granted in February 1862 showed that most of these detainees were eventually released after a few months—albeit thoroughly unpleasant months—in prison. Now, however, not only was *habeas corpus* suspended but also, instead of being merely detained, those arrested for a variety of vaguely defined offenses were subject to martial law and to trial, and possible sentencing, by courts-martial or military commissions. Such people faced, in other words, stringent penalties for actions that were often not offenses by normal civilian standards, and faced them, moreover, without the right to jury trial or other procedural protections customarily attending a criminal trial in a civil court. Lincoln's order underwent two court tests—one in Wisconsin and the other in Ohio—and incurred criticism even from some who fully supported the northern war effort.

.   .   .

WISCONSIN WAS THE last of the states to be carved out of the old Northwest Territory. It was admitted to the Union in 1848, and by 1860 its population was nearly eight hundred thousand, half of whom had arrived during the previous decade. The largest city, Milwaukee, had a population of forty-five thousand, and its citizens fancied it as a rival to Chicago as the foremost port on Lake Michigan. Wisconsin's population was concentrated in the southeastern part of the state; the northern half was still an unsettled primeval forest. More than a third of the state's population had been born abroad, and nearly half of that number came from Germany. These immigrants were concentrated in the lakeshore counties and were a remarkably literate group. The 1860 census reported that no fewer than twenty German-language newspapers were published in the state. There were also substantial numbers of immigrants from Scandinavia and Ireland.

Lincoln had carried the state handily in the election of 1860, receiving some eighty-six thousand votes to sixty-five thousand for Douglas. Governor Alexander Randall, elected to a two-year term in 1859, was a Republican who believed that the southern states had no right to secede; but until the attack on Fort Sumter, opinion in the state, as elsewhere in the North, was divided as to what course the Union should pursue. But when Lincoln called for volunteers, the state quickly responded with three regiments, and more would follow.

When Congress enacted the first military draft law in 1862, Wisconsin was assigned a quota of nearly forty-three thousand. Edward Salomon, who had succeeded Randall as governor, distributed this number proportionally to population among the state's counties. The draft, not surprisingly, was unpopular with many of those eligible for it. Opposition centered in those counties that had a substantial number of German-born immigrants. Many of these had little understanding of the long-simmering dispute over the extension of slavery in their adopted country. The majority of them were Democrats and tended to blame the war on "black abolitionists."

There were draft protests and disorder in Milwaukee and Sheboygan. These, however, paled beside the riot that occurred in Port Washington, the county seat of Ozaukee County, located about twenty-five miles north of Milwaukee. Governor Salomon had shrewdly postponed the actual draft until after the election of November 1862. William A. Pors, the draft commissioner for Ozaukee County, had set November 10 as that county's draft date.

> Early that morning a crowd of Germans and Luxembourgers gathered before the steps of the county courthouse. There were shouts of "No Draft." Some said they were opposed to a war to free the slaves. By grumbling and complaining they gave courage to each other. When Pors began the lottery some emboldened rioters pushed forward, protesting and shouting. The mob joined in the protest. A couple of burly fellows seized the draft commissioner and pushed him down the steps of the courthouse. Others pummelled him severely or kicked him. Women rained abuse and blows on him. He lay at the bottom of the steps, bloodied and bruised.
>
> The mob then turned its attention to the machinery of the draft. Mobsters destroyed the box containing the names of those who could be drafted. They seized other enrollment records and started a fire in the street. While the mob was venting its rage against the draft machinery, Commissioner Pors got up and ran for his life. He was chased by women and children. He escaped into the basement of the building which housed the Post Office. There he locked himself in the cellar and listened anxiously to the noise outside.
>
> The mob, meanwhile, sought additional outlets for its anger. Some of the rioters led a portion of the rabble to the "handsome, well-furnished dwelling" which Commissioner Pors called home. They invaded the house, tore clothes to ribbons, spread jams and jellies over the rugs and carpets, and wrecked the furniture. The vengeful mob visited four more homes, all owned by prominent Republicans who had endorsed the draft, and destroyed what they could handle. Sometimes they made bonfires out of furniture and furnishings dragged out of the homes. . . .[3]

Nicholas Kemp, one of the leaders in the riot, was taken to Madison and imprisoned in Camp Randall (the present site of the University of Wisconsin football stadium). His attorney obtained a writ of *habeas corpus* from the Wisconsin Supreme Court; the response of Kemp's military custodian was that the President, by his September proclamation, had suspended *habeas corpus* throughout the country. The Wisconsin Supreme Court—then consisting of three members—was presented with the same question that Chief Justice Taney had been presented in *Merryman*. The Wisconsin court reached the same conclusion as Taney, but gave quite a different impression in doing so. Each of the three justices wrote a separate opinion, which was unusual and showed the importance that they attached to the case. The judges decided that the President did not have the authority by himself to suspend the writ of *habeas corpus* and that martial law could not prevail in areas where there was no insurrection or combat.

The Wisconsin court nonetheless refused to issue an attachment against the military custodian of Nicholas Kemp. In the words of Chief Justice Dixon,

> As the issuing of the attachment at the present time may lead to serious and most unfortunate collisions, which it is possible to avoid by a short delay, I deem it advisable, adhering to the precedent set by other courts and judges under like circumstances, and out of respect to the national authorities, to withhold [the attachment] until they shall have had time to consider what steps they should properly take in the case.[4]

Several months later, in the spring of 1863, Clement Vallandigham was arrested in the middle of the night at his home in Dayton, Ohio, and tried before a military commission in Cincinnati for expressing sympathy with the Confederates. He was charged with violation of General Order No. 38, which had been issued by General Ambrose Burnside, commander of the military district of the Ohio. This district included four states bordering the Ohio River— Ohio, Indiana, Illinois, and Kentucky—and embraced Michigan for geographical convenience.

Burnside was a seasoned combat veteran. He had commanded the Army of the Potomac in one of its worst reverses of the war, and was unlikely to have any tolerance for those who expressed sympathy with the Confederacy. Born in Indiana and educated at West Point, he graduated in 1847 as a lieutenant of artillery but was too late to

fight in the principal campaign of the Mexican War. In 1861 he organized and became the colonel of a Rhode Island regiment. This regiment was one of the first northern units to reach Washington after
Lincoln's call for volunteers, and Burnside made a good impression
on the President. In early 1862 he commanded the successful Union
expedition against the North Carolina coastal forts, and was
rewarded with the rank of major general.

On two separate occasions Lincoln, disappointed with the performance of General George McClellan as commander of the Army of
the Potomac, offered Burnside that command. Both times Burnside
refused it, deeming himself not sufficiently competent. Finally, when
McClellan again disappointed Lincoln by his failure to pursue the
Confederate forces after the battle of Antietam, the President simply
ordered Burnside to assume the command, and Burnside felt he had
no choice but to accept. Instead of pursuing the Confederate army,
he devised a plan to cross the Rappahannock River at Fredericksburg, Virginia, and thence march rapidly on Richmond. The ensuing
battle of Fredericksburg was a staggering defeat for the Union army.
Burnside had delayed crossing the river because the pontoon bridges
necessary for the effort had not yet arrived, and in the interim
the Confederates under Generals James Longstreet and Thomas
"Stonewall" Jackson had entrenched themselves on the heights above
the city. The Union efforts to cross the river were repulsed with
heavy losses. Early in 1863, General Joseph Hooker replaced Burnside as commander of the Army of the Potomac.

In March 1863, Burnside took over command of the Department
of the Ohio. He soon became concerned about disloyal persons
residing within the Union lines who were thought to be giving information and other aid and comfort to the enemy. In April, he issued
his General Order No. 38, which included this language: "The habit
of declaring sympathies with the enemy will no longer be tolerated in
this department. Persons committing such offenses will be at once
arrested with a view to being tried as above stated or sent beyond our
lines and into the lines of their friends."[5]

Clement Vallandigham was born in Ohio in 1820. He read law
and was admitted to the Ohio bar, and in 1845 he became the
youngest member of the state legislature. Only a year later, he was
chosen Speaker of the lower house by his fellow Democrats. Val-

landigham was handsome, vain, and impetuous, a strong believer in Jeffersonian states' rights, and very much opposed to the views of the Abolitionists. He became a member of the national House of Representatives in May 1858, after having successfully contested the official count in the election of 1856. He was a delegate to the Charleston convention of the national Democratic party in 1860, where he supported the candidacy of Douglas. He supported various efforts to compromise the dispute that led to the Civil War and vigorously opposed every military measure taken up by Congress when it convened in July 1861. He was defeated for reelection in 1862, largely because of his insistence that fighting the war was a mistake and that peace must be restored.

In April 1863, Vallandigham left his home in Dayton for Columbus in order to attend the state Democratic convention. He had hoped to receive the nomination for Governor, but was rejected by party leaders. He now apparently decided that he needed to become a martyr to the cause, have himself arrested, and ride a favorable tide of public opinion. On April 30, he spoke to a Democratic rally in Columbus, where he defended the right of people to assemble at any time to hear the policy of the current administration debated. He criticized Burnside's Order No. 38 and denied the government's right to try civilians before military commissions. The *Dayton Daily Empire*, a newspaper that Vallandigham had once owned and that was edited by his handpicked successor, William T. Logan, declared: "Prison bars and bolts have no terrors for a freeman in the conscientious discharge of his duty. Fortified behind the Constitution, he can bid defiance to the impotent threats of usurpers and would-be despots."[6]

The next day, Vallandigham appeared at a Democratic rally in the small county seat of Mount Vernon. Burnside got word of Vallandigham's itinerary, and sent a dozen "observers" to the rally to take notes. Before the rally there was a parade, in which nearly five hundred wagons so jammed the roads that it took two hours for any one vehicle to complete the parade route. After the parade, Vallandigham was the first of three speakers. As he rose to speak, he received thunderous applause from the assembled multitude. He described Burnside's Order No. 38 as a usurpation of arbitrary power. He closed—nearly two hours later, with complete disregard of what must have been the feelings of the other two scheduled speakers—with a plea to citizens who valued their rights to exercise the franchise and hurl "King Lincoln" from his throne.

Vallandigham returned to Dayton, and Burnside was ready with elaborate plans to arrest him. A special train was commandeered, and was scheduled to be ready to leave Cincinnati for Dayton at midnight. Burnside's aide-de-camp, Captain Charles G. Hutton, was put in charge of a company of sixty-seven men to effectuate the arrest. About two hours after midnight on May 5, the special train arrived in Dayton. Hutton's company surrounded Vallandigham's house and after they were refused admittance, broke down the back door. Vallandigham was arrested and hurried off to a military prison near Cincinnati. Burnside later had him transferred to a first-class hotel in Cincinnati.

Burnside convened a military commission and set ten o'clock on the morning of May 6 as the time for the commencement of Vallandigham's trial. (Recall, he was arrested early in the morning on May 5.) When the trial began, the defendant protested to the presiding officer, Brigadier General Robert B. Potter, that the military commission had no authority to try him, a civilian. The Judge Advocate then proceeded to read to Vallandigham the charge against him: "publicly expressing, in violation of 'General Order No. 38 . . .' sympathies for those in arms against the Government of the United States, declaring disloyal sentiments and opinions, with the object and purpose of weakening the power of the Government in its effort to suppress the unlawful rebellion." The specification was that he had declared that "the present war is a wicked, cruel and unnecessary war, one not waged for the preservation of the Union, but for the purpose of crushing our liberty and to erect a despotism. A war for the freedom of the blacks and enslavement of the whites." The defendant refused to enter a plea, and so a plea of "not guilty" was entered for him.

Two of the "observers" whom Burnside had sent to Mount Vernon testified as to what Vallandigham had said in his speech there. Congressman S. S. Cox from Columbus spoke in Vallandigham's defense, saying he had not counseled resistance to the laws in his Mount Vernon address. At 5 p.m. on May 7, after hearing Vallandigham make a statement in his own behalf, the members of the court retired to deliberate.

The commission returned the verdict of guilty of the charge and of all but one of the specifications; it was unlikely that they would have done otherwise, since they were all Burnside's subordinates. After debating several penalties, the commission sentenced Vallandigham to imprisonment for the duration of the war.

Two days after the military commission's verdict and sentence, Vallandigham's attorney, George Pugh, sought a writ of *habeas corpus* for him in the United States District Court for the Southern District of Ohio. Pugh argued to Judge Humphrey H. Leavitt that *habeas corpus* had not been suspended in Ohio; the lawyer for the government argued to the contrary. The judge took the case under advisement, and a short time later ruled in favor of the government.

Back in Washington, Lincoln and Stanton knew only what they read in the newspapers of the Vallandigham affair, since Burnside had not immediately reported his actions to them. The President had inquired whether the newspaper stories about Vallandigham's arrest were correct, but had received a vague response. Stanton prepared an order suspending the writ of *habeas corpus* in Vallandigham's case, but Lincoln never signed it. Seward and Chase—the latter with considerable authority, since he was an Ohioan—warned that such a particularized measure would lose more support in the state than it would gain.

The Cabinet took up the Vallandigham case at its meeting on May 19, 1863. Most members seemed to agree with the assessment of Secretary of the Navy Gideon Welles that Burnside's summary action had been a mistake. But now that it had taken place, there was no way to back down. After this discussion, Lincoln changed Vallandigham's sentence from imprisonment for the duration of the war to banishment "beyond the Union lines" into the Confederacy. Over Burnside's protest, the sentence was carried out and the prisoner was turned over to General William Rosecrans, with instructions to deliver him to the Confederates in Tennessee.

Vallandigham sought to have the decision reviewed in the United States Supreme Court, but was unsuccessful; in February 1864, the Court held that it had no jurisdiction to review the decision of the military commission.[7] Meanwhile, Vallandigham escaped from the Confederate States by running the Union blockade to Bermuda, sailing from there to Halifax, Nova Scotia, and finally settling in Windsor, Ontario, across the Detroit River from Detroit.

In July 1863, the Peace Democrats of Ohio nominated Vallandigham as their candidate for Governor, even though he remained in Canada. He polled a substantial vote but was defeated by John Brough, who ran on a fusion ticket with endorsement by both the War Democrats and the Republicans. In June 1864, Vallandigham reappeared in the United States and spoke at several political meetings in Ohio. He was ignored by the government, and continued sporadic political activity until his death in 1871.

Vallandigham was not only tried by a military commission, rather than a jury, but the charge upon which he was tried was that he violated an order issued by Burnside—an order that forbade the expression of sympathy for the enemy. A criminal trial in a civil court must be based on a charge that the defendant engaged in conduct prohibited by an Act of Congress (in a federal court), or by an act of a state legislature (in a state court). Burnside's order had no such pedigree; it was not even based on an order of the President or the Secretary of War. It originated with Ambrose Burnside, the commanding general of the military district of Ohio. Members of the armed forces are naturally accustomed to being governed by such orders. But Vallandigham was not a soldier; he was a civilian.

The justification for convicting Vallandigham was Lincoln's proclamation of September 1862, invoking martial law. But what is martial law? Much has been written both before and after this time in an effort to describe this regime, but in fact the nation had only limited exposure to it between the close of the Revolutionary War and the Civil War.

The first instance occurred in the last stage of the War of 1812, when General Andrew Jackson commanded the military district headquartered in New Orleans. Jackson had fought the British at Pensacola and Mobile and arrived in New Orleans to take command on December 1, 1814. Two weeks later, British forces landed and captured all of the American gunboats on Lake Borgne, thus giving them access to New Orleans by way of Lake Pontchartrain. On December 16, Jackson proclaimed martial law throughout the city and imposed drastic restrictions on any movements in or out of it. In the Battle of New Orleans on January 8, 1815, he defeated the British troops under the command of Lieutenant General Sir Edward Pakenham. Ironically, the Treaty of Ghent, which concluded the War of 1812 (or so the ministers plenipotentiary of both the United States and Great Britain thought), had been signed more than two weeks earlier on December 24, 1814.

But news of the treaty did not reach New Orleans in time to preclude the one great American victory of the war. Not knowing what disposition the British would make of their defeated army, Jackson continued to maintain martial law after he had successfully defended New Orleans. The treaty's existence did not become known on the east coast until the middle of February, and rumors of it filtered into New Orleans shortly afterwards. But Jackson was determined to maintain martial law until he was officially advised that a treaty had concluded hostilities. Indeed, he sought to muzzle newspapers from circulating accounts of such a pact before the "official" news was received.

During this period, an anonymous article appeared in the French-language press of New Orleans saying that:

> It is high time the laws should resume their dominion; that the citizens of this state should return to the full enjoyment of their rights; that, in acknowledging that we are indebted to General Jackson for the preservation of our city and the defeat of the British, we do not feel much inclined, through gratitude, to sacrifice any of our privileges, less than any other, that of expressing our opinion of the acts of Jackson and his administration.[8]

Jackson forced the editor of the paper to reveal the name of the writer, and the latter was arrested for inciting mutiny and disaffection among the troops. The author, Louis Louailler, obtained a writ of *habeas corpus* from the New Orleans federal district judge, Dominick Agustin Hall. Hall issued a writ, returnable before him the next day at 11 o'clock. But Jackson, instead of responding to the writ, ordered Hall himself to be arrested and locked up in the same prison as Louailler. Louailler was acquitted by the military court set up to try him, quite surprisingly on the basis that he was not in the armed forces and therefore could not be tried before such a body. But Jackson disregarded the court's decision and kept Louailler in prison. Judge Hall, on the other hand, was escorted several miles out of the city of New Orleans by a detachment of troops and set free.

On the following day—March 13, 1815—the long-awaited official announcement of the ratification of the Treaty of Ghent arrived from Washington, and Jackson unhesitatingly revoked his proclamation of martial law. Louailler was released, Hall returned to the city, and celebration ensued. But now it was Judge Hall's turn, and on March 21 he issued an order to show cause why Jackson should not be held in contempt of court for refusing to respond to the writ of *habeas corpus* he had earlier issued on behalf of Louailler. This time Jackson obeyed the court's order, and on Friday, March 24, appeared before Hall with an aide and two attorneys. The court heard argument of counsel, granted a continuance for one week, and then found the general in contempt. He was fined $1,000, an action that the judge took reluctantly in view of the general's services to his country. Jackson paid the fine as ordered, but thirty years later, when he lay mortally ill, Congress voted to remit the fine to him.

The second instance in which martial law was invoked before the Civil War arose as a result of Dorr's Rebellion in Rhode Island in 1842. Rhode Island was a peculiar state in more ways than one. It was the last of the original thirteen states to ratify the Constitution, doing so only in 1791, after the new national government was a going concern. And, unlike almost every other of the original thirteen, Rhode Island never enacted a constitution upon obtaining its separation from Great Britain. It retained as its organic act the charter issued to the colony by King Charles II in 1663. This charter allowed only those who owned land to vote, and although the legislature could alter that requirement, it chose not to do so. Understandably, considering the fact that the charter had been issued by one of England's Stuart kings, there was no method provided for its amendment by any sort of popular vote or convention.

During the Jacksonian era and even before, most states extended their franchise to allow all male residents of age to vote, and there was public demand for such a change in Rhode Island. But the legislature turned a deaf ear to such requests. Finally, a large group of citizens took matters into their own hands and by a series of local meetings elected delegates to a state convention, which produced a new constitution. That document extended the franchise to all male residents of the state who had resided there for one year. The constitution was submitted to a vote of the people, and a majority of those voting ratified it.

But none of this activity had been approved or authorized by the sitting legislature, representing the charter government. When a government was formed under the new constitution, Thomas Dorr was elected Governor, and other officers were likewise selected. The charter government declared the new government illegal, and Dorr and his followers decided to resort to arms to uphold their claim to govern. The charter government called out the militia to repel Dorr's forces and declared a state of martial law. Dorr's men were repelled by the state militia when they made an effort to seize the state arsenal, and they were finally dispersed by the militia in June 1842.

In the course of the rebellion, the home of a man named Martin Luther was broken into without a warrant, and he sued Luther Borden, who had been in charge of the offending group. Borden defended this action for trespass on the grounds that Luther was suspected of aiding the rebels and that under the existing state of martial law the break-in was justified.

This suit began in the federal court in Providence but ended up in the United States Supreme Court in 1849. In an opinion by Chief Justice Taney, the Court held that the break-in did not violate the United States Constitution. It was argued that a military government violated Article IV, Section 4 of the Constitution, which provides that the United States shall guarantee to every state in the Union a republican form of government. Taney's response to this argument was:

> Unquestionably a military government, established as the permanent government of the state, would not be a Republican government, and it would be the duty of Congress to overthrow it. But the law of Rhode Island evidently contemplated no such government. It was intended merely for the crisis, and to meet the peril in which the existing government was placed by the armed resistance to its authority. It was so understood

and construed by the State authorities. And, unquestionably, a state may use its military power to put down an armed insurrection, too strong to be controlled by the civil authority. . . . [I]n that state of things the officers engaged in its military service might lawfully arrest anyone, who, from the information before them, they had reasonable ground to believe was engaged in the insurrection; and might order a house to be forcibly entered and searched, when there were reasonable grounds for supposing he might be there concealed.[9]

The Court was not unanimous in upholding the actions of the charter government of Rhode Island, however. Justice Levi Woodbury vehemently protested that part of the Court's opinion upholding the regime of martial law in Rhode Island:

[In Rhode Island, martial law] exposed the whole population, not only to be seized without warrant or oath, and their houses broken open and rifled, and this where the municipal law and its officers and courts remained undisturbed and able to punish all offences, but to send prisoners, thus summarily arrested in a civil strife, to all the harsh pains and penalties of courts-martial or extraordinary commissions, and for all kinds of supposed offences. By it, every citizen, instead of reposing under the shield of known and fixed laws as to his liberty, property, and life, exists with a rope around his neck, subject to be hung up by a military despot at the next lamp-post, under the sentence of some drum-head court-martial.[10]

The administration's treatment of Clement Vallandigham became a cause célèbre with the Peace Democrats, who viewed it as one more step in the direction of a military dictatorship. But War Democrats too—and some Republican editors—were disturbed by the outcome of the Vallandigham case. A mass meeting was held in Albany, New York, presided over by Erastus Corning, the president of the New York Central Railroad. The attendees denounced the arrest and trial of Vallandigham as a violation of his constitutional rights, and a copy of the letter was sent to the President. Lincoln carefully prepared his response and read it to the assembled members of his Cabinet, who approved it. He then sent it to Corning, with a copy to Horace Greeley's *New York Tribune*. Lincoln agreed that in normal times Vallandigham should not have been tried by a military commission, but pointed out that the country was then in the throes of a rebellion. Even though the rebels had not come anywhere near Dayton, Ohio, where Vallandigham was arrested, he had been charged with undermining the effectiveness of the draft upon which army manpower to suppress the rebellion depended. Lincoln went on to employ what are now the most familiar words from that letter: "Must I shoot a simple-minded soldier boy who deserts while I must not touch a hair of a wily agitator who induces him to desert?"

Lincoln's defense of his actions, as might be expected, was addressed to the general public, and not to constitutional lawyers. It was an able defense, made in a difficult case. The argument for detaining someone like John Merryman, who had helped to burn the railroad bridges that would bring troops through Baltimore to Washington, was much stronger than that for arresting and trying Vallandigham, who had simply expressed views strongly critical of the administration.

Another pre–Civil War consideration of martial law occurred in 1857, when the opinion of the United States Attorney General was sought with respect to the action of the Governor of Washington Territory in proclaiming martial law in order to detain persons who had been arrested on a charge of treasonable intercourse with hostile Indians. Caleb Cushing, who was Franklin Pierce's Attorney General, issued a very learned discussion of authorities from ancient law and English and Continental experts, but concluded that "we are without law on the subject." He was apparently unaware of the Supreme Court's decision in *Luther v. Borden*, decided only eight years earlier. Cushing took the view that the "proclamation" of martial law was simply a recognition of the existing fact that the civil authority is no longer able to effectively function and has been superseded by military power.

Whatever the theory of martial law might be, its consequences at New Orleans in 1815, in Rhode Island in 1842, and in Ohio and Wisconsin during the Civil War were quite apparent. Statements critical of the government, whether appearing in the press or made in the course of political oratory, were punished by fine and imprisonment. Homes of suspects could be broken into without warrants. And none of this was in accordance with laws enacted by any legislature or city council. Martial law was the voice of whichever general was in command.

CHAPTER 6

Copperheads in the Heartland

THE INDIANAPOLIS TREASON trials, out of which the Supreme Court case of *Ex Parte Milligan* arose, took place in Indiana's capital city in the fall of 1864. The defendants were charged with a conspiracy against the United States government, including a plan for an armed uprising to seize Union munitions, free Confederate prisoners of war in Illinois, and abduct the staunchly Republican Governor of Indiana. With the benefit of hindsight, such charges, if proven, would have made the defendants seem fatuous indeed. Before another year had elapsed, the Confederate forces would have surrendered to the victorious Union armies. Why would any rational plotters in the summer of 1864 have thought such a plan would be successful? This sort of conspiracy would have seemed more believable in the dark days before the Union victories at Gettysburg and Vicksburg in the summer of 1863. And its site would have appeared more logical in one of the border states than in Indiana or Illinois, which Lincoln had carried handily in 1860.

But the timing of the plot was not as perverse when viewed from the perspective of the summer of 1864. This was a presidential election year, and Lincoln, although renominated for the presidency on a "Union" ticket, was viewed even by many Republicans with mixed feelings. The Emancipation Proclamation, which converted the war to preserve the Union into a war to abolish slavery as well, was not popular in the states of the old Northwest. At the same time, Lincoln's announced policy of liberal terms for readmission of seceded states to the Union alienated the radical wing of the Republican party. That wing not only desired slavery abolished but also wanted the seceded states to be treated like "conquered provinces" when the war was over.

By now it was apparent that the South could not win the war. But many Northerners questioned nevertheless whether the costs in human lives and money that the North would be paying for victory were worth the price. General Ulysses S. Grant had engaged General Robert E. Lee in a series of bloody battles near Richmond, essentially fighting to a draw with shockingly high casualties on both sides. General William T. Sherman, commanding Union troops laying siege to Atlanta, appeared to be stalled in his effort to capture that vital railhead. A spirit of war-weariness settled over much of the North in the summer of 1864.

This weariness manifested itself in different ways. Horace Greeley had written Lincoln in July 1864, urging him to make peace overtures to the South. He told the President that "our bleeding, bankrupt almost dying country . . . longs for peace . . . shudders at the prospect of fresh conscriptions, of further wholesale devastations, and of new rivers of human blood."[1]

Greeley was not just another newspaper editor. Since the founding of the Republican party in the Midwest in 1854, he had been the party's principal editorial voice. Greeley's first job was as a typesetter for a New York City printshop, where by working up to fourteen hours a day he was able to earn six dollars a week. Four years later, he started a weekly newspaper, and in 1840 he began publishing the *New York Tribune*. It was a daily paper and sold for a penny. After a slow start, the paper had in ten years bested all of its established rivals and boasted a circulation of fifty thousand.

Angered by congressional passage of the Kansas-Nebraska Act in 1854, which repealed the Missouri Compromise of 1820, Greeley urged the formation of a "Republican" party. Groups in Wisconsin and Michigan soon obliged, and a new political party was born. Its adherents were united in their opposition to the extension of slavery into the territories, but by little else. Thus the editorial voice of the *Tribune* had an influential role in the development of the new party. By the time of the Republican convention that nominated Lincoln in

1860, the paper had a circulation in the hundreds of thousands; it was read not just by New Yorkers, not just by Easterners, but by thousands who subscribed by mail from as far away as Oregon and California.

Greeley was a master political publicist, as well as an inveterate political intriguer. He had fallen out with Seward in the 1850s, and attended the 1860 convention to make sure that his fellow New Yorker did not get the nomination. After Lincoln was elected with Greeley's enthusiastic support, the publisher showered the President with advice. But Greeley was volatile and fickle, swinging wildly between urging that the southern states be allowed to go in peace and, after Fort Sumter, carrying a daily banner on the paper urging "On To Richmond." He was not satisfied with Lincoln's performance as President, and when, in his letter of July 1864, he spoke of the nation's desire for peace, he was speaking as the editor of the principal organ of the Republican party.

Henry J. Raymond, editor of the *New York Times*, chimed in with a similarly gloomy assessment a month later. "The tide is setting strongly against us," Raymond wrote to Lincoln on August 22, adding that "nothing but the most resolute and decided action on the part of the Government and its friends can save the country from falling into hostile hands."[2] Lincoln himself now joined in this dreary assessment. On August 23, he prepared and signed a memorandum:

> This morning, as for some days past, it seems extremely probable that this administration will not be re-elected. Then it will be my duty to so co-operate with the President-elect, as to save the Union between the election and the inauguration; as he will have secured his election on such ground that he cannot possibly save it afterwards.[3]

Lincoln sealed the memorandum in such a way as to make its contents invisible, and at the next Cabinet meeting asked each member to sign his name on the back of the document. He later said that he had planned to show it to General George McClellan, the Democratic presidential candidate in 1864, if McClellan had won the election.

The war-weariness, then, was recognized by the President himself in the summer of 1864. Nor was it unusual that this sentiment would be more prevalent in Indiana than in other states of the North. Indiana was the second of the territories making up the old Northwest Territory to be admitted to statehood; Ohio had been the first, in 1802, and Indiana followed in 1811. Illinois was admitted in 1819.

A look at how these states were settled will show the population mixture that gave Illinois, Ohio, and Indiana their volatile status during the Civil War. Glancing at a map of these three states today, one might assume that their northern portions were settled first. It is here that the principal east–west highways and railroad routes run. But in fact, the states were largely settled from their southern borders by immigrants coming down the Ohio River, the southern boundary of each of them. Cincinnati was an important commercial center long before Cleveland was. Centrally located Indianapolis was but the third capital of Indiana. The first was Vincennes, located in the southwestern part of the state, and the second was Corydon, in the southeast, directly across the Ohio River from Louisville, Kentucky.

The ancestors of the Indianans were German and Scotch-Irish immigrants who settled in the Cumberland Valley of Pennsylvania and the Shenandoah Valley of Virginia after having made their way west from the Atlantic ports. Their way of life depended on farming, hunting, and fishing, and they were used to having their cabins near streams with timber readily available.

The Midwest to which they emigrated had been scoured by glaciers, which carried with them precious topsoil. The northern portions of Indiana, Illinois, and Ohio, as a result, were extraordinarily fertile and suitable for agriculture. But the glaciers had penetrated only sporadically into the southern belt of the region, and these parts were markedly less fertile, less suitable for farming.

In the first part of the nineteenth century, the principal avenue by which farmers in most of the Midwest got their products to market was the Mississippi River and its tributaries, such as the Ohio, Illinois, and Wisconsin rivers. Steamboats and flatboats journeyed down the Mississippi to New Orleans, and the agricultural products of the Midwest were transshipped on oceangoing vessels bound for east coast or foreign ports. Thus, the commercial ties of Ohio, Indiana, and Illinois were at first almost entirely with the South.

The northern water route whereby agricultural products might be shipped was, of course, the Great Lakes. But Niagara Falls blocked access from Lake Erie to Lake Ontario, and the St. Lawrence River through which the Great Lakes emptied into the Atlantic Ocean belonged to England, not to the United States. This situation was dramatically altered in 1825, with the completion of the Erie Canal, which joined the Mohawk and Hudson rivers to Lake Erie above Niagara Falls. Other canals were built to overcome the lack of navigable rivers to bring the agricultural products raised by the farmers to the shores of the Great Lakes, and the northern water route began to compete with the Mississippi Valley route as a way for midwestern farmers to send their products to market.

Beginning about 1850, the railroads, which had first started along the east coast twenty years earlier, had reached over the Appalachian Mountains and headed for the midwestern terminus of Chicago. With the settlement of the upper Midwest, it became virtually inescapable that Chicago would be a great railroad center. The three-hundred-mile water barrier created by Lake Michigan between these states and those farther east meant that Chicago, at the foot of Lake Michigan, would have unique advantages as a transportation hub. In 1850, there were no railroad tracks in Chicago; five years later there were twenty-two hundred miles of track coming into the city and a hundred trains departing and arriving each day. Thus, farmers in the upper Midwest, including the northern portions of Illinois, Indiana, and Ohio, now had an alternate method by which to ship their products to eastern markets.

Conforming to the improvement of transportation routes to the Northeast, the previously small stream of settlement from that portion of the country into the Midwest sharply increased. Farmers who toiled in the shallow, rocky soil of New England soon realized that they were at a distinct disadvantage in competition with those who had emigrated to the Midwest and farmed the fertile loam found there. The same was true to a lesser extent in upstate New York; it was not uncommon for a family to move from New England to upstate New York, from upstate New York to Michigan, and from Michigan on to Wisconsin or Minnesota. Added to this stream of Americans going west were the immigrants coming from Germany and Ireland in the middle years of the century. Many of the Germans were skilled laborers, while most of the Irish worked on construction projects. The Germans and the Irish tended to settle in the northern parts of Ohio, Indiana, and Illinois, and in the upper midwestern states.

The result of these migrations was that the southern portions of Ohio, Indiana, and Illinois had been settled by immigrants from the upland South, while the northern portions were populated by immigrants from the Northeast and from Germany, Ireland, and Scandinavia. Indiana, as of the middle of the nineteenth century, had a larger southern-born population, both as a percentage of the whole and in absolute terms, than any of the other states carved out of the Northwest Territory. These factors of climate, emigrant population, and trading practices made Indiana a volatile mixture of wartime sympathies and a logical place for the events leading up to the Indianapolis treason trials.

IN THE ELECTION of 1856, John C. Frémont, the first Republican candidate for President, lost to his Democratic rival, James Buchanan. Buchanan carried both Indiana and Illinois. In 1860, Lincoln won those states, along with every other state in the Midwest. Stephen A. Douglas's strength was concentrated in the southern parts of Indiana and Illinois.

Opinion in Indiana, just as elsewhere in the Midwest, was divided as to how the North should deal with the secession of the southern states. But when, after the firing on Fort Sumter, Lincoln called for volunteers to put down the rebellion, Indiana responded enthusiastically and sent more than its share of soldiers to fight for the Union. Many of the Indiana regiments participated in the major battles of the first part of the Civil War.

The war did not go well for the Union during this time. Union forces had been routed at the first Battle of Manassas in the summer of 1861. General George McClellan, appointed commander-in-chief of the Army of the Potomac, successfully reorganized the dispirited troops but was reluctant to deploy his army in battle.

The Peninsular Campaign which McClellan finally undertook in the spring of 1862 was a failure. He moved his army by water to the lower end of the peninsula between the James and York rivers below Richmond and successfully marched to within a few miles of the Confederate capital. But he was driven back by the Confederates and

President Abraham Lincoln, 1863

Left: Chief Justice Roger Taney rebuked Lincoln for
suspending the writ of *habeas corpus.*
Right: William Henry Seward, Lincoln's Secretary
of State, spearheaded the government's internal-security
program for the first year of the Civil War

Secretary of War
Edwin M. Stanton
arrested and detained
some 13,000 civilians
between 1862 and
1865

General Ambrose Burnside issued General Order No. 38 directing the arrest of anyone who publicly expressed sympathy with the Confederacy

David Davis, appointed to the Supreme Court by Lincoln in 1862, wrote the majority opinion in the *Milligan* case

John Wilkes Booth assassinated Lincoln at Ford's Theater in April 1865

Mary Surratt was found guilty of conspiracy in Lincoln's assassination and hanged on July 7, 1865

Thomas Woodrow Wilson, President of the United States during World War I

Justice Oliver Wendell Holmes wrote the Supreme Court's unanimous opinion holding that anyone counseling draft evasion could be criminally punished

Judge Learned Hand's ruling that World War I draft resisters' cartoons were not in violation of the Espionage Act was reversed by the Court of Appeals

Franklin Delano Roosevelt, President of the United States during World War II, authorized the evacuation of more than 100,000 persons of Japanese origin from strategic areas on America's west coast

Henry L. Stimson, Secretary of War during World War II, recommended that the President approve the Japanese evacuation

Chief Justice Harlan F. Stone wrote the Court's opinion in the *Hirabayashi* and *Masui* cases of 1943

Associate Justice Hugo Lafayette Black wrote
the opinion in the *Korematsu* case that upheld the
forced relocation of the Japanese

Lieutenant General
Robert Richardson,
Commander of the
Military Department
of Hawaii, ordered the
detention without
charges of two
naturalized Germans,
Glockner and Seifert

Judge Delbert Metzger, United States district court judge
in Hawaii, ordered General Richardson held in contempt
for his failure to free Glockner and Seifert

ultimately evacuated his troops by water. On the heels of this defeat came the second Battle of Manassas in August 1862, another Union defeat. A month later the Battle of Antietam in western Maryland left the Union forces in possession of the battlefield, but McClellan's failure to follow Lee back across the Potomac pretty much deprived the Union forces of any of the fruits of victory. The Union's fortunes of war in the East were at a low ebb in the fall of 1862.

Northern troops had had more success in the West. General Ulysses S. Grant led an army to capture Forts Henry and Donelson, and his arrival at the Battle of Shiloh saved the Union from a major defeat. But after Shiloh, the Union forces proceeded very slowly toward the Confederate fortress of Vicksburg on the Mississippi River.

It was immediately after Antietam that Lincoln issued his Emancipation Proclamation, in which he declared that all slaves in Confederate territory were to be free as of January 1, 1863. He had drafted the proclamation and presented it to his Cabinet during the summer, but had decided to await a Union victory before issuing it. Critics pointed out that it attempted to free slaves only in Confederate territory, where it could not yet be enforced, but liberated none of the slaves in the border states, where it might have been enforced. But the proclamation played a part in dissuading England and France from recognizing the Confederacy; particularly in England, it helped to swing the support of many working-class people to the North.

The proclamation produced a negative reaction, however, in midwestern states such as Indiana. Coming after the first draft law enacted by Congress during the summer of 1862, it helped to turn sentiment against Washington. Indiana descendants of immigrants from the upland South disapproved of slavery, but they also disliked blacks—partly from differences in race and in education, partly from fear of economic competition from freed blacks. They were willing to fight a war to preserve the Union, but not a war to free the slaves.

Adding fuel to this discontent was an economic depression that swept the Midwest at this time. Manufacturers in eastern cities were cashing in on the business of supplying the ever-increasing needs of the government for military supplies, but their prosperity was not shared by the largely agricultural Midwest. The Confederacy still controlled the lower Mississippi valley, and so this customary route for shipment of their products to market was cut off. The alternate route by rail to the east coast was more costly, and the farmers felt they were gouged by excessive freight rates charged by the railroads.

There was also discontent with the arbitrary arrests made by the administration, under the auspices first of Seward, then of Stanton. The result was a series of dramatic Democratic gains throughout the Midwest in the 1862 elections. In Indiana, Democrats obtained control of both houses of the legislature and succeeded in electing eight of the state's eleven members of Congress. Governor Oliver Perry Morton, who had been elected in 1860 to a four-year term, remained in office, but for the next two years he waged an extraordinary battle with the Democratic legislature. When the legislature refused to appropriate funds he regarded as necessary to support the war effort, Morton borrowed from private sources on his own account. Stanton found hundreds of thousands of dollars in War Department funds that he lent to the Governor. When the state supreme court declared this practice illegal in the absence of any legislative approval, Morton ignored the decision and went on doing what he felt was necessary to sustain the state government in its war effort. In Indiana, as well as in other parts of the Midwest, 1863 and 1864 were characterized by rabid political partisanship on both sides.

During this time, various secret societies were organized in parts of the Midwest. Some, such as the Loyal League and the Union League societies, were politically Republican and supported the national administration. Others were politically Democratic and hostile in varying degrees to the government. Historians disagree about the number of people involved in these societies, the scope of their activities, and the extent to which those aligned with the Democrats posed a realistic threat to the northern war effort.

In the mid-1850s, under the leadership of George W. L. Bickley of Cincinnati, the Knights of the Golden Circle were formed. At the beginning the group's purpose was to "colonize" Mexico, then revolt against the lawful government and make Mexico a slaveholding territory allied with the South. Its membership was almost entirely southern, both geographically and in regional loyalties. After the outbreak of the Civil War, the organization loosely expanded, becoming in some places an umbrella for small local groups. When some of the activities of the Knights came to public knowledge in 1863, it was thought desirable to change the name and some of its aspects. First, under the leadership of Phineas C. Wright, editor of the *New York News*, Easterners formed the Order of American Knights. The following year, further exposés required another name change, and this time the organization chose to call itself the Sons of Liberty. Clement L. Vallandigham, still then in Canada, became the supreme commander of this organization.

Some members thought it desirable that the Midwest—at that time referred to as the "Northwest"—should, like the southern states, separate from the Union and form its own confederacy. That confederacy could then ally with the seceded southern states against the remainder of the Union. High officials of the Confederate government sent agents with money to pay certain designated ringleaders to stir up trouble and possibly foment an uprising.

Many of these organizations were infiltrated by informers for the federal government, who reported back about their various activities. The Democratic National Convention was scheduled to meet in Chicago in the latter part of August 1864. A number of Confederate officers and agents, and members of the Sons of Liberty, planned to be in the city at that time, and vague plans were made to stage an uprising and free the eight thousand Confederate prisoners at nearby Camp Douglas. But a week before the convention, Governor Morton discovered evidence of arms shipments to Indiana members of the organization. The office of Harrison H. Dodd, its grand commander in Indiana, was searched. A cache of arms and incriminating correspondence were found. The planned uprising in Chicago was aborted.

Dodd, together with William Bowles, Lambdin P. Milligan, Stephen Horsey, Andrew Humphreys, Horace Heffren, and J. J. Bingham, was arrested by soldiers on orders from the commanding general of the District of Indiana, Henry Carrington. Although Carrington favored trying the defendants in the civil courts, Morton and Stanton resorted to the more expeditious mode of a military tribunal. On September 17, 1864, Dodd was brought to trial before a military commission sitting in Indianapolis. Dodd had obtained permission to be confined in the federal Post Office building in Indianapolis, rather than in the regular military prison, during his trial. But before the proceeding was completed, Dodd let himself down from an upper window and escaped to Canada. He was found guilty as charged by the military commission and sentenced to death.

J. J. Bingham, editor of the *Indianapolis Sentinel*, was released from prison, but the other five men arrested in September were brought to trial before the military commission in October. They were arraigned, as was customary in the case of military commissions, on general charges, followed in each case by more detailed specifications. The first charge was entitled "Conspiracy Against the Government of the United States," and the specifications recited the various hostile activities of the five defendants. The second was "Affording Aid and Comfort to Rebels Against the Authority of the United States." The third charge was "Inciting Insurrection," with two specifications dealing with efforts to induce persons to revolt against the authority of the United States and to cooperate with the armed enemies of the United States. The fourth was entitled "Disloyal Practices," and the fifth, and final, charge was entitled "Violation of the Laws of War."

At this point it may be well to step back a moment and compare the charges made against the defendants in this case with what would be found in a normal indictment or information used to bring a defendant to trial in a civil court. Today, it is the practice in all federal courts and in virtually all state courts for the charging instrument in a criminal prosecution—whether it be an indictment returned by a grand jury, or an information filed by the prosecuting attorney—to state not only the acts with which the defendant is charged but also the particular criminal laws which that conduct is said to violate. This practice is required by the Rules of Criminal Procedure which govern criminal proceedings in federal courts, and one of the grounds on which a defendant may move to have an indictment dismissed is that it "fails to charge an offense"—that is, even if the conduct alleged in the indictment is proved, that conduct does not violate any applicable criminal statute. If, for example, a defendant were charged with homicide, but the indictment alleged only that he attacked and beat the victim, a court would dismiss the charge of homicide because the death of the victim is a necessary element of that crime.

A criminal defendant in a civilian court, then, is never at any loss to know not only the criminal acts with which he is charged but also the exact laws that make those acts a crime. And these laws not only specify the *elements* of the crime—e.g., the classical common-law definition of murder as the unlawful killing of another human being with malice aforethought—but also the *punishment* to be imposed should the defendant be found guilty of the crime. In the federal courts, and in most state courts, the sentence is imposed by the judge, rather than by the jury, but the judge is bound to sentence within the limits set forth in the statute.

In England, whence the United States derived its legal system, the decision as to what acts are crimes came originally from the courts, rather than from Parliament. Parliament could and did change or add to the criminal law developed by the various English courts which administered it, but a prosecution did not have to be based on a law enacted by Parliament.

After the federal government was created by the Constitution in 1789, the question arose as to whether such common-law crimes could be prosecuted in federal courts without any act of Congress expressly making them a crime. The answer to the question remained in doubt until the decision of the Supreme Court in *United States v. Hudson*.[4] The answer that the Court gave to the question was in the negative, saying "the legislative authority of the Union must first make an act a crime, affix a punishment to it and declare the court that shall have jurisdiction of the offense," before such a crime might be prosecuted in federal court.

If we now turn back to the charges against the defendants tried before the military commission in Indianapolis, the question naturally arises as to what is the source of law that makes the acts charged against these defendants criminal. Unlike present-day indictments, the charges and specifications against the defendants in the Indianapolis treason trials made no reference to any federal statute which would have made the charged conduct a crime. "Conspiracy against the government of the United States," "affording aid and comfort to rebels," "inciting insurrection," "disloyal practices," and "violations of the laws of war"—the five general categories of charges—all sound evil and reprehensible, but were they violations of existing federal criminal statutes at that time? If not, is it simply left to the military commission to decide what acts are crimes?

As mentioned in an earlier chapter, a defendant before a military court at this time was not accorded some of the important procedural rights possessed by a defendant in a civil court. But if a military commission could simply decide for itself what acts were criminal, and what sentence was appropriate upon conviction, a defendant before such a commission suffered an additional and equally serious deprivation, compared with his counterpart in a civil court.

A prime example of a procedural right thus lost would be the Sixth Amendment's guarantee of the right of jury trial in a criminal prosecution. That amendment states in relevant part:

> In all criminal prosecutions, the accused shall enjoy the right
> to a speedy and public trial, by an impartial jury of the State
> and District wherein the crime shall have been committed. . . .

Thus, if the Indianapolis defendants had been tried in federal court in that city, they would have had a right to insist that all the jurors be residents of Indiana, and that the verdict of the jury be unanimous. Before the military commission, however, there was no right to insist that any of the officers constituting the commission be residents of Indiana, and the commission could impose any sentence but death by a simple majority vote. (A two-thirds majority was required for a sentence of death.)[5]

But even apart from this sort of procedural right—to have the trial conducted in a particular manner—a defendant in federal court also had the right to insist that he could only be punished for conduct that Congress had by law made a crime. This general principle can be traced back to the Roman legal maxim *Nulla poena sine lege:* no punishment except pursuant to established law. An analogous principle is found in Article I of the United States Constitution, which prohibits states from making ex post facto laws—laws that retroactively criminalize conduct or increase the punishment for a crime already on the books.

A comparison of the charges made against the defendants before the military commission with similar acts that Congress had made punishable shows that there are significant differences, particularly as to the authorized punishment. Section 5331 of the Revised Statutes provided that every person owing allegiance to the United States who levies war against them, or adheres to their enemies, giving them aid and comfort within the United States or elsewhere, is guilty of treason. Section 5332 provided that every person guilty of treason should suffer either death or, at the discretion of the court, imprisonment at hard labor for at least five years and a fine of not less than $10,000. None of the defendants in the Indianapolis treason trials were explicitly charged with treason.

Section 5334 of the Revised Statutes provided that "every person who incites, sets on foot, assists, or engages in any rebellion or insurrection against the authority of the United States, or the laws thereof, or gives aid or comfort thereto, shall be punished by imprisonment for not more than ten years, or by a fine of not more than $10,000, or by both. . . ." This statute, as might be suspected, was enacted during the war, in July 1862, in obvious response to the problem of disloyal citizens in the North as well as rebels in the South. Section 5336 of the Revised Statutes provided:

> If two or more persons in any state or territory conspire to overthrow, put down, or to destroy by force the Government of the United States, or to levy war against them, or to oppose by force the authority thereof; or by force to prevent, hinder, or delay the execution of any law of the United States; or by force to seize, take or possess any property of the United States . . . each of them shall be punished by a fine of not less than $500 and not more than $5,000; or by imprisonment, with or without hard labor, for a period not less than six months, nor more than six years, or by both. . . .

Three years after the Indianapolis treason trials, Congress would enact a general conspiracy statute providing that if two or more persons conspired to commit any offense against the laws of the United States, and one or more of them should do any act to effect the object of the conspiracy, the parties to the conspiracy should be deemed guilty of a misdemeanor, and on conviction thereof should be liable to payment of a fine of not more than $10,000 and to imprisonment not exceeding two years.

Thus, as of 1864, Congress had made criminal the inciting or engaging in rebellion against the authority of the United States, and the conspiracy to overthrow the government, to levy war against it, or to prevent or delay the execution of any law of the United States.

The charges before the military commission, on the other hand, included offenses covered by these statutes but swept more broadly in several instances. But the greatest contrast was not in the acts that were proscribed but in the maximum penalties authorized. Both of the statutes quoted above set maximum imprisonment terms at ten years and six years, respectively. But, as mentioned, the military was authorized by a two-thirds majority to impose a sentence of death.

CHAPTER 7

The Indianapolis
Treason Trials

FOLLOWING DODD'S ESCAPE to Canada, the trial of the remaining five defendants began on October 21, 1864. William Bowles, the oldest of the defendants, was then in his eighties. He had been a captain in the Mexican War, but his sympathies with the South were well known. His wife was from New Orleans, and after their marriage they brought with them to Indiana a number of slaves. Indiana laws forbidding slavery eventually required him to send his slaves back to Louisiana. Bowles by now was one of the wealthiest men in the state; he was a physician, and a large landowner in French Lick Springs, where he kept a second home.

Lambdin P. Milligan was a lawyer in Huntington, where his legal abilities were well recognized. He had been born in Ohio, but had moved to Indiana and become active in Democratic politics. He lost the Democratic nomination for Governor of Indiana in 1864 to J. E. McDonald, who in turn was defeated in the general election by the incumbent, Oliver P. Morton. Milligan had a firm belief in the correctness of his own opinions and vehemently insisted that he could be tried only in civil courts and not before a military commission.

Horace Heffren was also a lawyer and a prominent figure in the Democratic party. He opposed the war originally but then had a change of heart and raised a company of volunteers that he commanded in the Union cause. He left the service after a short time, and was elected to the Indiana legislature.

Andrew Humphreys and Stephen Horsey had not the prominence of the other three defendants. Humphreys was active in local politics in his part of the state, while Horsey engaged in farming and other odd jobs.

William M. Harrison was the first witness called by the government. He lived in Indianapolis and had been employed as grand secretary of the Grand Council of the Sons of Liberty of the State of Indiana, at a salary of $800 per year. He had first joined an organization called the Order of American Knights at a meeting in Terre Haute in late August 1863. He went to that meeting at the request of Harrison Dodd. At that meeting he, along with twelve or fifteen others, was initiated into a secret organization called the Grand Council of the Sons of Liberty. Dodd presided at the meeting.

Harrison next attended a meeting in Indianapolis the following month. Bowles, he testified, was initiated at that gathering. Harrison was elected "Grand Secretary," and a military committee was appointed to draft a resolution. The resolution divided the state into four districts, and each was subdivided by counties. Andrew Humphreys, William Bowles, and Lambdin Milligan were all appointed major generals under this resolution.

The next meeting, according to Harrison, was in November. Bowles and Milligan were present, but Horsey, Humphreys, and Heffren were not. There was discussion of the object of the military organization; it was said that it was necessary to have such an organization "to protect the rights of the members against the encroachments of the Administration."[1]

The next session of the Grand Council was held in Indianapolis in June 1864. There were, according to Harrison, thirty counties represented. Bowles, Horsey, Milligan, and Humphreys were among the forty or so who attended. Organizational matters were discussed, and an executive committee of thirteen—whose membership was to remain secret—was to be appointed to manage the affairs of the organization between meetings. A committee of five was appointed to journey to Hamilton, Ohio, to greet Clement Vallandigham on his return from Canada. There was also a discussion as to whether government spies were infiltrating the organization. Harrison stated that in June he had received reports from seventeen counties, which reported a total strength of over five thousand members. He estimated that there were another twelve thousand members in the counties that had not made reports and estimated that the total membership of the organization in June exceeded eighteen thousand.

Harrison seems to have been a thoroughly credible witness; none of the counsel for the defendants attempted to impeach his credibility on cross-examination. He was asked, "What do you know about the arms seized here?" He responded:

> I had no knowledge of the purchase or the shipment of the arms until about four or five days previous to their arrival. Mr. Walker came to my house one night between nine and ten o'clock. He asked me if I knew whether Mr. Dodd had informed Parsons that there would be some boxes coming here addressed to him. I told him I did not. [Harrison then left town for several days.] The morning after my return to the city, I went down to Dodd's office, and I saw on the sidewalk five or six boxes addressed "J. J. Parsons, Indianapolis, IND." Parsons was engaged in getting these boxes into the building. I asked him if they were the boxes spoken of, and he said they were. The boxes were taken up to the second floor, and put in a back room of the building. I went there as they had been placed there, and asked him if he knew what those boxes contained. He said he did. I asked him what they contained. He said pistols.

Harrison then testified that Parsons was a member of the Order of Sons of Liberty, and that ten boxes of arms were received at that time and twenty-two more boxes were obtained about two weeks later.

Towards the end of his testimony, Harrison was asked if any plan for an uprising by the Order ever came to his knowledge. He replied:

> I received my information from Harrison H. Dodd, that there was a design in progress, or in contemplation for the release of the prisoners of war confined at this point, at Chicago, and at Rock Island, Illinois. The plan had not been fully decided on; but if decided on, he was to have charge of the release of the prisoners at this point. He desired to have a

Democratic mass meeting called about the sixteenth of August, and use this influence to influence the Democratic State Central Committee to call that meeting. If they did so, he intended to send out circulars to the members of the order in the various counties, authorizing the members to come up to that meeting armed. If the meeting had been held at that time, there would have been an uprising.

Q. Did Dodd at that time state to you when and where this plan for revolution had been agreed upon?

A. He stated to me that he had been to Niagara Falls, and from there to New York City; that he returned again to Niagara Falls, and from there he went to Chicago. I understood him that this whole plot had been arranged at Chicago.

Q. Did he mention whom he had met at Niagara Falls?

A. He stated that he met there the parties representing themselves as Peace Commissioners.

Q. At what date and to whom did he refer?

A. It was about the time of the meeting of the Peace Commissioners at Niagara Falls. I suppose he referred to the Peace Commissioners on the part of the rebel States.

Q. Did he state what the rebel prisoners were to do after the uprising on the sixteenth?

A. He stated, in an informal way, that they were to aid and assist in the uprising here.

Q. What were they to do after the uprising?

A. If successful in the uprising, they were to be taken South.

Q. What was that success to consist in?

A. In revolution.

Q. What was to be revolutionized?

A. The government, as far as the state was concerned.

Q. Did he have reference to the General Government?

A. He said nothing about the General Government. It was a revolution which was to take place in this State.

Q. How is this uprising to take place, and at whom was it aimed?

A. By the aid of the rebel prisoners, who were to be released through his instrumentality, and that of the persons who came into the meeting to be held here on the sixteenth. They would have an uprising and overturn the State Government.

Q. Who was to be Governor after that revolution?

A. He did not state.

Q. Did he state particularly his plan for the release of the rebel prisoners, and how the guards were to be overpowered?

A. He said if the thing was decided on, he was to release the prisoners here. He was to surprise the camp, and seize the artillery here, and in the confusion and excitement of the moment effect the success of the plan. He thought he could do this with about one hundred and fifty men. That was his idea which he communicated to me.

Harrison's testimony was damning as to Dodd, but Dodd had escaped and had been convicted in absentia. His testimony as to the defendants on trial in this proceeding—Milligan, Bowles, Heffren, Humphreys, and Horsey—simply showed that they had been at various meetings of the society and had accepted high-ranking military titles from the Order. If the other defendants were to be explicitly tied to the Dodd plan for the overthrow of the state government and release of rebel prisoners, it would have to be by other witnesses.

During this part of the trial, a letter from Milligan to Dodd dated May 9, 1864, was introduced in evidence by the Judge Advocate. Most of it was devoted to discussing the possibility of Milligan's contesting the Democratic nomination for Governor against Joseph E. McDonald, and examining the support McDonald received from people sympathetic to the principles Milligan believed in. He went on to say:

When men of so much seeming patriotism are willing for mere temporary purposes to abandon the great principles of civil liberty, what will those of less pretentions do, when the real contest comes, when life and property all depend on the issues, when bullets instead of ballots are cast, and when the *halter* is a preamble to our platform? For unless Federal encroachments are arrested in the states by the effort as well of the legislatures as the executive, then will our *lives* and *fortunes* follow where our honors will have gone before.

I am willing to do whatever the cause of the North-West may require, or its true friends may think proper, but I am as well convinced that upon mature reflection they will not ask me to obtrude myself upon the public, nor will they ask me to be McDonald's contingent. . . .

Harrison concluded his testimony by saying he had been arrested in Indianapolis on August 20. He stated that he had become dissatisfied with the Order and had resolved to abandon it before his arrest. He was, however, by no means a northern sympathizer; in a letter that he had written (but not sent) to the secretary of a county organization and that had been found upon his person when he was arrested, he advised the addressee that he would send no information by mail: "Written communications are *played out*, as all letters are opened and read by Lincoln spies and hirelings during their transmission through the mails."[2]

The government's next witness was Wesley Tranter, a sawmill operator in the southern part of the state who had been solicited to join the Order by Stephen Horsey. He joined in May 1863. Asked the purpose of the organization, he replied:

> *A.* Its purpose came out toward the last, that we were to support Jeff Davis; that we were to have our guns fixed; that we did not know what hour we should be called on to have a general turn-out to support Jeff Davis, either North or South. This is what they said in the Knights of the Golden Circle; but in the Circle of Honor they did not go so far.
> *Q.* You say this meeting in the woods was in the latter part of summer; when was the next?
> *A.* About the twenty-seventh or twenty-eighth of January 1864, when the order was changed to the Knights of the Golden Circle.

Tranter testified that there were about thirty people present at the January meeting, including Horsey. Ten or fifteen people were sworn in, and a different oath taken, including "something said about putting Governor Morton out of the way."

Q. Was Horsey present during this speech?

A. Yes, sir.

Q. Did he make any speech?

A. Not that I recollect.

Q. Was anything said at this meeting as to how these purposes were to be carried out?

A. Yes, sir; they stated that they were first to put Morton out of the way. A man who signed himself M.D. was to pay Governor Morton a visit, and he was to live but a short time afterwards. This visit was to be made about the twenty-sixth or twenty-seventh of March. There was to be a raid made on this place about five days from the first of April.

Q. Who were to make this raid?

A. The men of the lodge, and we were to arm ourselves to be ready. We were to take this place, wear out the soldiers, and release the prisoners.

Q. What was to be done with the rebel prisoners?

A. Nothing that I recollect; only that we were to go at blue coats.

Q. Was anything said about the invasion of Ohio or Indiana by the rebels?

A. They said that when we made the raid on this place, that members of the Order in Illinois were to make a raid on Springfield, and those in Missouri on St. Louis. Washington was to be attacked, and Forrest was to make a dash into Kentucky. He did make a raid a few days from the Fifth of April.[3]

The government's next witness was J. J. Bingham, editor of the daily and weekly *Indiana State Sentinel*. He had published that newspaper since August 1856, and joined the American Knights in the fall of 1863 in Indianapolis. Dodd and Harrison, among others, were present at that time.

Bingham testified that he was opposed to all secret political organizations, and at first declined to join the Order. Other Democrats in the city were solicited, but most of them also demurred. Then Dodd, who had been a friend for many years, again urged him to join, and told him that the organization would uphold the principles of the Democratic party. Finally, Bingham agreed to enroll on an informal basis, in order to help unify the different elements in the state opposed to the Lincoln administration. He attended another meeting in Indianapolis on February 16, but after that told Dodd he wished to withdraw. Bingham went on to say that in early August 1864, Dodd had come to him and said that he wanted to have a talk in secret. Bingham agreed. According to Bingham, Dodd "said that arrangements had been made to release the prisoners on Johnson Island; at Camp Chase, near Columbus, Ohio; at Camp Morton, and also at Camp Douglas, and that the prisoners at Camp Douglas, after their release, were to go over and release those at Rock Island. At the same time there was to be an uprising at Louisville, at which the Government stores, etc., were to be seized."

According to Bingham, Dodd asked him, as chairman of the Democratic State Central Committee, to call a mass meeting of the party on August 16. Bingham refused. Dodd then requested a district mass meeting to nominate a candidate for this congressional district, but Bingham again turned him down. Bingham then began to investigate the matter on his own, because he felt he might be obliged to break his vow of secrecy to Dodd. At a meeting of prominent Democrats in McDonald's office a few days later, Bingham counseled that the whole program of the Secret Order should be stopped.

He went on to testify that he had been informed that a Council of Sixteen had decided upon the scheme for an uprising when it had convened in Chicago in late July 1864. He was likewise told that Bowles was a member of the Council but had not been notified that Heffren, Horsey, Milligan, or Humphreys were members. He said that until Dodd let him know of the scheme in early August, he had thought the organization was purely political.

The government's next witness was Felix Stidger, who today would be called a "government informant"—that is, an undercover agent employed by the government to infiltrate an organization believed to be engaged in criminal activities. Stidger had had the good fortune to seek out and talk to two of the defendants who proved to be remarkably indiscreet in their conversations with him. He had been variously, over the previous several years, a soldier in the Northern army, a carpenter, and a dry-goods merchant. When discharged from the army for physical disability in February 1864, he had been told by the Adjutant General's office of his division that Dr. Bowles was a dangerous man. He set out for Bowles's home in French Lick, Indiana, hoping to elicit damaging statements from him.

En route to French Lick, Stidger met Horace Heffren in Salem. Heffren, apparently a rather loquacious conspirator, told Stidger that he, Heffren, could call together, within twenty-four hours, between one thousand and fifteen hundred armed men in that part of the state in connection with a secret organization. The following day Stidger went to Bowles's house and introduced himself as J. J. Grundy. It was not until the evening of the following day that he had a conversation with Bowles, who asked him if he knew anything about the Democratic organization. Stidger replied that he was a member, and Bowles then told him he was the military chief of the "Order." Bowles said that the forces of Indiana would march into Kentucky and make it a battleground, while Illinois counterparts would concentrate on St. Louis. The "Order" was an offshoot of the Knights of the Golden Circle, and it would act in conjunction with rebel forces. Bowles informed Stidger there was to be a meeting in Indianapolis, and that he, Stidger, should go to Kentucky and "see what could be done."

Stidger returned to Indiana later in May and again met with Heffren, who said that the Indiana organization was now about complete, and that it numbered between seventy-five thousand and eighty thousand people. Still going under the name of Grundy, Stidger reported this conversation to the office of the Adjutant General in Louisville. From Salem, Stidger went on to see Bowles at French Lick. Bowles now told him that thirty thousand from Missouri and fifty thousand from Illinois would cooperate with Confederate General Sterling Price for a campaign in Missouri. He also said that Indiana had pledged forty thousand, who were to concentrate near Louisville and cooperate with whatever troops the Confederate army could send into Kentucky under General Buckner or General Breckenridge.

Understandably, Stidger was vigorously cross-examined by counsel for the defendants. He testified that he had been initiated into the first level of the Order of the Sons of Liberty in early May and that he entered it for the purpose of disclosing its secrets to the government. He reported to the Adjutant General as often as twice a week.

Colonel A. J. Warner, commander of the Indianapolis post of a volunteer regiment, was then called as a witness. He had been in charge of the detail that seized the arms and papers from the office of Dodd at the beginning of August. Twenty-six boxes of arms and ammunition were taken; the boxes had been shipped to "J. J. Parsons" and on the waybill were described as "stationery." Twenty-four of the boxes contained fixed ammunition for large-sized revolvers; the other two had the revolvers themselves. There were between 350 and 400 such guns.

The following day, the Judge Advocate, much to everyone's surprise, announced that all the proceedings against Horace Heffren were withdrawn and that he was released from arrest, and would now appear as a witness for the government. Thus Heffren alone of the conspirators would take the witness stand; the law at that time prohibited a defendant in a criminal case from testifying on his own behalf. He said he was a lawyer who had resided in Salem since March 1857. He had joined an order called the American Knights in the latter part of 1863; he had never belonged to the Order of the Golden Circle. He had attended a meeting of the Grand Council in Indianapolis in the middle of February 1864. Dodd had presided, Harrison was secretary, and there he met Bowles and Milligan. With respect to the Order generally, Heffren testified that no one would have been admitted unless he professed to be a Democrat. The following colloquy occurred between the Judge Advocate and Heffren:

Q. What proportion of the members belonged to the military portion of the organization?

A. Only the leaders; they were to control the matter through a Committee of Thirteen, who were to be known only to the Grand Commander and themselves. They were to so control us as to bring us into their trap. That was why I said it was a humbug, and said I would have nothing to do with it.

Q. Have any of the schemes of the Order come to your knowledge since then?

A. Yes, sir. The schemes of a few of the leaders of this military part of the Order, and the schemes of these were unknown to the great mass of the Order.

Q. Do you say that it was to their military leaders alone this was confined?

A. Yes, sir; I think so.

Q. Was Dodd considered a military leader?

A. He was; but there was a man over him.

Q. Who was that?

A. It was Dr. Bowles.

On cross-examination, Heffren testified that he had met Humphreys at a railroad junction en route to Indianapolis, and that they had talked about the Order and the organization. Humphreys, he said, "said it would not do. . . . He said he was for his country, right or wrong, and would have nothing to do with it. He advised me to quit the Order, and I said I had quit it, and would have nothing more to do with the Order." Humphreys, according to Heffren, had also said that it would not do to resist the law.

The testimony of other government witnesses was merely cumulative of that already given, with one exception. W. L. Bush, a reporter for the *Cincinnati Gazette*, testified about speeches made at a Democratic convention in Fort Wayne, Indiana, in August 1864.

Q. State to the court what was said by Mr. Milligan on the state of the country, whether it was prosperous or otherwise?

A. He referred to the country as desolated by this war, and the oppressions of the Administration. That was the general tenor of his remarks on that point.

Q. What did he state in reference to the freedom of the press and of speech?

A. He spoke of the freedom of speech allowed as simply that granted by a Lincoln mob—as a freedom in name rather than in fact.

Q. What did he say in reference to the draft or conscription?

A. ... He stated, if the war was right, the draft was right, and if they considered the war right, and were good citizens, they would not grumble about the draft.

Q. What else did he say about the rightfulness of the war?

A. He denied that the war was right, and proceeded to argue, that under the Constitution the President had no power to coerce a State, and asked if those who entered the army would look in the future for their laurels to such battles as Bull Run, Chickamauga, and Red River. He also appealed to them to consider the condition of their wives and children at home, destitute and dependent on the charity of their neighbors, if they entered the army, and asked whether they considered it a duty to make such a sacrifice.

Q. ... What did he say about the President of the United States?

A. He spoke of him as a tyrant, and an usurper, I think.

Q. Did he denounce arbitrary arrests?

A. I think he did. ...

Q. I will ask you now this general question, whether his speech at that time was loyal, and in favor of the Government, or whether it was disloyal, and against it?

At this point counsel for Milligan objected, and argued the admissibility of the testimony to the commission. The commission withdrew, and on returning, announced that the objection was sustained.

The examination of witnesses before the commission concluded on December 1, and the trial recessed for several days to give counsel time to prepare their closing arguments. These were presented on December 6, and the case was thereupon submitted to the commission for decision.

REVIEWING THE TESTIMONY received by the commission at this point, one might simply say that yes, these defendants had made some likely treasonable, albeit fatuous, plans, but nothing had ever come of them. At most, Dodd had been caught red-handed when the search of his establishment turned up weapons and ammunition, but the other defendants had engaged in little more than talk. But the law of conspiracy is not so forgiving. As understood in the federal courts in the mid-nineteenth century, conspiracy consisted of an agreement among two or more persons to commit an offense forbidden by the criminal law, together with an overt act by one or more of those persons in furtherance of the conspiracy. The conspiracy need not have been successful, and indeed need not ever have come to fruition.[4]

The law of conspiracy is equally unforgiving in relation to the evidence that may be admitted against a defendant at trial. The "general rule" as to "hearsay"—that is, statements purportedly made by a person not present in court to be cross-examined—is that it is not admissible. If, say, a man named Green is on trial for a given offense, and the government calls Jones as a witness and seeks to have him recount that Smith said to him, Jones, "I was in the Kit Kat Club on Thursday night with Green," Jones's testimony on this point would be hearsay and so not admissible under the general rule; for while Green's lawyer has an opportunity to cross-examine Jones, he cannot cross-examine Smith. In a trial with multiple defendants, out-of-court statements that Jones reports by one defendant concerning the actions of his co-defendants are under ordinary circumstances similarly classified as hearsay, since (unless the given defendant turns state's evidence) those statements are also not subject to cross-examination. Jones may, of course, legitimately testify as to actions of Green that he personally witnessed or statements that Green made directly to him concerning his, Green's, own conduct.

Thus Bowles's foolish statements to Felix Stidger, whom he barely knew, were in any case admissible against him as an individual. But when the charge is conspiracy, and an agreement among the defendants has been proved in court, the statements of one conspirator in furtherance of the conspiracy are admissible not just against the one but against each of the other conspirators as well. So an out-of-court statement by Bowles could be admitted not just against him but also against the other conspirators.

From this perspective, there can be little question that a jury could have found Harrison Dodd guilty as charged on several of the counts; he was the kingpin of a conspiracy that was planning an uprising, and he was well advised to have fled to Canada. Bowles, though not as central a figure, seems to have been party to an agreement to engage in the planned uprising in the summer of 1864, and the shipment of arms and ammunition to Dodd was an overt act in furtherance of the conspiracy. The evidence as to Milligan, Humphreys, and Horsey tails off dramatically. These three were at times present at meetings of an organization to which they belonged, when rather vague military plans were discussed, but the discussion never focused on any particular object. Milligan's speech at Fort Wayne should not have been admitted against him because it was nothing more than entirely permissible criticism of the Lincoln administration's decision to make war against the Confederate states.

Early in January 1865, it became publicly known that the commission had found Bowles, Milligan, and Horsey guilty on all charges and specifications except one, and sentenced each of them to be hanged. It found Humphreys guilty, but sentenced him only to confinement at hard labor for the duration of the war.

General Alvin Hovey, the commandant of the Military District of Indiana, whose approval was required to carry out any of the sentences, had been before the war a Justice of the Indiana Supreme Court. He approved each of the sentences but commuted that of Humphreys to limited release on parole because he concluded that the evidence did not show that this defendant had taken any active part in the conspiracy. The record of the proceedings against Horsey, Bowles, and Milligan was then sent to President Lincoln, whose approval was required for any death sentence imposed by a military court.

By now, both the political and military situations had changed dramatically since the summer of 1864. Lincoln had been reelected in November; Sherman had taken Atlanta and was marching through Georgia. It was evident that the end of southern resistance was but a matter of a short time. Joseph McDonald, a former Attorney General of Indiana and a leader of the Democratic party, now took over as chief counsel for Milligan, Bowles, and Horsey. McDonald was a person of unquestionable loyalty to the Union, unlike other Democrats who had become "Copperheads"—the term for Northerners who were sympathetic to the South, and who manifested overt disloyalty to the Union. He had practiced law with Lincoln on the Illinois circuits, and he set out for Washington to seek clemency for his clients. McDonald wrote to a friend in 1883 to describe his meeting with Lincoln:

> Much to our surprise we found Mr. Lincoln in a singularly cheerful and reminiscent mood. He kept us with him until almost eleven o'clock. He went over the history of my clients' crimes as shown by the papers in the case, and suggested certain errors and imperfections in the record. The papers, he said, would have to be returned for correction, and that would consume no little time. "You may go home, Mr. McDonald," he said, with a pleased expression, "And I'll send for you when the papers get back; but I apprehend and hope there will be such a jubilee over yonder," he added, pointing to the hills of Virginia just across the river, "we shall none of us want any more killing done."[5]

The corrected papers in the case of the Indiana conspirators, however, did not reach the White House again until after Lincoln had been assassinated on April 14 at Ford's Theater and been succeeded by Andrew Johnson. Johnson's first instincts on becoming President were draconian, and in May 1865, General Hovey issued an order reciting that the President had approved the sentences and directed that they be carried into execution without delay. The order stated that each of the prisoners "will be hanged by the neck until he be dead on Friday, the 19th of May 1865 . . . on the parade grounds between Camp Morton and Burnside Barracks, near the city of Indianapolis, Indiana." Hovey then sent a personal letter to Colonel A. J. Warner, who would be responsible for carrying out the executions:

> . . . From the language of my orders, I am compelled to fix Friday, the 19th instant (between the hours of twelve o'clock noon and three o'clock P.M.) as the most remote day within which the same can be properly obeyed. You will give the condemned every facility within your power, consistent with their safe-keeping, to settle up their worldly affairs, and prepare for the future. These are sad duties for both of us, and more trying

than the field of battle, but they are stern duties, that must be obeyed for our country's safety and future welfare.

I need not say to you to extend the families of the condemned any courtesy you can, consistent with your duty as an officer. A man who has served and suffered as you have for your country, can execute justice in mercy, though it may cost you tears of blood. With a high appreciation of your past services, I am, yours truly,

Alvin P. Hovey

Meanwhile, on May 10, counsel for the three condemned men had filed petitions for *habeas corpus* in the United States Circuit Court in Indianapolis. Public opinion had now shifted, and newspapers such as the *Cincinnati Daily Gazette*, which had strongly supported the Union during the war, expressed the hope that the sentences would be commuted and the prisoners turned over to the civil courts. Even Governor Morton, whose death had been one of the objects of the conspiracy, took up the cause and wrote Johnson requesting him to commute the sentences to life imprisonment. At first, Johnson was adamant, but then he too had a change of heart. On May 16 he telegraphed Hovey commuting the sentence of Horsey, who was surely the smallest cog in whatever conspiracy there was, to life imprisonment. He also granted a reprieve to Bowles and Milligan until June 1. Two weeks later he issued a general amnesty proclamation and commuted the sentences of Horsey, Bowles, and Milligan to imprisonment at hard labor for life.

But the commutation did not moot the petition for *habeas corpus* that they had filed in the federal court. Their contention was that no sentence could be properly imposed on them by a military court because they were civilians and Indiana was not a theater of war. Their petition would be heard by David Davis, now a Justice of the U.S. Supreme Court, and David McDonald, the federal district judge in Indianapolis. It is Davis in particular who attracts our interest, because he would write the opinion of the Supreme Court in the case that decided Milligan's fate.

CHAPTER 8

David Davis and the Supreme Court

D AVID DAVIS WAS born in Cecil County, Maryland, in 1815. His mother, widowed while pregnant with him, lived on her father's plantation in the northernmost part of Maryland's Eastern Shore. When the boy was five, his mother remarried, and he went to live with his uncle, an Episcopal rector, in Annapolis. For the next few years, he alternated between residing with his uncle and with his mother and stepfather. At age thirteen, he was placed on a stagecoach headed to Kenyon College, in Gambier, Ohio. After graduating from Kenyon in 1832, at the age of seventeen, he began the study of law for three years with an attorney in Lenox, Massachusetts. He then migrated westward to central Illinois and purchased a law practice in Bloomington, which would be his home for the rest of his life. In 1838, he married Sarah Walker, to whom he had become engaged while clerking in Lenox.

Bloomington was part of what was called the Eighth Judicial Circuit in central Illinois. No one city in the circuit had enough legal business to justify the full-time presence of a judge, and so the judge and lawyers "rode circuit" together. Springfield, where Abraham Lincoln lived, was also in the circuit, and so Lincoln and Davis came to know each other. Indeed, those who rode the circuit at that time came to know one another intimately—they would eat and sleep, often two to a bed, at the same boardinghouse in the city where court was being held. At the age of thirty-three, Davis was elected judge of this circuit and held that position until Lincoln appointed him to the United States Supreme Court fourteen years later, in 1862. Davis, unlike Lincoln, became a wealthy man during his time in Bloomington—not from his law practice but from his buying up of vacant land at tax sales.

Lincoln and Davis were both admirers of Henry Clay, and both members of his Whig party. When the Republican party was formed in Illinois in 1856, Lincoln and Davis were among its prominent adherents. That year the Republicans nominated their first presidential candidate, John C. Frémont. In the November election, Illinois gave its electoral votes to Democrat James Buchanan.

Four years later, the Democratic party, meeting in Charleston, South Carolina, split wide open. Eventually the northern wing nominated Stephen A. Douglas for President, and the southern wing chose the sitting Vice President, John C. Breckenridge of Kentucky. The Republican presidential nomination suddenly became very attractive. Lincoln had gained national recognition from his debates with Douglas during the 1858 senatorial campaign in Illinois, and from his Cooper Union speech in New York City in February 1860. But while he was more than just a dark horse candidate, Seward was the preeminent Republican and a heavy favorite to win the nomination. When the Illinois state Republican convention overwhelmingly endorsed Lincoln as its choice, David Davis became a chief manager in the effort to secure the nomination for the "Rail Splitter" at the national convention.

Davis's strategy of the convention was to ingratiate Lincoln with all of the state delegations, and to secure promises of support from them for Lincoln as their second choice if they were pledged to another candidate on the first ballot. His greatest success was in obtaining such a commitment from the feuding Pennsylvania delegation, at the price of assuring its leaders that Pennsylvania would have a place in Lincoln's cabinet.

On the convention's first ballot, Seward received 173 1/2 votes and Lincoln 102. The second ballot showed a notable swing to Lincoln, who now had 181 votes to Seward's 184 1/2. Pennsylvania had cast 48 votes for Lincoln. On the third ballot, Lincoln wrapped up the nomination. A cannon on the roof boomed, and David Davis wept.

Lincoln's nomination was a moment of supreme triumph for Davis. A trial judge from downstate Illinois had bested Thurlow Weed, Seward's canny and experienced manager from New York. After the convention, Davis worked with Lincoln to placate Weed and other Seward partisans; their support was essential if Lincoln was to carry New York in the November general election. Davis also acted as intermediary for Lincoln in various party disputes within Illinois during the summer. In August, he journeyed to Pennsylvania to attempt to get the warring factions of the Republican party there to pull together. On his return to Illinois, he stopped in Indiana, another doubtful state, to mend fences there. Most of Davis's summer was devoted to this sort of political activity, and in September, when the Illinois courts reconvened from their summer recess, he persuaded one of his colleagues to hold court in his place. On election day, he voted in Bloomington, and then went to Springfield to be with Lincoln when the returns came in that evening. Good news from the East—Lincoln had carried both New York and Pennsylvania—was followed by good news from Illinois and Indiana. Abraham Lincoln had been elected President of the United States.

Davis, among others, was consulted by Lincoln about Cabinet appointments. Some of Lincoln's friends thought that at least one post should go to an old and trusted friend on whom he could confidently rely. Davis agreed with the idea but refused to let his own name be proposed. Lincoln decided against such an appointment; he would take with him to Washington as personal secretaries two young men, John Nicolay and John Hay, but the members of his Cabinet were virtually unknown to him at the time of their selection.

A few days before he was to leave for Washington, Lincoln asked Davis to join the presidential party on the train trip to Washington. On February 11, 1861, Davis saw Lincoln off in Springfield, wearing a "great white hat," but because of court commitments he could not join the presidential party until it reached Indianapolis. Meanwhile, he was besieged by supplicants urging him to support their claims for federal jobs.

As the presidential party passed through Philadelphia on February 21, the *Philadelphia Inquirer* reported:

> Judge David Davis, of Bloomington, Ill., will probably attract more attention than any other member of the suite, by virtue of his rotund corporation, the inexpressible humor of his broad, good-natured countenance, and the roar-like laughter in which he all but constantly indulges. Without the mirthfulness of the Judge, the trip would have been like a body without a soul. The Judge is also a most distinguished Republican leader of his State, and a most intimate friend and former partner of the President-elect who places great confidence in his judgment and discretion. He is a man of great talent, penetrating mind, and first-class legal and other acquirements.[1]

Davis was present at Lincoln's inaugural on March 4 and remained in Washington for two weeks afterward. When he returned to Bloomington, he felt some bitterness and dejection. He had made a point of publicly seeking no office, and yet his private view was much more ambivalent. He had played a major part in advising Lincoln on the appointment of Cabinet members and other slightly less exalted federal officials, but had received nothing himself. Lincoln had refused the request of their mutual friend Ward Lamon to make Davis Commissioner of Patents, and the President had been unable to clear the way for his selection as Commissary-General of the War Department, a position which would have engaged Davis's shrewd business instincts. In the heavy work of setting up the new administration, correspondence between Davis and Lincoln all but ceased. One of Davis's letters to the President asking after a cousin of Sarah's who had been reported missing in action, was answered by a brief note from a secretary. Lincoln, of course, had matters of much greater moment on his mind at the time, but the point of view in Bloomington was understandably different from that in Washington. The President, however, had not forgotten his old friend, and soon found a temporary post for Davis. In due time he would appoint him to the Supreme Court, but Davis's first public service for Lincoln was as chairman of the Frémont Commission.

JOHN C. FRÉMONT, the Republican candidate in 1856, went on to become a Union general commanding troops in the bitterly divided border state of Missouri. In the late summer of 1861, he issued a proclamation freeing slaves of rebel owners in that state. Lincoln revoked the proclamation, fearing for the loyalty of other border states, and determined that if any such politically charged step were to be taken, it should be only by him. But the abolitionist wing of the Republican party vehemently protested the President's action. Indeed, Jessie Benton Frémont took a train to Washington, where she confronted Lincoln in his bedroom to argue her husband's case. Lincoln coolly rebuffed her, and that October he removed Frémont from his command because of reports of his incompetence and mismanagement. The President then appointed Davis as chairman of a three-man commission to review unsettled claims against the government incurred by Frémont's extravagant and undisciplined practices. The commissioners struggled for four months with more than six thousand claims and issued a report highly critical of Frémont in March 1862.

At the time of Lincoln's election, there was one vacancy on the nine-member Supreme Court. Shortly afterwards, Justice John McLean of Ohio, a perennial Whig and a former Republican presidential hopeful, died, and John Campbell resigned to follow his state of Alabama into the Confederacy. With only six members, and Chief Justice Taney frequently ill, the Court had difficulty maintaining a quorum for its deliberations. Lincoln explained to Congress, in his message of December 1861, that two of the vacancies were from southern states, and he had been loath up to then to appoint only Northerners to fill them. He urged Congress to get on with the process of realigning the federal judicial circuits, a matter that made more difference in Supreme Court appointments then than it does today.

Around the time of the Civil War, the Justices customarily met together in Washington for only part of the year; the rest of the time they sat as trial judges in the respective geographic circuits to which they were assigned. The great majority of cases tried in the lower federal courts at this time were in federal court simply because the plaintiff was a citizen of one state and the defendant of another. There were no issues of federal law involved, and the judges were required to apply the law of the state in which the federal court sat. Because of this, it was thought essential that a Supreme Court Justice have practiced law in one of the states comprising the circuit to which he was appointed.

Lincoln, of course, was besieged with claims for the three appointments at his disposal, and finally, in January 1862, he filled the first vacancy by nominating Noah Swayne of Ohio. Swayne was fifty-seven years old and had had a distinguished career at the bar of his home state. He had been McLean's own choice to succeed him.

Swayne was born in Frederick County, Virginia, of Quaker heritage. He began the study of law in Warrenton, Virginia, but after he was admitted to the bar there he moved to Zanesville, Ohio. In 1830, Andrew Jackson appointed him United States Attorney for Ohio, a position that he held for nine years, after which he returned to private practice and became active first in Whig politics and then in the organization of the Republican party.

In December 1861, Congress took up the realignment of the federal judicial circuits. But so diverse were the views as to how this should be done that no law would be enacted until the summer of 1862. Senator John P. Hale of New Hampshire proposed that the existing Supreme Court be abolished and a new one be substituted in its place. The present Court, he argued, was simply a part of the machinery of the Democratic party and could never regain the confidence of the public after the *Dred Scott* decision. Some senators sympathized with Hale's position, but cooler heads prevailed. Senator Orville Browning of Illinois said: "If you repeal the Supreme Court out of existence today for the purpose of getting rid of obnoxious judges, and reorganize it, and have new judges appointed, the very moment there is a change in the political complexion of Congress the same 'town meeting proceeding' recurs and the court is again abolished, and it will be abolished as often as the political complexion of Congress changes."[2]

Finally, a bill realigning the circuits was enacted into law. Ohio was lumped together with Michigan, Illinois with Indiana and Wisconsin, and the trans-Mississippi states were linked in a circuit of their own.

As soon as this bill became law, Lincoln appointed Samuel Freeman Miller of Iowa as an Associate Justice of the Supreme Court. Miller had been born in Richmond, Kentucky, in 1816 and received a medical degree from Transylvania University. He settled in Barbourville, in the eastern part of the state, and practiced medicine there for nearly ten years. But in 1845 he commenced the study of law while continuing to practice medicine, and in 1847 he was admitted to the Kentucky bar.

Three years later, at the age of thirty-five, he moved from Kentucky to Keokuk, Iowa, largely because he wanted to live in a free state rather than in a slave state. In Iowa, Miller opposed the repeal of the Missouri Compromise in 1854 and became an early member of the Republican party. He was head of the party county organization during the 1850s, and in 1860 he was a member of the state central committee. At the Chicago convention in 1860, he played an active role in securing Iowa's votes for Abraham Lincoln.

Two of the three vacancies were now filled, and no one from Illinois had been nominated. If the other Justice were to come from that state, Davis was certainly a contender, but not the only one. Davis at first had considerable misgivings about his qualifications. He wrote his wife that "I appreciate fully that I am not fit for Supreme Judge even if I could get it," and wrote to his protégé, William W. Orme, that "I often doubt, Orme, whether I could sustain myself on the Supreme Bench. . . . I certainly could not without hard study. . . . I have but little legal learning. . . ."[3]

Gradually, however, as he saw rivals who he felt were no more qualified than himself making claims to the position, he changed his mind. Among them were Secretary of the Interior Caleb Smith from Indiana and Senator Orville Browning from Illinois. Smith prevailed upon John Usher, an old friend of Davis, to suggest an appointment to a newly created vacancy on the Court of Claims for Davis. Davis replied that he did not wish to be an applicant for any position and felt that the President knew him so well that he, Lincoln, could best determine what service he might render to the country.

Hearing that Lincoln was about to name Thomas Drummond, the federal district judge in Chicago, to the Supreme Court vacancy, Davis inquired of Ward Lamon, now U.S. Marshal in the District of Columbia, whether he, Davis, might be appointed to the district court vacancy should Drummond be elevated. Davis still had misgivings, which his biographer Willard King feels were justified:

> Davis' misgivings were understandable: his experience had been confined to a trial court—he had never even argued a case in the Supreme Court of Illinois—and he doubted his ability to fill a place in a higher tribunal. It is fair to assume that Lincoln shared his doubts. He himself had handled more cases before the Illinois Supreme Court than almost any lawyer in the state and he knew that an excellent trial judge might not necessarily make the best Supreme Court Justice.[4]

But if Lincoln did have such doubts, they had been dispelled by late August 1862, when he advised Davis that "my mind is made up to appoint you Supreme Judge." Davis expressed his gratitude, and Lincoln by letter of October 19 sent him a commission making him a recess appointee to the Supreme Court.

Under the Constitution, the President may, when Congress is not in session, appoint persons to office without the normal requirement of the advice and consent of the Senate. These recess appointments last until the final day of the next session of Congress. Today it is thought highly undesirable for a President to make such an appointment to the Court, because it is all but inevitable that a Justice so appointed will have had to participate in decisions, and write opinions, before the Senate gets around to accepting or rejecting him or her; and this situation can inhibit the Justice in question from exercising independent judgment on questions that come before the Court. In Davis's case, however, there was no such difficulty, because he was confirmed by the Senate in early December, shortly before he took his seat at the far left of the bench in the newly remodeled courtroom of the Supreme Court.

Chief Justice Taney, now eighty-five, continued to preside over the Court. The senior Associate Justice was James Wayne of Georgia, who had been appointed by Andrew Jackson in 1835. Wayne had been born in Savannah, Georgia, in 1790 but went north to attend what was then the College of New Jersey at Princeton, where he graduated in 1808. He returned to Savannah to read law and was admitted to practice in 1811. He served as an officer in the War of

1812, as a state legislator, and as mayor of Savannah before becoming a trial judge in that city. He was elected to Congress in 1829 and loyally supported Jackson and Taney in their struggle with the Bank of the United States during Jackson's second term.

In spite of his southern roots, Wayne remained a Unionist throughout his life. During the Civil War, he gave up his home in Savannah and took up permanent residence in Washington.

> He was apparently highly influential in the councils of the Court, finding there outlet for most of his political energies, instead of engaging in maneuvering for the Presidency, as did his colleague McLean. . . . He was handsome, courtly, and convivial. When eventually the Justices began as a matter of course to bring their wives to Washington, the Waynes took a prominent part in the social life of the capital.[5]

John Catron of Tennessee was nominated to the Court by Andrew Jackson on March 3, 1837, his last full day as President. The Senate did not consider the nomination until March 8, by which time Martin Van Buren had succeeded Jackson. Van Buren could have withdrawn the nomination, but it appears that he and Jackson were in complete accord on the matter. Catron had been born in Pennsylvania in 1781 and spent his boyhood on farms first in Virginia, then in Kentucky, and finally in Tennessee. He served in one of Jackson's military campaigns and began the practice of law on the Tennessee frontier. In 1818 he moved to Nashville, became a successful lawyer there, and finally Chief Justice of the state Supreme Court. The *New York Commercial Advertiser,* commenting on his nomination to the United States Supreme Court, said: "He is a well-informed, industrious man, and a tolerably good lawyer, but not exactly the person to be put on the bench of the Supreme Court."[6]

Samuel Nelson of New York was appointed to the Court by John Tyler during his last month in office. The Senate had refused to agree to two of Tyler's earlier nominees for vacancies, but Nelson was confirmed only ten days after his name was sent to the Senate. He had been born in upstate New York in 1792, attended Middlebury College, read law in an office, and was admitted to the bar in 1817. He began practicing in Cortland, a town located in the southeastern part of the Finger Lakes district. In 1831 he was appointed as an Associate Justice of the highest court of New York, and in 1837 he was promoted to be Chief Justice of that Court.

Robert C. Grier was sent to the Court by James K. Polk in 1846. Grier attended Dickinson College—likewise the alma mater of Roger Taney and James Buchanan—and graduated in 1812. While teaching at a private academy, he studied law in his spare time and was admitted to practice at the Pennsylvania bar in 1817. He was made a presiding judge of the state trial court in Pittsburgh in 1833 and served in that capacity until he was appointed to the Supreme Court by Polk. The definitive historical work of this era says of Grier: "Through most of his career . . . he served with industry and vigor, both in Washington and on circuit, taking time off each year for his favorite sport of trout fishing. . . . At once generous of heart and rough and outspoken in manner, he probably found himself closer to Justice Catron, whom in these respects he resembled, than to any of his other colleagues."[7]

The most recent of the Democratic appointees was Nathan Clifford of Maine. Clifford's predecessor, Benjamin Curtis of Massachusetts, had been one of the two dissenters from the *Dred Scott* decision in March 1857. He and Taney had an acerbic disagreement over access to the Court opinions in that case, and Curtis resigned in a fit of pique. Buchanan, a "doughface"—a Northerner with southern sympathies—had just become President, and would surely appoint a successor quite sympathetic to the views of the *Dred Scott* majority. One wonders whether Curtis might not have better served the cause in which he believed by remaining on the Court, even as a dissenter.

Buchanan chose Clifford to succeed Curtis. Clifford had been born in New Hampshire in 1803 and was admitted to the bar of that state in 1827. Shortly afterward he moved to western Maine and began a practice there. In 1830 he was elected as a Democrat to the Maine legislature and was at one time state Attorney General. He later served two terms in the House of Representatives. In 1846, President Polk named him Attorney General; at the close of the Polk administration in 1849, Clifford returned to practice law in Portland, Maine, for eight years. His nomination was submitted to the Senate on December 9, 1857, and was confirmed by a narrow margin the following month.

Horace Greeley's *New York Tribune*, never sympathetic to dough-faces, commented that Clifford was "just about equal to the trial of a case of assumpsit upon a promissory note in the court of a Justice of the Peace." But he was defended in other quarters on the grounds that he had not only had experience as a practicing lawyer but also in the Executive Branch of the national government. Carl Swisher describes Clifford: "Stocky and phlegmatic, and meticulous and thorough in his work, he never stood out as a leader of the Court. He wrote no majority opinions on important constitutional questions. . . . He remained a firm Democrat on a Court which before his death became largely Republican."[8]

This, then, was the Supreme Court as it was constituted when Davis took his seat on the bench in December 1862. But several changes would occur in its composition between that time and four years later, when it heard the *Milligan* case. In 1863, Congress created a tenth federal judicial circuit to serve the Pacific Coast states. This meant, under the practice that then obtained, an additional seat on the Supreme Court had to be created. This was because each judicial circuit was thought to be entitled to its own Justice. Lincoln nominated Stephen J. Field, an active War Democrat, to this newly created vacancy.

Field was born in Connecticut in 1816, but in 1819 his family moved to Massachusetts, where he grew up as one of nine children. One of his brothers, David Dudley Field, would become a prominent New York lawyer and the author of the "Field Code," a system of pleading and practice that was adopted not only in New York but in other states. Another brother, Cyrus Field, would, after the Civil War, lay the transatlantic cable linking the United States to Europe. Field attended Williams College, then studied law in the New York office of his older brother and was admitted to practice in New York in 1841. He practiced in New York for eight years, until he was attracted by the lure of the California gold rush in 1849 and sailed there by way of the Isthmus of Panama. He landed in San Francisco, but ultimately settled in Marysville, a frontier town located above Sacramento on the Sacramento River. He engaged in a successful law practice during the 1850s, and in 1857 was elected to the Supreme Court of California, giving up his law practice. He was serving in that position when Lincoln appointed him.

In the summer of the following year, 1864, Taney died at the age of eighty-seven, giving Lincoln the opportunity to pick a new Chief Justice. At this time, the constitutionality of the so-called "greenback legislation," which the government had used to finance the war effort, was headed for a Court test, and Lincoln was very much aware of this fact. He said to a confidant: "We wish for a Chief Justice who will sustain what has been done in regard to emancipation and the legal tenders. We cannot ask a man what he will do, and if we should, and he should answer us, we should despise him for it. Therefore, we must take a man whose opinions are known."[9]

In an act of true magnanimity, Lincoln appointed his Secretary of the Treasury, Salmon P. Chase, to succeed Taney. In the early part of 1864, Chase had shamelessly allowed a campaign to be carried on whereby he would supplant Lincoln as the Republican party's presidential nominee that year, and he had unhesitatingly used his Treasury patronage to bolster this effort. Owing to his cold personality and his enemies within the party, the campaign ultimately failed. Lincoln had finally accepted his resignation as Treasury Secretary in June 1864, over a dispute about patronage. Nonetheless, Lincoln thought Chase would make a good Chief Justice because he would uphold the constitutionality of the greenback legislation that Chase himself had authored and submitted to Congress. His only doubt about Chase was whether he could finally give up his ambition for the presidency if he were appointed Chief Justice.

Then, in May 1865, John Catron died at the age of seventy-eight. The remaining nine Justices—Chief Justice Chase and Justices Wayne, Nelson, Grier, Clifford, Swayne, Miller, Davis, and Field would constitute the Court that heard the *Milligan* case.

On May 10, the petition of Milligan and the other defendants for *habeas corpus* was filed in the federal court in Indianapolis. It would be heard by Davis, the Circuit Justice, and David McDonald, the District Judge. The next day, Davis and McDonald wrote a letter to President Johnson urging him to stay the execution of the death sentences until the question of whether a civilian could be tried by a military commission was decided by the Supreme Court. They pointedly expressed no view on the constitutional question but added a paragraph toward the end of the letter that by today's standards of judicial conduct would be thought a highly unusual bit of political pleading: "We beg leave also most respectfully to state that, aside from the legal question, which we press most earnestly, we doubt the policy of the proposed execution. We fear its effect upon the public mind in Indiana. By many, these men will be regarded as political martyrs. Everything now, in this state, is quiet and peaceable. . . ."[10]

After hearing arguments in the case, Davis and McDonald certified that they differed in opinion on the legal question, which enabled them to certify the question to the Supreme Court. On February 5, 1866, the Supreme Court agreed to take up the case out of order, and set arguments for the first Monday in March.

CHAPTER 9

The Arguments in the *Milligan* Case

B Y ADVANCING THE *Milligan* case on its calendar, the Supreme Court indicated that the issues presented were of extraordinary importance. The Court announced on March 5 that four attorneys might appear for the petitioners, that the Attorney General and two associates would be heard in opposition, and that three hours would be allowed each counsel. As a result, the Court heard argument in the *Milligan* case for more than six consecutive days.

Such extended oral arguments are unknown in the Supreme Court today. Almost without exception, half an hour is allowed counsel on each side. On rare occasions, in cases of extraordinary complexity, the time is extended to an hour and a half or at most two hours. But at the time of *Milligan*, the Court was accustomed to relying much more heavily on oral argument, and less on comprehensive briefs. Even so, the Court then usually permitted each side of a case two hours to argue, and thus the much greater allowance of time in *Milligan* showed the importance that it attached to the case.

The actual arguments began on March 6, 1866. Until 1860, the Court had sat in a small chamber in the basement of the Capitol, a location that the Justices criticized as both cramped and unhealthful. But in that year, the Court moved into new quarters previously used as the Senate chamber:

The chamber, like the basement chamber previously occupied, was semi-circular. It was forty-five feet long and the same distance wide at the widest point. The ceiling was a low half-dome, architecturally figured, with a suspended chandelier. . . . Ionic columns of marble formed a colonnade along the eastern side of the room, while pilasters of marble decorated the circular wall. Marble busts of former Chief Justices were arranged around the walls. From above the seat of the Chief Justice looked down the gilded eagle which had previously sat above the presiding officer of the Senate, while over the door facing the Justices was a white marble clock.[1]

On each day the justices entered the courtroom in a procession at 11 a.m. and stood behind their chairs on the bench while the crier intoned very much the same "cry" as the marshal does today: "O Yea! O Yea! All persons having business before the Honorable, the Judges of the Supreme Court of the United States, are admonished to draw near and give their attendance, for the Court is now in session. God save the United States, and this Honorable Court."[2]

The government was represented by Attorney General James Speed, by Benjamin Butler, a Massachusetts lawyer and a general in the Civil War, and by Henry Stanbery, an Ohio attorney. Of these, only Stanbery was regarded as a truly first-rate advocate.

Speed, born in Kentucky in 1812, had been named Attorney General by Lincoln in late 1864 to succeed Edward Bates. Speed's brother, Joshua, had been a close friend of Lincoln's during the time they had both lived in Springfield, Illinois, and Lincoln had visited the Speed family in Kentucky after Joshua returned to his native state. James Speed had been a Kentucky Unionist during the War, and Lincoln relied on him for information about that critical state. After Lincoln's assassination, Andrew Johnson retained Speed and the other members of Lincoln's Cabinet, and Speed had issued an opinion in the summer of 1865 justifying trials of civilians before military commissions. Unfortunately for the government, Speed was not a first-class lawyer or advocate. As witness the comments of Justice Miller, in a letter written shortly before the commencement of argument in *Milligan:* "This session of the Court has developed his

[Speed's] utter want of ability as a lawyer—He is certainly one of the feeblest men who has addressed the Court this term."[3]

Butler had grown up in Lowell, Massachusetts, where his widowed mother ran a boardinghouse for women factory workers. He was admitted to the bar of that state in 1840, at the age of twenty-two, and practiced intermittently until his death more than fifty years later. Early in his career, he established a reputation as a shrewd and successful defender of accused criminals. He started out in politics as a Democrat, and at the party's presidential conventions in 1860 he sided with its southern branch, which favored Breckenridge as the party's nominee. In response to Lincoln's call for volunteers after the capture of Fort Sumter, however, he spent his own money to equip a regiment which departed for Washington immediately. Finding the rail lines from Baltimore impassable because of the destruction of bridges, his regiment sailed down Chesapeake Bay to Annapolis, and the troops came overland to Washington by this route.

> Thereupon began one of the most astounding careers of the war. Butler was, until Grant took control, as much a news item as any man except Lincoln. He did many things so clever as to be almost brilliant. He moved in a continual atmosphere of controversy which gradually widened from local quarrels with Governor Andrew of Massachusetts until it included most of the governments of the world. . . .[4]

The reputation that Butler brought to *Milligan* was one of considerable ability marred by lapses in propriety and ethics throughout a checkered career.

Stanbery was a well-respected Ohio lawyer who made up for both Speed's lackluster skills and Butler's tarnished personal reputation. But his role was limited to argument of a jurisdictional point on the fringes of the case.

One may wonder why the government would have assigned two such weak links to the team it chose to argue a case that was of extraordinary importance. But the fact that Speed was not a leader of the bar did not distinguish him from many of his predecessors as Attorney General. The government did not have much litigation before the Supreme Court at this time, and the post of Attorney General was generally regarded as one to be filled on the basis of political and patronage considerations rather than of legal distinction. Speed may have been picked for much the same reasons as was Edward Bates. Bates, however, was aware of his own inadequacy as an oral advocate. When, in 1863, litigation involving the legality of Lincoln's proclamation of a blockade of Confederate ports reached the Supreme Court in the *Prize Cases*, Bates took no part in the argument himself and instead employed outstanding counsel from the private bar to represent the government. Speed, unfortunately, was not similarly aware of his own limitations, and argued the case himself.

When, later in the nineteenth century, the government began to have more litigation before the Supreme Court, the problem was solved by creating the office of Solicitor General, to whom was delegated the responsibility of conducting its cases.

Why Speed chose Butler is difficult to explain; as already noted, Butler was an able lawyer and advocate, but he had surrounded himself with controversy. Perhaps it was because until very recently he had been a Democrat, and might be thought to appeal to the Democratic appointees on the Court that heard *Milligan*.

The official reports of Supreme Court decisions at this time contained not only the opinion of the Court in the case but often excerpts or, in some cases, verbatim reports of the arguments of counsel, depending on the idiosyncrasies of the reporter. The arguments of counsel for the government in *Milligan* were merely summarized, and judging from the summary, they were not particularly good. The government's brief put forth that the military commission derived its powers from martial law, and that the proceedings of the commission could be reviewed only by military authority. To make the matter even more explicit, it was suggested that "the officer executing martial law is at the same time supreme legislator, supreme judge, and supreme executive. As necessity makes his will the law, he only can define and declare it. . . ." As for the Bill of Rights, the government argued that these were "peace provisions of the Constitution, and like all other conventional and legislative laws and enactments are silent amidst arms, and when the safety of the people becomes the supreme law."

Joseph E. McDonald led off for the petitioners in an argument that was not reported. Next came James A. Garfield, who would later be elected the twentieth President of the United States. At first blush, he would have seemed an odd choice, since his colleagues Jeremiah Black and David Dudley Field were preeminent members of the Supreme Court bar and Garfield was not; he was only thirty-five years old at the time and was admitted to the Court bar only the day before he argued *Milligan.*

But Garfield had risen to the rank of major general in the Union forces during the Civil War, proving himself one of the few successful commanders in that conflict with no previous military experience. He was also closely identified with the Republican party, serving at the time of the argument as a Congressman from Ohio. Such an advocate could not be tarred with any suspicion of kinship with the Peace Democrats such as Milligan and his cohorts.

Garfield had been born in a log cabin in northeastern Ohio—the last American President to enjoy that distinction—and worked his way through Williams College. He was elected to the Ohio Senate before he reached the age of thirty, and at the outbreak of the Civil War had championed the right of the national government to coerce the seceding states. In the late 1870s, he would become Republican leader in the United States House of Representatives. He was elected President on the Republican ticket in 1880. Only a few months after his inauguration, he was shot by a disappointed office-seeker in a Washington railroad station, and died of his wounds in September 1881.

Garfield's argument was the most down-to-earth of the three made on behalf of Milligan. He offered an able and exhaustive review of English and American practice with respect to martial law, concluding that it could only exist by necessity, and then could only be established by Congress. He made it clear he was not seeking any decision that would limit Congress in its authority to govern the previously seceded states. During his discussion of martial law, he was interrupted by Benjamin Butler. Such an interference would be regarded as extraordinary in present-day practice. (This author, in his more than twenty years of service as a member of the Court, cannot recall a single instance in which such an interruption has occurred.) Butler's breach is perhaps more understandable in the context in which *Milligan* was argued—each counsel being allowed three hours, and rarely if ever being questioned by the Justices—than it would be today, when counsel are allowed only a half hour and are steadily peppered with questions from the bench.

Garfield denounced the government's claim that civil liberties were suspended during wartime:

> Such a doctrine, may it please the court, is too monstrous to be tolerated for a moment; and I trust and believe that, when this cause shall have been heard and considered, it will receive its just and final condemnation. Your decision will mark an era in American history. The just and final settlement of this great question will take a high place among the great achievements which have immortalized this decade. It will establish forever this truth, of inestimable value to us and to mankind, that a republic can wield the vast enginery of war without breaking down the safeguards of liberty; can suppress insurrection, and put down rebellion, however formidable, without destroying the bulwarks of law; can, by the might of its armed millions, preserve and defend both nationality and liberty.

Next for the petitioners came Jeremiah Black. He had been Chief Justice of the Pennsylvania Supreme Court, and then successively Attorney General and Secretary of State in the Cabinet of James Buchanan. Indeed, had Buchanan had his way, Black would have been on the bench listening to the arguments of counsel in *Milligan* rather than in the well of the Court making the arguments. Shortly before his term expired, Buchanan had nominated Black as an Associate Justice of the Supreme Court to succeed Peter V. Daniel. This, however, was the period when southern states were beginning to secede from the Union, and Black had advised Buchanan that while secession was morally wrong, the President had no power to do anything about it. By the time Buchanan sent Black's nomination to the Senate, twelve southern senators—who might have been expected to support Black—had resigned their offices and returned to their home states. Black's advice to Buchanan was as displeasing to northern senators as it had been pleasing to the southerners. In late January 1861, the Senate, by a vote of 26–25, refused to take up the nomination, and it died.

Part of Black's opening statement gives a feel for the kind of argument he made:

> In performing the duty assigned to me in this case, I shall necessarily refer to the mere rudiments of Constitutional law, to the most common place topics of history, and to those plain rules of justice and right which pervade all our institutions. I beg your honors to believe that this is not done because I think that the court, or any member of it, is less familiar with these things than I am, or less sensible of their values; but simply and only because according to my view of the subject, there is no other way of dealing with it. If the fundamental principles of American liberty are attacked, and we are driven behind the inner walls of the Constitution to defend them, we can repel the assault only with those same old weapons which our ancestors used one hundred years ago. You must not think the worse of our armor because it happens to be old-fashioned and looks a little rusty from long disuse.

Senator Orville H. Browning of Illinois sat in court throughout the *Milligan* arguments and said of Black: "He did not look at a book or a note, but made, I think, the finest argument, and the most magnificent speech, to which I ever listened."[5] While Black was describing and condemning the position of the government, he too was interrupted by Butler, who declared, "We do not take that position"—whereupon Black replied, "Then they can take no ground at all, for nothing else is left. I do not wonder to see them recoil from their own doctrine when its nakedness is held up to their eyes. But they must stand upon that or give up their cause. They may not state their proposition precisely as I state it; it is too plain a way of putting it."

Black also resorted to irony. He inquired as to why, under the government's theory, the authority to try and imprison citizens for political offenses should be restricted to army officers:

> Why should it be confined to them? Why should not naval officers be permitted to share in it? What is the reason that common soldiers and seamen are excluded from all participa-

tion in the business? No law has bestowed the right upon Army officers more than upon other persons. If men are to be hung without that legal trial which the Constitution guarantees to them, why not employ commissions of clergymen, merchants, manufacturers, horse dealers, butchers, or drovers, to do it? It will not be pretended that military men are better qualified to decide questions of fact or law than other classes of people; for it is known on the contrary, that they are, as a general rule, least of all fitted to perform the duties that belong to a judge.

David Dudley Field, the last of the four counsel for Milligan, was the older brother of Stephen J. Field, who now sat on the Court. Like his brother, David Dudley Field attended Williams College, but he left without a degree in 1825. He was admitted to the New York bar in 1828 and practiced in New York City until his death more than sixty years later. He supported Lincoln for the Republican nomination in 1860 but later switched his allegiance to the Democratic party. He argued one side or another of many of the important constitutional cases before the Supreme Court in the decade following the Civil War, and he represented Samuel Tilden, the Democratic claimant to the Presidency in the election of 1876, before the Hayes-Tilden Electoral Commission. Field also had clients of more questionable propriety, such as Jay Gould, James Fisk, and "Boss" Tweed of New York City fame.

But it was as a champion of the idea of codifying the common law—enacting into written statutes what had previously been principles deduced from judicial decisions—that Field left his most lasting mark on the American legal system. He originally proposed the idea of codes in New York, but was opposed by the entire organized bar of that state. Eventually his scheme was accepted, not only in New York, but in more than twenty other states. His brother Stephen, while practicing in California, was instrumental in bringing the code system to that state. The two brothers were alike in many respects—both were able, opinionated, and occasionally abrasive and overbearing.

David Dudley Field judiciously pointed out to the Court that the *Milligan* case involved no issue of how Congress might govern the recently seceded states, and also no question of the authority of Congress to establish martial law, since it had not done so.

Field's description of martial law was particularly cogent:

The source and origin of the power to establish military commissions, if it exists at all, is in the assumed power to declare what is called *martial law*. I say what is called martial law; for, strictly there is no such thing as martial *law*. . . .

On this subject, as on many others, the incorrect use of a word has led to great confusion of ideas and to great abuses. People imagine, when they hear the expression, martial law, that there is a system of law known by that name, which can upon occasion be substituted for the ordinary system; and there is a prevalent notion that under certain circumstances a military commander may, by issuing the proclamation, displace one system, the civil law, and substitute another, the martial. . . .

But what is ordinarily called martial law is no law at all:

Let us call the thing by its right name; it is not martial *law*, but martial *rule*. And, when we speak of it, let us speak of it as abolishing all law, and substituting the will of the military commander, and we shall give a true idea of the thing, and be able to reason about it, with a clear sense of what we are doing. Thus explained, the proposition for which the counsel on the other side argue, and against which we argue, is that the President, in a time of war, has the power to abrogate all law, and substitute his own will in its place. . . .

What, it may be asked, may a general never in any case use force but to compel submission in the opposite army and obedience in his own! I answer, yes; there are cases in which he may. There is a maxim of our law which gives the reason and the extent of the power: "Necessitas quod cogit defendit." [Necessity justifies what it compels.]

Butler replied for the United States. He, too, made a telling point:

It is much insisted on, that the determining question as to the exercise of martial law, is whether the civil courts are in session: but civil courts were in session in this city during the whole of Rebellion, and yet this city has been nearly the whole time under the martial law. There was martial law in this city, when, in 1864, the rebel chief, Jubal Early, was assaulting it, and when, if this court had been sitting here, it would have been disturbed by the enemy's cannon. Yet courts—ordinary courts—were in session. It does not follow, because the ordinary police machinery is in motion for the repression of *ordinary* crimes, because the rights between party and party are determined without the active interference of the military in cases where their safety and rights are not involved, that, therefore, martial law must have lost its power.

CHAPTER 10

The *Milligan* Decision

T HE ARGUMENTS in the *Milligan* case were concluded on March 13, 1866. On April 3—the last day of the term—the Court entered an order directing that the writ of *habeas corpus* sought by Milligan and others should issue, because the military commission had no jurisdiction to try and sentence them. Chief Justice Chase also announced that the opinion of the Court in the cases would be read at the next term—beginning in December 1866— "when such of the dissenting judges as see fit to do so will state their ground of dissent." This order did not receive wide publicity at the time, because without any opinions the basis for the Court's decision could not be ascertained. But on December 17, the opinion of the Court for five members was delivered by Justice Davis, with a concurring opinion by Chief Justice Chase for four members.[1]

As previously noted, five of the nine members of the Court had been appointed by Lincoln: Chase, Swayne, Miller, Davis, and Field; while Wayne, Nelson, Grier, and Clifford had been chosen by Lincoln's Democratic predecessors. Joining Davis's opinion for the majority of the Court were three of the four Democratic appointees, together with Field, a War Democrat. Joining the concurring opinion of Chief Justice Chase were Justices Swayne and Miller, Lincoln appointees, and Wayne, picked by Jackson. The two opinions were in accord on the fundamental issues of the case. Both found that the trial and sentencing of Milligan and his cohorts by the military commission were contrary to law, and that they should be discharged from custody; both opinions rejected the government's contention that the Bill of Rights was suspended in time of war or rebellion. On other points, however, the two opinions were in sharp disagreement.

Davis wrote that several provisions of the Constitution prohibited the trial of civilians even during time of war if the civil courts were open in a state such as Indiana. It stated that neither the President nor Congress could authorize such trials of civilians. Chase's opinion for the four concurring Justices said that the Habeas Corpus Act of 1863 represented a determination by Congress that civilians were to be tried in civil courts, and not by military commissions. He strongly criticized the Court majority for saying that Congress could not authorize such trials, since Congress had clearly not tried to do so. But since the majority had resolved otherwise, the concurring Justices dealt with that question and decided that Congress did have the power to authorize trials by military commission of Milligan and his cohorts.

Davis's opinion is far from a model of logical organization. It begins with reference to the Fourth Amendment, forbidding unreasonable searches and seizures; the Fifth Amendment, requiring indictment by a grand jury and forbidding the denial of life, liberty, or property except by due process of law; and the Sixth Amendment, preserving the right to jury trial in criminal cases. The opinion then continues with the somewhat rhetorical passage for which it is justly famous:

> The Constitution of the United States is a law for rulers and people, equally in war and in peace, and covers with the shield of its protection all classes of men, at all times, and under all circumstances. No doctrine, involving more pernicious consequences, was ever invented by the wit of man than that any of its provisions can be suspended during any of the great exigencies of government. Such a doctrine leads directly to anarchism or despotism, but the theory of necessity on which it is based is false; for the government, within the Constitution, has all the powers granted to it, which are necessary to preserve its existence; as has been happily proved by the result of the great effort to throw off its just authority.[2]

The majority went on to say that every trial involves the exercise of judicial power, and that that power is vested by the Constitution "in one Supreme Court and such inferior courts as Congress may from time to time ordain and establish." It is not pretended, said Davis, that the commission was a court ordained and established by Congress under Article III of the Constitution, which requires that judges of such courts hold office during good behavior—that is, unless removed by impeachment for serious misconduct. Nor could the President establish such a court under executive authority, because his authority is to "execute, not to make, the laws."

The Court majority thereupon went on to attack the government's contention that the military commission had jurisdiction under the "laws and usages of war":

> This court has judicial knowledge that in Indiana the Federal authority was always unopposed, and its courts always open to hear criminal accusations and redress grievances; and no usage of war could sanction a military trial there for any offence whatever of a citizen in civil life, in no wise connected with the military service. Congress could grant no such power. . . . One of the plainest constitutional provisions was, therefore, infringed when Milligan was tried by a court not ordained and established by Congress, and not composed of judges appointed during good behavior.

If the Constitution required that Milligan be tried before a court composed of judges holding office for life, clearly the military commission was not such a court, and the opinion might well have ended there. But the majority went on to say that the trial was void as well because Milligan had been denied the right to trial by jury guaranteed by the Sixth Amendment to the Constitution. It rejected the argument that in time of war the commander of an armed force had the authority to suspend civil rights and remedies; this argument was rejected because it "destroys every guarantee of the Constitution, and effectually renders the 'military independent of and superior to the civil power'—the attempt to do which by the King of Great

Britain was deemed by our fathers such an offence, that they assigned it to the world as one of the causes which impelled them to declare their independence."

The majority asserted that only the privilege of the writ of *habeas corpus*, among the liberties guaranteed by the Constitution, could be suspended in accordance with the provisions of Article I, Section 9 of the Constitution. But suspension of the writ, said Davis, simply permitted detention of suspected persons by the government, not their trial outside of the normal judicial process so long as civil courts were open. He observed that on Indiana soil, "There was no hostile foot; if once invaded, that invasion was at an end, and with it all pretext for martial law. Martial law cannot arise from a *threatened* invasion. The necessity must be actual and present; the invasion real, such as effectually closes the courts and deposes the civil administration."

Chase's concurring opinion agreed that Milligan and the other petitioners should be discharged, because the Act of Congress of March 3, 1863, required that result. That law, according to him, allowed detention of suspects only until a grand jury had met in the district where they were held; if they were not indicted by the time the grand jury adjourned, the Act of Congress required their discharge from custody. Thus, to the concurring Justices, Congress had affirmatively provided that prisoners in the position of Milligan be either indicted by a grand jury and tried in the civil courts, or else discharged from custody if there was no indictment.

There was no occasion for the Justices, under this view, to deal with the question of what might have been the result had the Act of Congress not so provided, or, more particularly, if Congress had by law provided for the trial of these particular defendants before a military commission. But, the majority's opinion having concluded that Congress could not so provide, the concurring Justices proceeded to explain why they thought that Congress did have the power to authorize such a trial:

> Congress has the power not only to raise and support and govern armies but to declare war. It has, therefore, the power to provide by law for carrying on war. This power necessarily

extends to all legislation essential to the prosecution of war with vigor and success, except such as interferes with the command of the forces and the conduct of campaigns. That power and duty belong to the President as commander-in-chief. Both these powers are derived from the Constitution, but neither is defined by that instrument. . . .

In Indiana . . . the state was a military district, was the theater of military operations, had been actually invaded, and was constantly threatened with invasion. It appears, also, that a powerful secret association, composed of citizens and others, existed within the state, under military organization, conspiring against the draft, and plotting insurrection, the liberation of the prisoners of war at various depots, the seizure of the state and national arsenals, armed cooperation with the enemy, and war against the national government.

We cannot doubt that, in such a time of public danger, Congress had power, under the Constitution, to provide for the organization of a military commission, and for trial by that commission of persons engaged in this conspiracy. The fact that the Federal courts were open was regarded by Congress as a sufficient reason for not exercising the power; but that fact could not deprive Congress of the right to exercise it. Those courts might be open and undisturbed in the execution of their functions, and yet wholly incompetent to avert threatened danger, or to punish, with adequate promptitude and certainty, the guilty conspirators.

In Indiana, the judges and officers of the court were loyal to the government. But it might have been otherwise. In times of rebellion and civil war it may often happen, indeed, that judges and marshals will be in active sympathy with the rebels, and courts their most efficient allies.

Charles Warren, in his work, observed that "This famous decision has been so long recognized as one of the bulwarks of American liberty that it is difficult to realize now the storm of invective and opprobrium which burst upon the Court at the time when it was first made public."[3]

A respected lawyer wrote to Chief Justice Chase:

If, as the public begin to fear, [the Court's] denial of the powers of Congress is any index to the view they are prepared to take of the great questions that will come before them in reference to Reconstruction, our situation is certainly a grave one. . . . I cannot yet consent to believe that we are brought into this dilemma, and that appointees of Mr. Lincoln are ready to imitate the late Chief Justice, in making the Court the chief support of the advocates of slavery and the Rebellion.[4]

The *New York Times* opined:

In the conflict of principle thus evoked, the States which sustained the cause of the Union will recognize an old foe with a new face. It is the old dogma of rigid construction as applied to the National Government and liberal construction as applied to the states on the one hand, and on the other, the common sense doctrine that the Constitution provides for the permanence of the Union, and for such exercise of authority by Congress as may be necessary to preserve the National Existence. . . . The Supreme Court, we regret to find, throws the great weight of its influence into the scale of those who assailed the Union and step after step impugned the constitutionality of nearly everything that was done to uphold it. . . . The whole Copperhead press exults over the decision. . . .5

James Gordon Bennett's *New York Herald* entered the fray on an even more strident note:

This two-faced opinion of Mr. Justice Davis is utterly inconsistent with the deciding facts of the war, and therefore utterly preposterous. These antediluvian Judges seem to forget that the war was an appeal from the Constitution to the sword. . . . The constitutional twaddle of Mr. Justice Davis will no more stand the fire of public opinion than the *Dred Scott* decision.[6]

The *Springfield* (Illinois) *Republican*, which had supported the administration during the war, took a different view.

The *Milligan* decision is simply a reaffirmation of the sacred right of trial by jury. To deny principles so well established and so essential to liberty and justice would not be progress, but a long step backwards towards despotism.[7]

Democratic newspapers were all but unanimous in their approval of the decision. "The fact that the Supreme Court has escaped the servile contamination of the times, and pronounces an independent opinion which vindicates a party so traduced and maligned as the Democracy, is full of encouragement," said the *New York World*. "[The Court] fast anchored in the affections of the American people . . . will resist the assaults directed against it, and continue the tranquil and sure arbiter of right."[8]

The Court's traditional approach to deciding a claim that a law passed by Congress was unconstitutional had been first enunciated by Chief Justice John Marshall. It was Marshall who was largely responsible for transforming the Supreme Court of the United States from a court of last resort for the resolution of disputes between individuals into a genuinely coequal third branch of the federal government. He observed, in *Fletcher v. Peck*, that the act of declaring a law of Congress unconstitutional was "a question of much delicacy, which ought seldom, if ever, to be decided in the affirmative, in a doubtful case." The Court's traditional approach required that it render a decision declaring an Act of Congress unconstitutional only if there were no other ground for deciding the case. This sound advice, repeated again and again in subsequent decisions throughout its two-hundred-year history, was simply ignored by Davis's opinion in *Milligan*.

The *Milligan* majority, confronted with no effort on the part of Congress to enact such a law, nonetheless proceeded to suggest that Congress could not constitutionally do so even if it chose. David Dudley Field had been at pains to point out the Court was confronted with no such question.

The construction put on the Habeas Corpus Act of 1863 by the concurring Justices was not the only way in which that law might have been read. Entitled as it was, an Act dealing with *habeas corpus*, it would have been reasonable to say that Congress was dealing only with persons detained for the purpose of trying them in civil courts and did not by implication preclude trial of some arrested suspects by military commission. If the law had been given this meaning, it would have been necessary to decide whether the *President, acting on his own,* could authorize trials of civilians by military commissions in time of war. But the one interpretation that the Act simply will not bear is that Congress affirmatively authorized such trials.

The majority opinion deals only obliquely with the Act of 1863. It neither adopts nor rejects the construction placed on the Act by the concurring Justices, nor does it offer any alternative construction of its own. For the Court to unnecessarily decide such an important question at that particular time was peculiarly unfortunate. It was still laboring under the cloud of the *Dred Scott* decision, where it had gone out of its way to hold an Act of Congress unconstitutional on highly dubious grounds. With the end of the Civil War and the assassination of Lincoln, conflict loomed between Andrew Johnson, who attempted to carry out Lincoln's relatively lenient policy of restoring the seceded states to their position in the Union, and the radical Republicans in Congress who wished to treat these states as "conquered provinces." The Court might soon enough face the actual question of whether Congress could provide for military commissions to try civilians in the states that had seceded—indeed, it would face just such a question in the case of *McCardle*, which came to it less than two years after it decided the *Milligan* case.

But to reach out and attempt to decide the question in a case where it was not presented was not only unsound constitutional adjudication but also doubly unwise in the political atmosphere of the country at the time. A respected law review of the time cogently made this point:

> Had [the Court] in truth simply adhered to their plain duty as Judges, they could have united in one opinion on this most important case. We deem the course they saw fit to adopt matter for great regret. Instead of approaching the subject of the powers of the coordinate branches of the government as one of great delicacy, which they were loathe [*sic*] to consider . . . they have seemed eager to go beyond the record, and not only to state the reason of their present judgment, but to lay down the principles on which they would decide other questions, not

now before them, involving the gravest and highest powers of Congress. They have seemed to forget how all-important it is for the preservation of their influence that they should confine themselves to their duties as Judges between the parties in a particular case; how certainly the jealousy of the coordinate departments of the government and of the people would be excited by an attempt on their part to exceed their constitutional functions; and how, the more a case before the Supreme Court assumes a political aspect, the more cautious should the Judges be to confine themselves within their proper limits. . . .[9]

The primary reason for the Supreme Court's practice of refraining from deciding a constitutional question unless necessary, is the "delicacy" of one branch of government declaring invalid the action of a coordinate branch of that government. But an additional reason for caution is that unnecessary *obiter dicta*—statements made in the course of a judicial opinion that are not pertinent to the decision of the point in question—come back to haunt the Court in future cases. This is just what happened with some of the *dicta* in the *Milligan* opinion when the case of *Quirin*[10] arose during the Second World War.

While the United States and Germany were at war in 1942, Richard Quirin and seven other men in the German armed forces were trained in the use of explosives and secret writing at a sabotage school near Berlin. Four of them were later transported by German submarine to Amagansett Beach on Long Island, New York. They landed under cover of darkness in June 1942, carrying a supply of explosive and incendiary devices. At the moment of landing they wore German uniforms, but immediately afterwards they buried their garb on the beach and went in civilian dress to New York City. The other four trained at the sabotage school were taken by another German submarine to Ponte Vedra Beach, Florida. They went through the same procedures and traveled to Jacksonville in civilian dress. All were ultimately arrested by the FBI in New York and Chicago; all had been instructed to destroy war industries in the United States.

President Franklin Roosevelt appointed a military commission to try Quirin and his cohorts for offenses against the laws of war and the Articles of War enacted by Congress, and he directed that the defendants have no access to civil courts. While they were being tried by the military commission, which sentenced them to death, they petitioned the United States Supreme Court for review of the procedures under which they were being tried. The Court convened in a special term on July 29, 1942, to hear arguments in their case.

One of the principal arguments made by lawyers for the petitioners was that the civil courts were open at this time, there had been no invasion of any part of the country, and therefore under *Milligan* there could be no resort to trial by a military commission. Counsel noted that one of the petitioners, Herbert Haupt, had been born in the United States and was an American citizen. At the conclusion of the arguments in the case, and after deliberation, the Court on July 31 upheld the government's position, but its full opinion did not come down until October. In that opinion the Court stated:

> Petitioners, and especially petitioner Haupt, stressed the pronouncement of this Court in the *Milligan* case . . . that the law of war "can never be applied to citizens and states which have upheld the authority of the government, and where the courts are open and their process unobstructed." . . . We construe the Court's statement as to the inapplicability of the law of war to Milligan's case as having particular reference to the facts before it. From them the Court concluded that Milligan, not being a part of or associated with the armed forces of the enemy, was a non-belligerent, not subject to the law of war save as . . . martial law might be constitutionally established. The Court's opinion is inapplicable to the case presented by the present record. We have no occasion to define with meticulous care the ultimate boundaries of the jurisdiction of military tribunals to try persons according to the law of war. It is enough that petitioners here, upon the conceded facts, were plainly within those boundaries. . . .[11]

The *Milligan* decision is justly celebrated for its rejection of the government's position that the Bill of Rights has no application in wartime. It would have been a sounder decision, and much more widely approved at the time, had it not gone out of its way to declare that Congress had no authority to do that which it never tried to do.

Lincoln Is Assassinated

BRAHAM LINCOLN was fatally shot by John Wilkes Booth at Ford's Theater on the evening of Good Friday, April 14, 1865. He died in the early morning hours of the following day.

The President, known for his periods of "melancholy," had been in particularly good spirits that day. Less than two weeks before, the Confederate capital of Richmond had fallen to Union forces, and Lincoln had visited the troops occupying the city. A week later, Robert E. Lee had surrendered his Army of Northern Virginia to U. S. Grant at Appomattox Courthouse. Grant had just arrived in Washington, and the Lincolns invited the Grants to join them in their box at the theater on the evening of April 14. Lincoln thought that an appearance at the theater, which seated hundreds of people, would be a good opportunity for the public to see the victorious general. But Julia Grant was anxious to go on to New Jersey to see their children, and the Grants declined. The Lincolns had also invited Secretary of War and Mrs. Edwin Stanton, but Stanton did not enjoy the theater, and they too begged off.

On the afternoon of April 14, before he had received the regrets of General Grant, Lincoln notified Ford's Theater of his planned attendance that evening along with the general. The manager immediately inserted notices to that effect in the two evening newspapers. Good Friday evening was notoriously bad for theater attendance, and this news might stimulate patronage.

One person who took particular interest in the news was John

Wilkes Booth. Booth, a well-known actor, had been plotting to abduct or kill Lincoln for some time. That afternoon, taking advantage of the professional courtesy afforded to actors, he watched a dress rehearsal of the play, *Our American Cousin,* to be given that night, and noted that at a point a little more than two hours into the play, there would be only one actor on stage. This, he decided, would be a propitious moment for the assassination. His plan was to sneak into the unoccupied box next to the President's, shoot him, and then jump from the box to the stage and flee out the back door. Shortly before the performance was to begin, Booth entered the deserted theater and checked out the empty box next to the President's in minute detail. He had also planned his escape route across the Navy Bridge to southern Maryland.

Up to this time, no American President had been assassinated. Two had died in office of natural causes—William Henry Harrison in 1841 and Zachary Taylor in 1850—and Andrew Jackson had been assaulted by a cashiered naval officer. But the hatreds engendered by the Civil War changed the climate of American political life. What were once partisan differences to be submitted to the democratic process of legislation became reasons for going to war, with all of the deep-seated hatred that war brings.

Threats on his life were nothing new to Lincoln—such a warning was the reason he had changed his schedule on his way to Washington in February 1861. But he came to regret his having "sneaked" into the capital, and did not like the idea of being regularly under the watchful eye of guards assigned to protect him.

Nonetheless, by the end of his first term in office, four members of the Washington Metropolitan police force had been assigned to attend him around the clock, whether at the Executive Mansion or elsewhere. Two were on duty during a day shift, a third served during a swing shift, and a fourth overnight. At about the same time, Stanton assigned a troop of Ohio light cavalry to act as a presidential escort whenever Lincoln left the Executive Mansion. The President, somewhat irritated by all these security measures, remained fatalistic about the possibility of assassination.

The Lincolns dined with their sons Tad and Robert. Mary Lincoln told her husband that she had invited her friend Clara Harris and her fiancé, Major Henry Rathbone, to accompany them to the theater and sit in their box. The police guard at the Executive Mansion who had been supposed to go off duty at 4:00 P.M. remained on duty because the officer assigned to relieve him—John Parker—had not shown up. Finally Parker arrived, and accompanied the party to the theater. The Lincolns left the mansion shortly after 8:00 p.m., picked up their guests, and arrived at the theater during the first act of the play. Two cavalrymen rode behind the presidential coach. As the President and his party entered the theater, the audience as well as the actors on the stage applauded heartily and the band played "Hail to the Chief." Parker, having inspected the box before the party arrived, would later desert his post in favor of a neighboring tavern during the course of the play.

John Wilkes Booth arrived at Ford's Theater at about 9:30 p.m., dismounted from his horse, and left it with a stagehand whom he knew. He entered the back door of the theater and conversed briefly with some of the actors he knew. He then went to a tavern for a drink—the same place where Parker was imbibing. He reentered the theater by the main entrance at about 10:00 p.m. and was admitted as a matter of courtesy without a ticket. He went upstairs to the dress circle, and from there he walked through the unguarded door of the box adjoining the presidential party. After a momentary surveillance through a hole in the door of that box, he swung the door inward; Lincoln was the nearest to him, but a few feet away and facing away from him toward the stage.

Booth fired his derringer pistol at the back of the President's head. Exclaiming *"Sic semper tyrannis"* ("Thus always to tyrants"—the motto of the state of Virginia) and "revenge for the South," he then pushed his way between the mortally wounded President and his wife. Major Rathbone tried to halt him, but Booth slightly wounded the Major with a knife. He climbed over the edge of the box, in order to drop to the stage, eleven feet below. The spur of his right foot caught in some bunting decorating the stage, and as he landed, he broke his left leg. He limped across the stage and was heading out the back door before the audience realized what had happened. Booth mounted his horse and rode down Ninth Street to Pennsylvania Avenue, where he turned eastward, heading south of the Capitol toward the Navy Yard Bridge over the Anacostia River.

At about the same time, two men on horseback rode into Madison Place, across Pennsylvania Avenue from the Executive Mansion, and stopped at the residence of Secretary of State William H. Seward. One of them was Lewis Payne, a large, muscular young man with jet-black hair. The other was David Herold, a slow-witted onetime druggist's assistant. While Herold held Payne's horse, the latter went up to the front door of the Seward residence and knocked. Seward, seriously injured in a carriage accident a few days before, was confined to bed with a broken arm and a fractured jaw.

Payne told the servant who answered the door that he brought medicine from Doctor Verdi, Seward's physician, and that he had been instructed to deliver it personally to the patient. The attendant said he had strict orders to allow no visitors, but Payne pushed by him and started up the stairs for the second floor. There he was met by Frederick Seward, the Secretary's son, who said that he would see that the Secretary got the medicine. Payne turned momentarily as if to go down, then pulled out a pistol with which he severely beat young Seward. By now the servant was crying for help, and Herold, waiting outside the house, mounted his horse and rode away. Payne gained entry to the Secretary's darkened sickroom and with a knife slashed at the invalid. The household now aroused, Payne fled, knifing a State Department messenger on his way out. William Seward had been slashed in each cheek but would eventually recover.

Meanwhile, at Ford's Theater, Charles Seale, a young assistant surgeon of a volunteer regiment, responded to the calls for medical help. He at first thought the President was dead, but then discovered a weak pulse and shallow breathing. Other doctors arrived on the scene, and it was determined that the ball from Booth's derringer had lodged in the President's brain. The doctors concluded that the wound was bound to be fatal. Soldiers removed Lincoln to the house of William Peterson, across the street from Ford's Theater.

Stanton and Secretary of the Navy Gideon Welles, having heard first the news of the attack on Seward, had gone to the latter's house, and then, learning of the shooting of the President, had driven to Ford's Theater and then to the Peterson home. From the time Lincoln was moved there until he died about 7:00 a.m. the next morning, the house was a scene of constant activity. Mary Lincoln, grieving and nearly hysterical, stood watch with their son Robert. Stanton, always energetic and disciplined, took charge of matters as soon as he arrived at the house.

As Secretary of War, he had the resources of the army at his disposal; General Christopher C. Augur, Commander of the Military Department of Washington, was there to assist him. The Metropolitan Police were also pressed into service. But knowing only of the attacks on Lincoln and Seward, there was bound to be confusion as to what should be done. Was this a widespread plot, which had yet to fully unfold? High government officials who might be targets of the plotters had to be protected. Booth and whoever had acted with him must be apprehended. To add to the confusion, the commercial telegraph linking Washington to the rest of the country had gone dead at about 10:30 p.m.

An army corporal who could take shorthand, James Tanner, was located, and Stanton began his interrogation. Chief Justice David K. Cartter of the local court of appeals administered oaths to witnesses, and Stanton proceeded to question them. He also ordered guards placed around the residences of Vice President Johnson and the members of the Cabinet. Many witnesses identified John Wilkes Booth as the guilty assassin; Corporal Tanner, taking shorthand notes, said that "in fifteen minutes I had testimony enough to hang Wilkes Booth higher than even Haman hung."

A few minutes after he had fled, Booth approached the Navy Yard Bridge over the Anacostia River on horseback. The bridge was routinely closed to traffic in or out of Washington after 9:00 p.m. Sergeant Silas Cobb, in charge of the bridge detail, let Booth pass after inquiring into the reason for his lateness. Shortly afterward, David Herold rode up to the same bridge and was also allowed to pass. John Fletcher, of the livery stable from which Herold had rented his horse, arrived at the bridge shortly afterward in pursuit of Herold and his now-overdue mount. Cobb told him that a man answering Herold's description had just crossed the bridge but that he, Fletcher, would not be allowed back into Washington before morning if he were to cross now. Fletcher turned back and reported his information to the police.

Herold overtook Booth near the village of Surrattsville (now Clinton), Maryland. It was a little after midnight when they stopped at a tavern at this crossroads. Herold dismounted and asked John Lloyd, the proprietor, for the "things" that had been left for them. Lloyd rented the tavern from a woman named Mary Surratt. He brought out two carbines, a cartridge box, and a pair of field glasses. Herold and Booth took them and rode off; Booth was now looking for a physician because of the pain in his leg.

At about 4:00 a.m. they reached the farm of Dr. Samuel Mudd, near Bryantown, thirty miles south of Washington. Mudd found that Booth had a broken leg, placed it in a splint, and gave Booth and Herold food and lodging for the rest of the night. The next day he pointed out to them the shortest route to the Potomac River and thence to Virginia. Lieutenant David Dana, who took part in the search for Booth, arrived in Bryantown shortly after noon on Saturday, April 15, and in answer to questions by some townspeople told them of the assassination—and of the search for Booth.

Booth was apparently sheltered for several days by Confederate sympathizers in southern Maryland, and eventually he and Herold crossed the Potomac into Virginia. On Monday, April 24, two Confederate soldiers and a companion were accosted by Booth and Herold at Port Conway, on the southern side of the Rappahannock River. Eventually these soldiers found a hiding place for the two fugitives in a barn belonging to Richard Garrett. Pursuing federal troops discovered the hiding place a day or two later, and in the ensuing gunfight Herold was captured and Booth was killed.

Obviously, Booth had not acted alone in this enterprise, and the stage was now set for the trial of those who were charged with having conspired with him. But in a sense the trial was an effort to stage *Hamlet* without the Prince of Denmark. There was, indeed, as Corporal Tanner had said, "testimony enough to hang Wilkes Booth higher than even Haman hung," but the evidence against the remaining defendants charged with conspiracy was a good deal murkier.

CHAPTER 12

Confederates in Canada

EDWIN STANTON PERSONALLY directed the investigation of Lincoln's assassination and the pursuit of the conspirators, but he was greatly assisted in that task by the Judge Advocate General of the Army, Joseph Holt. Holt was born in Kentucky in 1807, two years before Lincoln. He was educated at Centre College and began the practice of law at the age of twenty-one in the small town of Elizabethtown. Four years later, he moved to Louisville, and a few years after that to Mississippi, where he engaged in a highly successful legal practice. He returned to Kentucky at the age of thirty-five and resided there until he was appointed to public office by President James Buchanan as a reward for his support for the Democratic ticket in the election of 1856. He was made Commissioner of Patents in 1857, Postmaster General in 1859, and Secretary of War in January 1861. In this last office, he joined with Stanton and Jeremiah Black in an effort to prevent Buchanan from conceding vital points to the seceded states. After Lincoln was inaugurated in March, Holt returned to Kentucky and played an important part in keeping that border state in the Union. His views of the sectional conflict underwent the same sort of transformation as had those of Benjamin Butler and Stanton. All three had been partisans of Buchanan in 1856, and none had supported Lincoln in 1860. But with the coming of the Civil War, all three became strong partisans of the Union and, later, of the radical wing of the Republican Party. Lincoln appointed Holt to the newly created position of Judge Advocate General of the Army in September 1862, with the hope that Holt would find a way to utilize military commissions to try civilians suspected of disloyalty to the Union cause.

Three days after the assassination, Lewis Payne and Mary Surratt were arrested at the latter's boardinghouse in Washington. The same day, Samuel Arnold and Michael O'Laughlin, two minor figures in the alleged conspiracy, were arrested at Fortress Monroe, Virginia. At about the same time, Dr. Samuel Mudd was apprehended at his residence in southern Maryland. George Atzerodt, who would be charged with planning to assassinate Vice President Andrew Johnson, was taken into custody in Montgomery County, Maryland, and Edward Spangler, the stagehand who had held Booth's horse, was detained in Washington. The administration—spearheaded by Holt and Stanton—decided to try the alleged conspirators before a military commission rather than in the civil courts.

James Speed, the Attorney General who would the following year perform so poorly for the government in the argument of the *Milligan* case, issued a one-sentence opinion affirming the legality of such a trial. This opinion—the shortest ever issued by any Attorney General—was totally devoid of any reasoning or analysis. The arguments for and against this position—arguments that would ultimately be considered by the Supreme Court in *Milligan*—were very much bruited about at the time, and Speed's failure to deal with them at all is further evidence of his lack of professional ability.

On May 1, 1865—sixteen days after the assassination and less than a week after Booth was killed—President Andrew Johnson issued an order reciting the conclusion of Attorney General Speed and directing that the War Department detail nine military officers to serve as a commission for the trial of the conspirators. The order stated that the trials be "conducted" by Judge Advocate General Holt in person, aided by such assistance as he might designate. On May 6, the Adjutant General appointed seven general officers and two field-grade officers as members of the commission that would try the conspirators.

Major General David Hunter was, by virtue of seniority, the president of the Commission. Among its members was General Lew Wallace, who would later gain public recognition as the author of the historical novel *Ben Hur* and as governor of the Territory of New Mexico during the heyday of William Bonney (Billy the Kid). Hunter was an 1822 graduate of West Point and had served in the military for most of his adult life. He had various commands during the Civil War, including the Department of the South, which consisted primarily of Atlantic coastal areas under Union control. In March 1862, he issued an order liberating all the slaves within his department, only to have Lincoln revoke it as beyond the General's authority.

Unlike the case with the Indianapolis treason trials, the trial of the Lincoln conspirators was based on a single charge, and a single, though elaborate, specification. The eight defendants were charged with having

> maliciously, unlawfully, and traitorously, and in aid of the existing armed rebellion against the United States of America, on or before the sixth day of March A.D. 1865, and on divers other days between that day and the fifteenth day of April, A.D. 1865, combining, confederating and conspiring together with . . . John Wilkes Booth, Jefferson Davis . . . Jacob Thompson, Clement C. Clay . . . and others unknown to kill and murder, within the Military Department of Washington, and within the fortified and intrenched lines thereof, Abraham Lincoln, late, and at the time of said combining, confederating, and conspiring, President of the United States of America, and Commander-in-Chief of the Army and Navy thereof; Andrew Johnson, now Vice-President of the United States aforesaid; William H. Seward, Secretary of State of the United States aforesaid; and Ulysses S. Grant, Lieutenant-General of the Army of the United States aforesaid, then in command of the Armies of the United States, under the direction of the said Abraham Lincoln; and in pursuance of and in prosecuting said malicious, unlawful, and traitorous conspiracy aforesaid, and in aid of said rebellion, afterward, to-wit, on the fourteenth day of April, A.D. 1865. . . . Together with said John Wilkes Booth . . . maliciously, unlawfully, and traitorously murdered the said Abraham Lincoln, then President of the United States and Commander-in-Chief of the Army and Navy of the United States, as aforesaid; and maliciously, unlawfully, and traitorously assaulting with intent to kill and murder, the said

William H. Seward, then Secretary of State of the United States as aforesaid; and lying in wait with intent maliciously, unlawfully, and traitorously to kill and murder the said Andrew Johnson, then being Vice-President of the United States; and the said Ulysses S. Grant, then being Lieutenant-General, and in command of the Armies of the United States, as aforesaid.

To put it mildly, this was an ambitious charge. The defendants were accused not only of conspiring with one another, with Booth, and with persons unknown, but with, *inter alia*, Jefferson Davis, Clement C. Clay, and Jacob Thompson. Davis, of course, was President of the Confederate States of America. He and his cabinet decamped from Richmond when that city was taken by Union troops in early April, and he continued to be a fugitive. He was later captured and held in prison for several years until the government finally gave up hope of successfully prosecuting him. Clement C. Clay was a United States Senator from Alabama until his state seceded. Jacob Thompson was Buchanan's Secretary of War. He resigned in December 1860, disappointed with the President's refusal to grant all the demands of the seceded states. Both Clay and Thompson served as influential Confederate agents in Canada during the latter part of the Civil War, and a substantial part of the testimony at the trial would deal with their activities there.

The specification repeated much of the language of the charge but went into more detail with respect to each of the defendants. Spangler was charged with having aided Booth in gaining access to Ford's Theater on the night of the assassination and having aided and abetted him in making his escape from the theater after he had killed Lincoln. David Herold was accused of having aided and abetted Booth in making his escape from Washington and in concealing him after he had escaped. Lewis Payne was charged with having assaulted with intent to murder Seward and the others whom he confronted at the Seward residence.

George Atzerodt was accused of having on the same night lain in wait for Vice President Andrew Johnson with intent to kill him. Michael O'Laughlin was similarly charged with having, on the nights of April 13 and 14, lain in wait for General Grant with intent to kill him. Samuel Arnold was cited for giving aid and comfort to the other conspirators during the month of March and the first part of April. Mary Surratt was accused of harboring, concealing, and aiding Booth and others with knowledge of their "murderous and traitorous" conspiracy. Samuel Mudd was charged with having aided and assisted in the concealment of the other conspirators.

The decision to try the conspirators before a military commission was itself controversial at the time and has remained so. The findings and sentence imposed on Surratt and Mudd have likewise engendered controversy down to the present day.

The commission convened on May 9, adopted rules of procedure, and adjourned for several days in order that the defendants might obtain counsel. Attorneys were introduced to the commission on May 12, and Reverdy Johnson, representing Surratt, entered a plea challenging the jurisdiction of the military commission. He made essentially the same arguments that would be made later in *Milligan*. The commission overruled the argument, and all of the defendants pleaded not guilty.

The first witness, Richard Montgomery, was then called by the government. Montgomery and several of the other witnesses who followed him had no personal knowledge of any of the activities of the defendants. They testified to activities conducted by the Confederate agents in Canada and implicated Booth in these activities. They also discussed the involvement of those agents in a raid conducted by escaped Confederate prisoners of war on the post office and banks in the border town of St. Albans, Vermont. This testimony was wide-ranging and quite immaterial as to the defendants on trial, unless they could be linked to Booth, and through him to the Confederate agents in Canada. If that could be accomplished, and it could be shown that the conspiracy was not merely between Booth and the defendants before the commission, but extended to high officials of the Confederate government as well, that showing would have ramifications not only for defendants but also for the jurisdiction of the military commission.

Montgomery testified that he had spent most of his time in Canada since he first had gone there in the summer of 1864. He was in the service of the U.S. government, seeking to acquire information about Confederate activities north of the border. He testified that he had conversed with Jacob Thompson on several occasions:

> In a conversation I had with Jacob Thompson, in the summer of 1864, he said he had his friends (Confederates) all over the Northern States, who were ready and willing to go to any length to serve the cause of the South; and he added that he could at any time have the tyrant Lincoln, and any other of his advisers that he chose, put out of his way; he would have but to point out the man that he considered in his way, and his friends, as he termed them, would put him out of it, and not have let him know anything about it if necessary; and that they would not consider it a crime when done for the cause of the Confederacy.[1]

Montgomery had on several occasions been entrusted by the Confederate agents in Canada with dispatches to take to their government in Richmond; he would carry them to Gordonsville, Virginia, and arrange for them to be conveyed from there to Richmond. He would likewise receive dispatches at Gordonsville and take them to Thompson in Montreal. Montgomery testified that:

> Before the St. Albans' raid I knew of it; I was not, however, aware of the precise point aimed at, but I informed the Government at Washington that these men were about setting out on a raid of that kind. I also informed the Government of the intended raids upon Buffalo and Rochester, and by that means prevented them. I heard Mr. Clay say, in speaking about the funds for paying for these raids, that he always had plenty of money to pay for anything that was worth paying for. I know that they had funds deposited in several different banks. . . .[2]

Montgomery also testified that he had received for delivery to Richmond a long letter from Clement C. Clay to Judah P. Benjamin, the Confederate Secretary of State, and that although the letter was unsigned, he had watched Clay write most of it in his house in St.

Catherines, Canada West (the name then given to Ontario). The letter described the St. Albans raid in some detail:

> You have doubtless learned, through the press of the United States, of the raid on St. Albans, Vermont, by about twenty-five Confederate soldiers—nearly all of them escaped prisoners—led by Lieutenant Bennett H. Young; of their attempts and failure to burn the town; and of their robbery of three banks there of the aggregate amount of about $200,000; of their arrests in Canada by United States forces, their commitment, and the pending preliminary trial. There are twelve or fourteen of the twenty-five who have been arrested, and are now in prison at Montreal, where the trial for commitment for extradition is now progressing. . . .
>
> On showing me his commissions and his instructions from Mr. Seddon [the Confederate Secretary of War] which were of course vague and indefinite—he said he was authorized to do all the damage he could to the enemy in the *way of retaliation*. If this be true, it seems to me the Confederate States Government should not hesitate to avow his act was fully authorized as warrantable retaliation. If the Government do not assume the responsibility of this raid, I think Lieutenant Y. and his men will be given up to the United States authorities. If so, I fear the exasperated and alarmed people of Vermont will exact cruel [vengeance] upon them before they reach the prison at St. Albans.[3]

The next important witness for the prosecution gave his name as Sanford Conover and said he was a correspondent for the *New York Tribune* who had spent time in Canada during late 1864 and early 1865. Conover made some remarkable statements that tended to incriminate many people; long after the proceedings before the military commission were completed, serious doubt was cast on parts of his testimony, and it is not too much to say that he all but admitted perjury with respect to some of it.

Conover said that he had been drafted into the Confederate army, served as a clerk in the War Department in Richmond for six months, and then passed through Union lines to Canada by walking most of the way. While there, he was "intimately acquainted" with Jacob Thompson, Clement Clay, and other Confederate sympathizers. He said that he had seen Booth only once in Montreal: "That was in the latter part of October last. I think I saw him with Sanders, and also at Mr. Thompson's. I saw him principally about the St. Lawrence Hall. He was strutting about there, dissipating, playing billiards, etc."[4]

His first "interview" with Thompson had taken place in the latter's room in the St. Lawrence Hotel in Montreal in the early part of February 1865. Thompson told him that "some of our boys are going to play a grand joke on Abe and Andy." Thompson explained that it was to remove them from office by killing them and that everybody engaged in the effort would be commissioned in the Confederate army so that if they escaped to Canada after the assassinations they could not be successfully extradited. Conover went on to testify:

> I know of my own personal knowledge, that the commissions conferred on Bennett H. Young, the St. Albans' raider, was a blank commission, filled up and conferred by Mr. Clay. The name attached to it, when it came into the hands of these men from Richmond, was that of James A. Seddon, Secretary of War. I saw this commission, and I was asked by Mr. Thompson as to the genuineness of Seddon's signature, having been a clerk in his department. . . . I am well acquainted with the handwriting of James A. Seddon, and know that the blank commission was in his handwriting.[5]

Conover went on to testify as to a scheme whereby Confederate agents in Canada would bring goods infected with yellow fever to New York and Philadelphia in order to launch an epidemic. Another scheme about which Conover testified involved the destruction of the Croton Dam, which formed the reservoir that supplied drinking water for New York City. Conover also described a plan to poison the water in that reservoir. It was brought out that he had used the name James Watson Wallace while in Canada, and there appears to have been confusion between him and another person by the name of James Wallace.

Conover testified on May 20 and May 22 but was then sent back to Canada to obtain transcripts of the Canadian judicial proceedings in which he claimed to have participated. He was recalled to the stand on June 27, in an attempt to bolster his credibility. But meanwhile Holt apparently began to have doubts about his witness. He inquired of someone at the *New York Tribune* as to the general reputation of Conover for "integrity and truth." General John Dix, commanding in New York, wrote Stanton about Conover several days before Conover resumed the stand: The papers found in his trunk "show that he wrote for the *Montreal Telegraph*, a most atrocious and vindictive article on the assassination of Mr. Lincoln. His character, in other aspects, is bad; and his testimony, where he is known, will have no weight unless it is corroborated by witnesses of unquestionable credibility."[6]

Other government witnesses testified that they had spent time in Canada during the period of the alleged conspiracy and had heard various Confederate agents expatiate on the plan to kill Lincoln and others. Several testified to having seen Booth in Canada in company with known Confederate sympathizers. Henry Von Steinacker, an engineer in the Confederate service, said he had ridden on horseback in Virginia's Shenandoah Valley with three civilians for some eighteen or twenty hours. One of them, he said, was Booth, whom he identified on the stand from a photograph. He was asked by Booth, he said, what he thought of the probable success of the Confederacy; since this was immediately after the defeat at the Battle of Gettysburg, he said he thought "it looked very gloomy." Booth replied, he said: "That is nonsense. If we only act our part, the Confederacy will gain its independence. Old Abe Lincoln must go up the spout, and the Confederacy will gain its independence anyhow."[7]

Testimony was received as to a letter found by a woman named Mary Hudspeth while she was riding on the Third Avenue cars, in New York City. She overheard two other passengers conversing, and after they got out, her daughter picked up a letter that was lying on the floor and gave it to her mother. The letter was addressed to someone named Louis and bore the signature "Charles Selby." It spoke of the addressee as being the "Charlotte Corday of the nineteenth century," and said *"Abe* must *die,* and *now.* You can choose your weapons. The cup, the *knife,* the *bullet.* The cup failed us once, and might again." This letter, with virtually no other foundation having been laid, was admitted in evidence by the commission. Another letter was admitted, based on the testimony of Charles Dawson, a clerk at the National Hotel in Washington, where Booth had stayed. Following the assassination, he had come across a letter addressed "J.W.B." which had been left at the desk, and he took the letter unopened to Judge Advocate Bingham about May 24. He testified that the only guest at the National Hotel whom he knew to have the initials J.W.B. was John Wilkes Booth. The letter was offered in evidence:

> South Branch Bridge,
> April 6, 1865.
>
> FRIEND WILKES I received yours of March 12, and reply as soon as practicable. I saw French, Brady, and others about the *oil* speculation. The subscription to the *stock* amounts to $8,000 and I add $1,000 myself, which is about all I can stand. Now, when you *sink* your well go DEEP enough; don't fail, everything depends on you and your *helpers*. If you can't get through on your trip, after you *strike ile*, strike through Thornton Gap, and cross by Capon, Romney's and down the Branch and I can keep you safe from all hardships for a year. I am clear of all surveillance, now that infernal Purdy is beat. . . . I send this up by Tom, and if he don't get drunk, you'll get it the ninth; in all events, it can't be understood if lost. I can't half write. I have been drunk for two days. Don't write so much highfalutin next time; no more; only Jake will be at Green's with the funds. Burn this. Truly, yours, LON.[8]

Robert Purdy then testified that he knew someone living on the South Branch (one of the upper tributaries of the Potomac River in West Virginia) named Leonidas McAleer, who generally went by the name of "Lon." He testified that he had seen Lon's handwriting, and that the writing in the letter offered in evidence resembled that of McAleer.

This letter, of course, if properly authenticated, might have been admissible against Booth, but Booth was not on trial—he was dead. The testimony of the activities in Canada, and of Booth's doings in the United States, plainly incriminated him in a plot to kill Abraham Lincoln and perhaps other government officials. But there was no need for speculation on that point; there was no doubt that Booth had in fact assassinated Abraham Lincoln at Ford's Theater on the evening of April 14. The task of the government in the proceedings before the military commission was to show that the defendants on trial there had in some way conspired with Booth, or aided and abetted him.

CHAPTER 13

Booth's Accomplices

G EORGE H. ATZERODT was charged before the commission with having lain in wait for Andrew Johnson at his hotel with the intent to murder him. Atzerodt was from Port Tobacco, a hotbed of secessionist sympathy in southern Maryland, but he often traveled to Washington and to Montgomery County, where he was finally arrested. Robert Jones, who was a clerk at the Kirkwood House hotel at the time of Lincoln's assassination, identified a page from the hotel register which showed that Atzerodt had taken Room 126 in that hotel sometime before 8:00 a.m. on April 14. Jones identified Atzerodt in the dock at trial and testified that he had seen him around noon that day in the Kirkwood House.

John Lee, an officer of the military police, had been sent to the Kirkwood House by Major Obeirne, one of the officials directing the investigation into the assassination of Lincoln, on the morning of April 15. He had to break open the door to Atzerodt's room because no key was available. He testified that underneath the pillow on the bed was a revolver, and that there was a Bowie knife between the sheets and the mattress of the bed. In the pocket of a coat hanging on the wall, he found a bankbook made to the order of John Wilkes Booth, showing a credit of $450 and containing a map of Virginia. He also said that when going from Room 126 to the front office of the hotel, a guest would pass by the room occupied by Vice President Johnson.

Colonel W. R. Nevins stated that he had stopped at the Kirkwood House on April 12, two days before the assassination, and had seen

Atzerodt in one of the passageways. The latter asked him which room was occupied by Johnson, and the Colonel obligingly showed him.

John Fletcher told the commission that he was the foreman at Naylor's Livery Stable and that Atzerodt had begun keeping horses there in early April 1865. Fletcher had seen him in the early afternoon of April 14, when Atzerodt asked him to put up a horse, which he later reclaimed at about 10:00 p.m. Fletcher had spotted him riding back to the Kirkwood House at that time.

John Greenawalt testified that he kept the Pennsylvania House, another hostelry in downtown Washington. Atzerodt stayed there in late March and early April 1865, and during that time John Wilkes Booth called upon him frequently. John Caldwell stated that he met Atzerodt in a store in Georgetown around 8:00 a.m. on the morning of April 15, and Atzerodt tried to sell him a loaded and capped revolver for ten dollars. Caldwell refused but then lent Atzerodt ten dollars on the security of the revolver in question. James McPhail, Provost Marshal of the state of Maryland, said that Atzerodt, while he was in prison after his arrest, requested to see McPhail in order to make a statement. The statement was that he, Atzerodt, had thrown his knife away near the corner of 9th and F Streets on the night of the assassination.

William Doster, Atzerodt's defense attorney, offered through another witness a statement by Atzerodt giving his version of the events of the night of the assassination. Today, of course, a defendant would be perfectly at liberty to take the stand on his own behalf and present such an account. He would then be subject to cross-examination by the prosecution, and to possible impeachment for the purpose of showing that the defendant was not a truthful witness. But there is no doubt that the defendant would be able to take the stand if he so desired. This was not the case, however, at the time the Lincoln assassination conspirators were tried. The defendant in a case then could not take the stand on his own behalf, because of reasons largely veiled in antiquity; one of them was the belief that a defendant was bound to lie, and therefore allowing him to give testimony offered too much of a temptation to commit yet another crime: perjury.

But opinion on the subject began to change in the middle of the nineteenth century, and Maine, in 1864, was the first state to make defendants in criminal trials fully competent to testify. Within the next twenty years, every state except Georgia, as well as the federal government, permitted the criminal defendant the option of testifying on his own behalf.[1]

However, the Indianapolis Treason trials and the trials of the Lincoln conspirators both proceeded under the prevailing rule of their time. Even had these defendants been tried in civil courts, they still would have been disqualified from testifying on their own behalf.

It was perfectly clear from the evidence presented to the commission that David Herold had accompanied Booth as he fled Washington over the Navy Yard Bridge, was with him when they stopped at a tavern operated by John Lloyd in order to pick up weapons that had been previously deposited there, and continued to be in his presence throughout their time in southern Maryland and northern Virginia, until Herold was captured by federal troops outside of Garrett's barn. John Fletcher said that Herold had come with Atzerodt to his stable shortly after noon on April 14. Herold engaged a horse which he told Fletcher he would call for later in the afternoon, which he did. Fletcher informed Herold that he could keep the horse only until 9:00 p.m. at the latest, but after 10:00 p.m. Fletcher saw Herold spurring the horse up Fourteenth Street. Fletcher got another horse from his stable and followed Herold to the Navy Yard bridge, where he was turned back by the military sentry.

Sergeant Silas T. Cobb, who was in charge of sentry duty at the bridge on the night of April 14, said that a man looking very much like Herold had ridden up to the bridge and, after questioning, had been allowed to pass. John Lloyd, who rented the tavern owned by Mrs. Surratt in Surrattsville, Maryland, testified that five or six weeks before Lincoln's assassination, Herold, Atzerodt, and John H. Surratt, the son of Mary Surratt, had come to his tavern. After having some drinks, John Surratt called Lloyd into the front parlor and asked him to conceal two carbines, some ammunition, and a rope from sixteen to twenty feet in length, which would be reclaimed by them when needed.

That time came at about midnight on April 14, according to Lloyd. Herold rode up on horseback with Booth and went into the tavern, saying, "Lloyd, for God's sake make haste and get those things." Booth, whom Lloyd did not then know, remained outside on his horse. Lloyd produced the carbines and the ammunition, but Herold took only one of them, since Booth's broken leg prevented him from carrying his. Then this conversation ensued:

> Just as they were about leaving, the man who was with Herold said, "I will tell you some news, if you want to hear it," or something to that effect. I said, "I am not particular; use your own pleasure about telling it." "Well," said he, "I am pretty certain that we have assassinated the President and Secretary Seward." I think that was his language, as well as I can recollect. Whether Herold was present at the time he said that, or whether he was across the street, I am not positive; I was much excited and unnerved at the time.[2]

Other witnesses traced Herold's progress with Booth to Garrett's barn on the south side of the Rappahannock River in Virginia, where Booth was shot and Herold captured. At the time Herold was captured, he had with him a small schoolbook map of the northern neck of Virginia (the area between the Potomac and Rappahannock rivers).

Herold, who was represented by Frederick Stone, called several witnesses in his own behalf. The gist of their testimony was that although Herold was in his early twenties, he behaved more like a boy than a man; he was a "light and trifling" person who could be "easily led."

Edward Spangler was charged before the commission with having, on the night of Lincoln's assassination, aided Booth in obtaining entrance to the box of the theater and with having assisted him in making his escape after the assassination. Joseph Guy, who had been present outside of Ford's Theater, testified that Spangler, a "ruffianly looking man," conversed at some length with Booth outside the theater between 9:30 and 10:00 p.m. He also said that Spangler at that time had a mustache. Joseph Selichmann, the assistant property man at the theater, said that Booth came to the theater at about 9:00 p.m. and called for "Ned." He had also seen Booth, Spangler, and others drinking at the restaurant next to the theater before dinner that evening.

The testimony of Jacob Ritterspaugh was particularly damaging to Spangler. Ritterspaugh was a carpenter at Ford's Theater and was present on the night that the President was shot. He told the commission:

> I was standing on the stage behind the scenes on the night of the fourteenth, when someone called out that the President was shot, and directly I saw a man that had no hat on running toward the back door.
>
> He had a knife in his hand, and I ran to stop him, and ran through the last entrance, and as I came up to him he tore the door open. I made for him, and he struck at me with the knife, and I jumped back then. He then ran out and slammed the door shut. . . . I came back on the stage where I had left Edward Spangler, and he hit me on the face with the back of his hand, and he said, "Don't say which way he went." I asked him what he meant by slapping me in the mouth and he said, "For God's sake, shut up"; and that was the last he said.[3]

Ritterspaugh had repeated his account to others, some of whom said that he omitted Spangler's statement "Don't say which way he went," and only attributed the statement "For God's sake, shut up" to him.

John T. Ford, the proprietor of Ford's Theater, testified that Spangler had been in his employ three or four years at intervals, and continuously for the previous two years. He was a stagehand, and his job was to move the scenery from place to place as the script required. He gave the following account of Spangler as a person:

> Spangler, I know, considered Baltimore his home. He buried his wife there about a year ago, or less, while in my employ. He usually spent his summer months there, during the vacation of the theater, chiefly in crab-fishing. . . .
>
> Spangler seemed to have a great admiration for J. Wilkes Booth; I have noticed that in my business on the stage with the stage-manager.
>
> Booth was a peculiarly fascinating man, and controlled the lower class of people such as Spangler belonged to, more, I suppose, than ordinary men would. Spangler was not in the

employ of Booth, that I know, and only since the assassination have I heard that he was in the habit of waiting upon him.[4]

What Ford said of Spangler appears to have been likewise true of Herold, Atzerodt, and Payne; they were all men of limited ability and no education who were attracted to the charismatic Booth, and used by him.

Michael O'Laughlin and Samuel Arnold were two young men on the outer fringes of the events of April 14. Arnold was arrested at Fortress Monroe in Tidewater Virginia on April 17, a few days after the assassination. A search of his carpetbag turned up a pistol. Arnold made statements to the arresting officer that were introduced at the trial. He said he had attended a meeting in Washington with Booth, O'Laughlin, Atzerodt, John Surratt, and others in March. He had urged immediate action upon the group, whereupon Booth became angry and threatened him. At that point Arnold said he told the others he wanted nothing more to do with the affair and took a position as a clerk-accountant at Fortress Monroe, a couple of hundred miles from Washington. He said that the purpose of the conspiracy from which he withdrew was to kidnap Lincoln and take him to Richmond in order to force an exchange of prisoners. His role was to have been to catch the President when he was thrown out of the box at Ford's Theater. A letter from Arnold to Booth dated March 27 was introduced in evidence. It had been written in Hookstown, Baltimore County, and read in part as follows:

Dear John:
     Was business so important that you could not remain in Baltimore until I saw you? . . . When I left you, you stated we would not meet in a month or so. Therefore, I made application for employment, an answer to which I shall receive during the week. I told my parents I had ceased with you. Can I, then, under existing circumstances, come as you request? You know full well that the G-T suspicions something is going there; therefore, the undertaking is becoming more complicated. Why not, for the present, desist, for various reasons, which if you look into, you can readily see, without my making any

mention thereof. You, nor anyone, can censure me from my present course. . . .

Do not in anger peruse this. Weigh all I have said, and, as a rational man and a *friend*, you cannot censure or abrade my conduct. . . . Write me to Balto., as I expect to be in about Wednesday or Thursday, or, if you can possibly come on, I will Tuesday meet you in Balto., at B-. Ever I subscribe myself,

Your friend,

SAM[5]

O'Laughlin was likewise a resident of Baltimore, and Booth had sent him a telegram in March saying, "Don't fear to neglect your business. You had better come at once," and another on March 27 saying, "Get word to Sam. Come on, with or without him, Wed. A.M. we sell that day sure. Don't fail."

But there was no evidence that either O'Laughlin or Arnold had played any part in the activities of the night of April 14. O'Laughlin came down from Baltimore to Washington the day before with some friends to see the illumination planned for that evening and to spend a couple of nights "on the town." The friends said that he had been with them throughout the two days including the evening of April 14. There was conflicting testimony as to whether he publicly entered the house of Edwin M. Stanton on the evening of April 13, the night before the assassination, when General Grant was visiting the Stanton house. But there was no testimony placing him anywhere near either Ford's Theater or Seward's or Stanton's house on April 14.

Lewis Payne was damned by eyewitness testimony of the several people he had assaulted on the evening of April 14 at the home of Secretary of State Seward. His attorney tried to lay the groundwork for a defense of insanity, which was much more stringently limited then than it is at present. Special Judge Advocate John Bingham did not even mention the insanity defense of Payne in his lengthy closing argument, but pointed out that Payne had associated himself with the other conspirators numerous times before the assassination of the President and the wounding of Seward.

So far as factual guilt of *some crime* was concerned, Payne had undoubtedly attempted to murder Seward. Herold had been associated with the conspirators at various times in such a way as to incriminate him, and most certainly had assisted Booth in his escape from Washington. The evidence of Spangler's involvement was a good deal less clear, but if Ritterspaugh's testimony is to be believed, he made some slight effort to hinder the pursuit of Booth from Ford's Theater. Arnold and O'Laughlin seemed to have been involved in a conspiracy among the same group of people to abduct Lincoln from Ford's Theater and take him to Richmond—a truly ludicrous undertaking. With the capture of Richmond by Union forces, and the subsequent surrender of Lee's army at Appomattox, even the conspirators could see that such a scheme was no longer remotely feasible. Before the final plot to assassinate Lincoln was hatched, O'Laughlin and Arnold appear to have abandoned the enterprise.

After a trial in which the taking of testimony lasted from May 12 until June 13, the commission heard closing arguments and retired to deliberate on June 29. After several days, it found each of these six defendants guilty of at least part of the charges against them. It sentenced Herold, Atzerodt, and Payne each to be "hanged by the neck until he be dead," and O'Laughlin and Arnold to imprisonment at hard labor for life. It exonerated Spangler of the conspiracy charge but found him guilty of aiding and abetting Booth in his escape from Ford's Theater and sentenced him to imprisonment at hard labor for six years.

The greatest controversy as to the factual findings of the commission has centered around the two remaining defendants: Mary Surratt and Samuel Mudd.

Mary Surratt had kept a boardinghouse on H Street, in Washington, and also owned a tavern in Surrattsville, Maryland, which she leased to John Lloyd. It was at that tavern that Booth and Herold had stopped late on the night of April 14, after the assassination, to pick up guns and ammunition that had previously been left there by Mary's son, John. Mary Surratt was the first woman to be hanged in the United States, and controversy about her case stemmed both from that fact and from the unusual circumstances surrounding the commission's recommendation of the death sentence.

Surratt was rather unkindly described by the *New York Times* as "fair, fat, and forty." Lewis Weichmann, a young man who had known her son John at college, began boarding at her Washington home in November 1864. He shared a room, and often a bed, with her son, although John was often absent in either Canada or Richmond for considerable periods of time. Weichmann was employed as a clerk in the office of the Commissary-General of Prisoners, and he was one of the principal prosecution witnesses against Mary Surratt.

He testified that from January 1865 on, Booth called frequently at the boardinghouse; he would ask first for John Surratt, but in John's absence he would talk privately to Mary Surratt. Weichmann also stated that Lewis Payne, using the alias Wood, had called at the house on two occasions in March or April 1865. He remained overnight the first time and stayed three days the second. David Herold also called at the boardinghouse several times, according to Weichmann, and Atzerodt had been there ten or fifteen times since January 1865.

Weichmann said that on the Tuesday before the assassination, Mrs. Surratt had sent him to the National Hotel to borrow Booth's buggy. Booth told him that he had sold the buggy but gave Weichmann ten dollars to rent one. Weichmann then proceeded to drive Mrs. Surratt to Surrattsville so that she could see a man who owed her money. Just before they left the house, Weichmann said, she and Booth had a short, hurried conversation, which he did not overhear.

On the day of the assassination, Weichmann again hired a buggy for Mrs. Surratt and drove her to Surrattsville. They stopped at the tavern leased by Lloyd, and Mary went into the parlor and remained for some time. Weichmann stated that Surrattsville was a two-hour drive from the city of Washington and about ten miles from the Navy Yard Bridge.

John Lloyd, who resided at the Surrattsville tavern, said that five or six weeks before the assassination, John Surratt, David Herold, and George Atzerodt came to his house in Surrattsville and that during the course of the visit, Surratt called him into the front parlor and gave him two carbines, ammunition, and a sixteen-to-twenty-foot length of rope. Surratt told him to conceal them on the premises, which Lloyd reluctantly did. Surratt said that they would be picked up in a few days.

On the Tuesday before the assassination, according to Lloyd, he had met Mrs. Surratt on the road from Washington in a buggy. She inquired generally about some articles at his place, but when he professed not to know what she meant, she explicitly referred to "shooting irons." Lloyd told her where they were hidden, and she then said they would be needed soon. When she visited the tavern on the afternoon of the assassination, she asked him to have the "shooting irons" ready that night; some parties would call for them.

Finally, Lewis Payne showed up on her doorstep on April 17, when both of them were arrested by investigating officers.

Those investigating the assassination at first thought that Weichmann and Lloyd were possible culprits in the conspiracy, but instead they became witnesses for the prosecution. When there was opposition to this tactic by the government, the *San Francisco Alta Californian* quite properly commented: "Some objection was made that several of the witnesses themselves were participants in the crime, and therefore unworthy of credence; but if such testimony were not accepted, the punishment of great crimes would be rarer than it is."[6]

Weichmann apparently made a favorable impression on at least one member of the military commission. Lew Wallace, in his autobiography, commented that "I have never seen anything like his steadfastness. There he stood, a young man only twenty-three years of age, strikingly handsome, intelligent, self-possessed, under the most searching cross-examination I have ever heard."[7]

Weichmann, as well as witnesses called for the defense, portrayed Mary Surratt as a devout practicing Catholic of exemplary character. Lloyd, on the other hand, was described as apt to drink heavily and, in fact, was said to have been drunk at the time of the purported conversation between him and Mary Surratt on April 14.

One of the established principles of appellate review of trial proceedings is that the credibility of witnesses is best left to the judgment of the trial judge or the jury. The principle is often expressed in terms of the difficulty of determining from the cold record whether or not a witness spoke accurately and truthfully. In the case under consideration, the principle applies in spades to any attempt to evaluate the testimony of witnesses at the conspiracy trial on the basis of Benn Pitman's transcript of that trial. The transcript is not in the form of questions and answers, as the testimony surely must have been presented to the commission at the time. Instead, it is paraphrased entirely as answers, without any questions at all. There are no grounds for suggesting that Pitman in any way deliberately shaded the testimony, but it is nonetheless true that this method of reporting will often lose nuances that would be preserved by reporting the testimony verbatim in question-and-answer form.

That said, it is difficult to fault the commission for having found Mary Surratt guilty of conspiracy. The conspirators most heavily involved—Booth, Atzerodt, Herold, and Payne—frequently used her house as a meeting place, and she and Booth had numerous private conversations. These facts by themselves are not enough to convict anyone of criminal complicity, but when they are taken together with the comment she made to Lloyd about the "shooting irons," the picture takes on a different hue. Contemporary critics focused their attention not so much on the finding of guilt as on the decision to hang a woman.

On July 7, the day set for the execution, Mary Surratt's lawyers applied to Judge Andrew Wylie of the Circuit Court for the District of Columbia for a writ of *habeas corpus*, claiming that civilians could not be tried before a military commission where the civil courts were open. Judge Wylie issued the writ, but the government made its return shortly before noon in the persons of General Winfield Scott Hancock and Attorney General Speed. They showed the court the endorsement of President Johnson suspending the writ of *habeas corpus*, and Wylie declined to act further.

Though not known at the time, there was a wrinkle to Mary Surratt's case that was not present in those of the other defendants. Five members of the military commission had refused to concur in the death sentence against her unless the Judge Advocate General appended to the verdict their recommendation that the President commute her sentence to life imprisonment. This unusual addendum did not become public until 1867, during the trial of John Surratt in a civil court—a proceeding that ultimately resulted in a hung jury. It was also intimated during the course of John Surratt's trial that Judge Advocate General Holt had never shown the clemency recommendation to Johnson, who under the law had to give final approval to any capital sentence. But the matter lay largely dormant until 1873, when Holt published a pamphlet, with supporting affidavits, that the clemency recommendation had been with the other papers, where Johnson should readily have seen it. Johnson, now out of office, replied shortly afterward that he had never come upon the addendum urging clemency and had not otherwise learned of it. Various officials supported one version or another, with the matter never being clearly resolved. Nor is it at all certain that had Johnson known of the clemency plea, he would have refused to approve the sentence.

Samuel Mudd has had his name immortalized in the expression "His name is Mudd." The evidentiary debate in his case has been about whether he could properly be found guilty of either conspiring with Booth and the others or as accessory after the fact to Booth's crime: in effect, whether he helped Booth and Herold to escape detection and flee, knowing that they had committed a crime. Mudd was sentenced to life imprisonment at hard labor and spent nearly four years in prison on Dry Tortugas, a barren island off the west coast of Florida. He was pardoned by Johnson as the latter left office, not because of his innocence but because of his valiant service in connection with an epidemic of yellow fever that had broken out at the prison. Mudd returned to southern Maryland, where he farmed until his death in 1883.

One critical evidentiary inquiry in Mudd's case is whether he had recognized Booth when the latter came to his farm in the early morning of April 15, following the assassination. Mudd's defenders contend that he was simply doing his duty as a physician when he attended to Booth's broken leg. They admit that Mudd knew Booth but say that he did not recognize the actor when he appeared with Herold in the dead of night and that, at any rate, he did not know at that time that Booth had fatally shot Lincoln.

Mudd's guilt, according to the opposite view, may be inferred from his well-known sympathy for the Confederate cause, and his previous contacts with Booth. He met with Booth, John Surratt, and Weichmann in a hotel in Washington in January 1865. At that time, Booth had private conversations with Mudd and Surratt, during which Weichmann saw Booth draw a diagram or a map. Mudd had also visited Mary Surratt's house in Washington in March and had entered the room of Marcus Norton at the National Hotel, looking for Booth, at about the same time.

Mudd's detractors also point out that the doctor did far more than simply treat Booth for a broken leg. He gave Booth and Herold shelter and lodging until they left his house late in the day on April 15, and he showed them a little-used route through a swamp by which they could elude capture and eventually cross the Potomac River into Virginia. By the time the culprits left, say those supporting the guilty verdict, Mudd would have known that Lincoln had been assassinated and that Booth was being sought as the culprit.

The evidence against Mudd seems too sketchy to have convicted him as a conspirator in the plot to kill Lincoln. It is not at all certain that the conspiracy to abduct Lincoln had ripened into the conspiracy to kill Lincoln by the time of Mudd's last visit to Washington to see Booth. There is no basis in the evidence for thinking that Booth and Herold would have stopped at Mudd's farm, thirty miles south of Washington, if Booth had not broken his leg, and of course Booth did not *plan* to break his leg. But the evidence for Mudd's guilt "as accessory after the fact" is a good deal stronger. Under the common law as it existed at that time, an accessory need only have assisted the criminal in escaping from capture, knowing or having reason to believe that a crime had been committed.

Mudd and his descendants have energetically sought to vindicate the doctor down to the present day. They have sought to show his innocence of any crime and have also insisted that neither Mudd, nor any of the other conspirators, could properly have been tried before a military commission.

In July 1868—three years after his trial—Mudd applied to Thomas Boynton, a federal judge in the district of Florida, for a writ of *habeas corpus*. The application relied in large part on the decision of the Supreme Court in *Milligan*, which had been handed down more than a year after the trial of the Lincoln conspirators. If there could be no trials of civilians by military commission in Indiana while the Civil War was still being fought—as *Milligan* held—surely, Mudd argued, his trial and that of the other conspirators before a military commission after Lee's surrender must be unlawful.

Judge Boynton disagreed. In his opinion denying Mudd's application, he said:

> I do not think that *Ex Parte Milligan* is a case in point here. There is nothing in the opinion of the Court in that case, nor in the third article of the Constitution, nor in the Habeas Corpus Act of 1863, to lead to the conclusion that if an army had

been encamped in the State of Indiana, (whether in the immediate presence of the enemy or not), and any person, a resident of Indiana or any other state (enlisted Soldier or not) had, not from private animosity, but from public reasons, made his way within the Army lines and assassinated the Commanding General, such a person could not have been legally tried for his military offense by a military tribunal and legally convicted and sentenced.

The President was assassinated not from private animosity nor any other reason than a desire to impair the effectiveness of military operations and enable the rebellion to establish itself into a Government; the act was committed in a fortified city, which had been invaded during the war, and to the northward as well as the southward of which battles had many times been fought, which was the headquarters of all the armies of the United States, from which daily and hourly went military orders. The President is the Commander in Chief of the Army, and the President who was killed had many times made distinct military orders under his own hand, without the formality of employing the Secretary of War or Commanding General. It was not Mr. Lincoln who was assassinated but the Commander in Chief of the Army, for military reasons. I find no difficulty, therefore, in classing the offense as a military one and with this opinion arrive at the necessary conclusion that the proper tribunal for the trial of those engaged in it was a military one.[8]

More than a century after their ancestor's death, Mudd's descendants renewed their attack on his conviction. In 1992 they applied to the Army Board for the Correction of Military Records, a rather obscure tribunal devoted to the hearing of claims from aggrieved soldiers or veterans with respect to their grade, pay, or benefits. The board, apparently having no pressing current business, decided to look into the Mudd descendants' claim that a military commission could not lawfully have tried the physician in 1865. Since the board's role is only advisory, the proceedings before it are not contested; no one from the government appears in opposition to the claimant. The board took evidence on the question posed and concluded that

Mudd should have been tried in a civil court and not before a military commission.

The board's findings were forwarded to the Assistant Secretary of the Army, who brought the proceedings down to earth by observing that it was not the function of the board to settle historical disputes. He further pointed out that the same issue had been expressly addressed in Judge Boynton's opinion a century and a quarter earlier and decided adversely to Mudd. The Assistant Secretary accordingly, and very sensibly, rejected the board's recommendation.

CHAPTER 14

World War I

SOME OF THE pressures to abridge civil liberties in the North during the Civil War arose because one part of the country sought to separate from the rest of it. Though most of the fighting was done in the Confederate states, a great battle was fought at Antietam Creek, Maryland, and the following year the decisive battle of the war was fought at Gettysburg, Pennsylvania. In the same year, Chambersburg, Pennsylvania, was burned by Confederate troops, and the following year Confederate General Jubal Early brought his troops to Rockville, Maryland—now a part of the Washington metropolitan area. Kentucky and Missouri were both the sites of pitched battles, and even Indiana was briefly invaded. The enemy was not three thousand miles away across the Atlantic Ocean, or six thousand miles away across the Pacific, but often within an overland march of a day or two. Under these circumstances, those suspected of sedition or disloyalty appeared more menacing than they might have otherwise.

The Lincoln administration had no past history upon which to base its treatment of those it perceived to be either hostile or disruptive within the country. True, during the War of 1812, the British sailed into Chesapeake Bay, burned the capital, and briefly invaded Maryland. But that was only an episode in a war that was quite unlike the Civil War, and the national government under President James Madison was too weak and inert to abridge anyone's civil liberties.

The reaction of the Lincoln administration to conspiracy, disloyalty, and dissent was, therefore, without precedent. Lincoln and his Cabinet chose to suspend the writ of *habeas corpus*, interfere with freedom of speech and of the press, and try suspected political criminals before military commissions. Few of those so treated resorted to the courts to challenge these measures, and so they would remain as a sort of benchmark for future wartime presidents.

For more than thirty years after the Civil War, the United States was at peace with other nations during a remarkable period of industrial expansion. This peace was briefly interrupted in 1898 by the Spanish-American War, but that war was fought in the Caribbean and the Far East, not on United States soil. The only significant engagements between ground forces took place in Cuba, and the Far Eastern part of the conflict ended with Admiral Dewey's victory at the Battle of Manila Bay. The Spanish-American War lasted only a few months, and it was sufficiently short and one-sided as to pose little danger to civil liberties.

The First World War—the "Great War"—was, on the other hand, a conflict of much greater magnitude. It originated from a series of diplomatic maneuvers following the assassination in June 1914 of Archduke Franz Ferdinand, heir to the throne of Austria-Hungary, and his wife, Sophie, by a Serbian nationalist. A month of threats and counterthreats followed between the Allied Powers—Great Britain, France, and Russia—and the Central Powers—Germany and Austria-Hungary. In August 1914, Germany invaded France by marching through neutral Belgium, and Britain, France, and Russia went to war with Germany and Austria-Hungary.

The initial reaction of the United States public was to let Europe fight its own battles. President Woodrow Wilson concurred in this sentiment; he urged the American people to remain neutral "in fact as well as in name . . . and impartial in thought as well as in action." A number of important figures in the mainly Protestant eastern establishment were pro-British, but their views were not shared by the majority. They did not at first urge intervention in the war, but simply an increase in American military strength.

Wilson at first opposed this "preparedness" movement, fearing that it would increase the pressure for intervention in Europe. But in May 1915, a German submarine sank the British liner *Lusitania* off the coast of Ireland. The death toll exceeded twelve hundred noncombatants, of whom 128 were Americans. The United States sent a series of stiff diplomatic notes to Germany, and a few months later

Germany abandoned unrestricted submarine operations against passenger ships. But Wilson now approved a preparedness program for the country.

Nonetheless, in the presidential election of 1916, the Democratic party's slogan was "He kept us out of war," and Wilson was narrowly elected to a second term over Charles Evans Hughes. In February 1917, however, Germany announced that it would sink without warning all ships, belligerent and neutral, in a zone around the Atlantic and Mediterranean coasts of Europe. A few days later, the United States broke off diplomatic relations with Germany. In March, German submarines sank three American merchant vessels without warning and with a considerable loss of life. On April 2, Wilson went before Congress and asked for a declaration of war against the Central Powers. Within a few days, Congress obliged him. But American public opinion was by no means united on the question; there had been no invasion or attack on American territory to mobilize public opinion, and millions of Americans—Socialists, Progressives, German-Americans and Irish-Americans—opposed American participation in the war.

A month later, Congress enacted a conscription law, authorizing the President, by proclamation, to draft men between the ages of twenty-one and thirty. This law was challenged on the ground that it was a form of "involuntary servitude," forbidden by the Thirteenth Amendment to the Constitution, but the Supreme Court unanimously upheld its validity in January 1918.[1] The Court's opinion was written by Chief Justice Edward Douglass White, a Louisianan who himself had been a drummer boy in the Confederate Army more than a half century before.

This war was, of course, different from the Civil War in more ways than one. Not only were the battlefields three thousand miles away across the Atlantic Ocean, but the enemy was foreigners—Germans and Austrians. In the Civil War, the enemy was close at hand, and cousins and even brothers might be on opposing sides. Mary Todd Lincoln had relatives in Kentucky who fought for the Confederacy. The first troops of the American Expeditionary Force reached France in the fall of 1917, and between then and the Armistice in November 1918, nearly one and a half million Americans served abroad. They helped to repulse the final German offensive in 1918.

In June 1917, Congress enacted the Espionage Act, which took up fourteen pages in the Statutes at Large. Many of its provisions were directed against traditional espionage, exportation of arms, interference with maritime vessels, and the like—matters of obvious concern in wartime. But there were at least two parts that did affect civil liberties.

Section 3 stated that "whoever . . . shall wilfully make or convey false reports or false statements with intent to interfere with the operation or success of the military or naval forces of the United States or to promote the success of its enemies and whoever . . . shall wilfully cause or attempt to cause insubordination, disloyalty, mutiny, or refusal of duty, in the military or naval forces of the United States, or shall wilfully obstruct the recruiting or enlistment service of the United States . . . shall be punished by a fine of not more than $10,000 or imprisonment for not more than 20 years, or both."[2]

Title XII, Section 2, said that "every letter, writing, circular, postal card, picture, print engraving, photograph, newspaper, pamphlet, book or other publication, matter or thing of any kind, containing any matter advocating or urging treason, insurrection, or forcible resistance to any law of the United States, is hereby declared to be non-mailable."[3] The following section provided that anyone who used or attempted to use the mails for transmission of any matter deemed nonmailable could be fined up to $5,000 or imprisoned for not more than five years.

Even before he asked Congress to declare war on Germany, Wilson had been critical of foreign-born American citizens who opposed what they regarded as a pro-British foreign policy. In his message to Congress of December 7, 1915, Wilson said, "The gravest threats against our national peace and safety have been uttered within our own borders. There are citizens of the United States, I blush to admit, born under other flags but welcomed by our generous naturalization laws to the full freedom and opportunity of America, who have poured the poison of disloyalty into the very arteries of our national life."[4] He made similar statements during the 1916 presidential campaign.

Wilson's version of the Espionage Act which he submitted to Congress provided for a $10,000 fine and ten years' imprisonment for any person convicted of publishing such information as would be declared by a presidential proclamation to be useful or possibly useful to the enemy. He insisted that such censorship would be "absolutely necessary to the public safety" and that it was "imperative that powers of this sort shall be granted."[5] This provision, however, was defeated in the House by a vote of 184–144 and did not appear in the final bill.

The First Amendment to the United States Constitution provides that Congress shall make no law "abridging the freedom of speech, or of the press. . . ." Though this provision was adopted as a part of the Bill of Rights in 1791, the United States Supreme Court had, as of 1917, never had occasion to decide a case in which it was claimed that the federal government had violated it. But the Espionage Act finally provided just such an occasion.

Charles T. Schenck was convicted of violating the act by printing and distributing to draftees leaflets that urged them to resist the draft. Schenck took his case to the Supreme Court, arguing that his conviction violated the First Amendment's guarantee of freedom of the press. The Supreme Court, in a unanimous opinion authored by Justice Oliver Wendell Holmes, upheld his conviction. It said that "When a nation is at war many things which might be said in time of peace are such a hindrance to its efforts that their utterance will not be endured so long as men fight. . . . No court could regard them as protected by any constitutional right."[6] The Court said that since the leaflet could be found to have been intended to obstruct the recruiting for the armed forces, it was not protected by the First Amendment; its words created "a clear and present danger" of bringing about conduct that Congress had a right to prevent.

This notable opinion put some flesh and bones on the First Amendment, but Holmes's formula, like most formulas, raised questions of its own. Few doubted that draft evasion was conduct that Congress had a right to prevent, but how was a court to know whether pamphlets such as these posed a "clear and present danger" of bringing it about? Schenck had of course distributed the pamphlets to draftees, and while their effect might be debated, there could be no doubt as to his intent.

Even though Congress had refused to grant the administration the express authority to censor that the President requested, Postmaster General Albert Burleson managed to achieve much the same results by use of the provision in the Espionage Act making certain matter "non-mailable." Burleson, a seven-term Texas congressman, had been one of Wilson's advisors at the marathon Democratic Convention in Baltimore in 1912, the convention that had finally given the New Jersey governor its nomination for the Presidency. Wilson appointed Burleson Postmaster General upon taking office, and the Texan held the post throughout Wilson's two terms as President. Wilson's most recent biographer describes Burleson as "diligent, narrowly and stubbornly diligent, in carrying out what he conceived to be his duties."[7] The President was uneasy about Burleson's zealous approach to barring dissident publications from the mails, but he rarely interfered.

One month after the enactment of the Espionage Act, Burleson directed the Postmaster in New York City to deny use of the mails to a publication called *The Masses*, and the Postmaster acted accordingly. Burleson's order was based on the contents of the August issue of the magazine, which contained four cartoons and four pieces of text that he found violated Section 3 of the Espionage Act. The publishers sought an injunction upholding their right to mail their magazine in the federal court in New York City. The case was heard by Learned Hand, then a district judge. Hand was later a judge of the federal court of appeals in New York and is generally regarded as one of the ablest jurists ever to have occupied the federal bench. He ruled in favor of the publisher.

The four cartoons were entitled "Liberty Bell," "Conscription," "Making the World Safe for Capitalism," and "Congress and Big Business." In the words of Judge Hand:

> The first is a picture of the Liberty Bell broken in fragments. The obvious implication, taking the cartoon in its context with the number as a whole, is that the origin, purposes and conduct of the War have already destroyed the liberties of the country. It is a fair inference that the draft law is an especial instance of the violation of the liberty and fundamental rights of any free people.
>
> The second cartoon shows a cannon to the mouth of which is bound the naked figure of a youth, to the wheel that of a woman, marked "Democracy," and upon the carriage that of a

man, marked "Labor." On the ground kneels a draped woman marked "Motherhood" in a posture of desperation, while her infant lies on the ground. The import of this cartoon is obviously that conscription is the destruction of youth, democracy, and labor, and the desolation of the family. No one can dispute that it was intended to rouse detestation for the draft law.

The third cartoon represents a Russian workman symbolizing the Workmen's and Soldiers' Council, seated at a table, studying a paper entitled, "Plan for a Genuine Democracy." At one side Senator Root furtively approaches the figure with a noose marked "Advice," apparently prepared to throw it over the head of the workman, while behind him stands Mr. Charles E. Russell, the Socialist member of the Russian Commission, in a posture of assent. On the other side a minatory figure of Japan appears through a door carrying a raised sword, marked "Threat," while behind him follows a conventional John Bull, stirring him up to action. The import again is unambiguous and undisputed. The Russian is being ensnared and bullied by the United States and its Allies into a continuance of the war for purposes prejudicial to true democracy.

The fourth and last cartoon presents a collection of pursy magnates standing about a table on which lies a map, entitled "War Plans." At the door enters an apologetic person, hat in hand, diffidently standing at the threshold, while one of the magnates warns him to keep off. The legend at the bottom runs as follows: "Congress: 'Excuse me, gentlemen, where do I come in?' " "Big Business: 'Run along, now! We got through with you when you declared war for us.' " It is not necessary to expatiate upon the import of this cartoon.

Hand, in discussing these items, said:

Yet to assimilate agitation, legitimate as such, with direct incitement to violent resistance, is to disregard the tolerance of all methods of political agitation which in normal times is a safeguard of free government. The distinction is not a scholastic subterfuge, but a hard-bought acquisition in the fight for freedom, and the purpose to disregard it must be evident when the power exists. If one stops short of urging upon others that it is their duty or their interest to resist the law, it seems to me one should not be held to have attempted to cause its violation. If that be not the test, I can see no escape from the conclusion that under that section every political agitation which can be shown to be apt to create a seditious temper is illegal. I am confident that by such language Congress had no such revolutionary purpose in view.[8]

. . . The inquiry is narrowed to the question whether any of the challenged matter may be said to advocate resistance to the draft, taking the meaning of the words with the utmost latitude which they can bear.

As to the cartoons it seems to me quite clear that they do not fall within such a test. Certainly the nearest is that entitled "Conscription," and the most that can be said of that is that it may breed such animosity to the draft as will promote resistance and strengthen the determination of those disposed to be recalcitrant. There is no intimation that, however hateful the draft may be, one is in duty bound to resist it, certainly none that such resistance is to one's interest. I cannot, therefore, even with the limitations which surround the power of the court, assent to the assertion that any of the cartoons violate the act.[9]

The government appealed Hand's ruling to the Court of Appeals, which took a different view of the matter when it reversed his decision four months later. Judge Rogers, writing the opinion for that court, said:

The cartoon entitled "Conscription" seems to us to say: this law murders youth, enslaves labor to its misery, drives womanhood into utter despair and agony, and takes away from democracy its freedom. Its voice is not the voice of patriotism, and its language suggests disloyalty. If counsel wish the court to understand that in his opinion the effect of the cartoon would not be to interfere with enlistment, we are not able to agree with him. That it would interfere, and was intended to interfere, was evidently the opinion of the Postmaster General; and this court cannot say that he was not justified in his conclusion.[10]

Notice the difference between Hand's opinion and that of the Court of Appeals. The former distinguishes between strongly worded "unpatriotic" criticism of the draft and the actual advocacy of unlawful resistance to it. The latter says that because the effect of the cartoon might be to interfere with enlistment, that is enough. But if freedom of speech is to be meaningful, strong criticism of government policy must be permitted even in wartime. And, as the Supreme Court recognized many years later, good cartoonists necessarily speak in hyperbole.[11] Advocacy which persuades citizens that a law is unjust is not the same as advocacy that preaches disobedience to it.

The part of the Espionage Act making some matter nonmailable was also challenged in the Supreme Court. That act provided that any newspaper that violates its provisions could be denied second-class mailing privileges—privileges that were essential to the commercial success of any newspaper relying on the mails for circulation. In 1917, Burleson revoked the second-class mailing privileges of the *Milwaukee Leader* because he found that it published articles in its daily issues that were intended to interfere with the success of United States military operations and tended to obstruct the recruitment and enlistment services of the United States military. The Supreme Court upheld the action of the Postmaster General against a challenge based on the First Amendment in *United States v. Burleson*.[12] The articles described the United States' involvement in the war as dishonorable, and the war as a capitalist war, and the United States government as a plutocratic republic. The President was called an aristocrat, and the draft law denounced as unconstitutional, arbitrary, and oppressive. Justices Holmes and Louis D. Brandeis dissented, saying that Congress had not given such broad authority to the Postmaster General.

Probably the most extreme example of Burleson's reach under the Act was barring the *Nation*, an influential liberal magazine, from the mails. Its editor, Oswald Garrison Villard, was informed that the reason for this action was an article criticizing Samuel Gompers, long-time leader of the American Federation of Labor. The post office solicitor advised Villard that "Mr. Gompers has rendered inestimable services to this government during the war in holding Union labor in line. . . . While this war is on, we are not going to allow any newspaper in this country to attack him."[13] This was one of the rare occasions in which the President countermanded his Postmaster General.

Perhaps the best-known individual prosecuted under the Espionage Act was Eugene V. Debs, perennial Socialist candidate for President. Debs has the unusual distinction of having on two separate occasions unsuccessfully appealed to the Supreme Court against prison sentences imposed upon him by the lower federal courts. In 1895 he was sentenced to six months for violating an injunction issued by the federal court in Chicago against strikers in connection with the Pullman Strike of 1894. His sentence was upheld by the Supreme Court in *In Re Debs*.

Immediately after the declaration of war in April 1917, the Socialist party issued a manifesto denouncing America's entry into the war. The following year, at a convention of the Ohio State Socialist party in Canton, Debs bitterly assailed the administration for the prosecution of persons charged under the Espionage Act. He said he had just returned from a visit to the workhouse where three of their most loyal comrades were paying the penalty for their devotion to the working class—these being three men who had been convicted of aiding and abetting one another in failing to register for the draft. Debs said he was proud of them. He also praised a woman convicted of obstructing the enlistment service, and went on to say that the master class always declared the war and the subject class always fought the battles—that the working class, who furnished the corpses, had never yet had a voice in declaring war and had never yet had a voice in declaring peace.

Four days later, Debs was indicted by a grand jury in Cleveland and was found guilty after a four-day trial. He was sentenced to ten years' imprisonment, and appealed his case to the U.S. Supreme Court. The Court, in a unanimous opinion by Justice Holmes, upheld his conviction under the Espionage Act. The Court said that a jury could have found "that one purpose of the speech, whether incidental or not does not matter, was to oppose not only war in general but this war, and that the opposition was so express that its natural and intended effect would be to obstruct recruiting. If that was intended and if, in all the circumstances, that would be its probable effect, it would not be protected by reason of its being part of a general program and expressions of a general and conscientious belief."[14]

Even though imprisoned, Debs was again the Socialist party nominee for President in 1920, and he received nearly one million votes—more than twice the number he polled on previous occasions when he was not incarcerated. (A part of this increase may have resulted from the fact that with the enactment of the Nineteenth Amendment to the Constitution, women now had the vote in every state.) Wilson refused to pardon Debs, but President Warren G. Harding did so in 1921.

In two other cases brought to the Supreme Court under the Espionage Act, the Court divided, although it upheld both convictions. In *Pierce v. United States*, the defendants were charged with having circulated in Albany, New York, in August 1917 a pamphlet entitled *The Price We Pay*. One statement in the pamphlet was that "our entry into [the war] was determined by the certainty that if the allies do not win, J. P. Morgan's loans to the allies will be repudiated, and those American investors who bit on his promises would be hooked." The Court majority held that a jury could find that this statement was false, on the basis of "common knowledge," and the jury's verdict against the defendants was upheld. Justice Brandeis, writing a dissent in which Justice Holmes concurred, made the point that this was an expression of opinion on a matter of great public importance and interest. "The fundamental right of free men to strive for better conditions through new legislation and new institutions will not be preserved, if efforts to secure it by argument to fellow citizens may be construed as criminal incitement to disobey the existing law—merely, because the argument presented seems to those exercising judicial power to be unfair in its portrayal of existing evils, mistaken in its assumptions, unsound in reasoning or intemperate in language."[15]

In the spring of 1918, Congress amended the Espionage Act to make it even more draconian; these amendments were referred to as the Sedition Act, and they were repealed in 1921. In *Abrams v. United States*, five defendants, born in Russia but residents of the United States for five to ten years, were charged and convicted under the terms of the Sedition Act.[16] They lived in New York City and met there in a room rented by one of them under an assumed name. Jacob Abrams purchased a printing kit and installed it in a basement room, and there pamphlets urging opposition to the intervention by the Allies against the Bolshevik regime that had come to power in Russia were printed. Of the five thousand turned out, some were distributed secretly, and others by throwing them from the window of a building where one of the defendants worked.

One of the pamphlets was printed in Yiddish; translated, it said:

> Workers, Russian emigrants, you who had the least belief in the honesty of *our* [emphasis added] Government must now throw away all confidence, must spit in the face of the false, hypocritical military propaganda which had fooled you so relentlessly, calling forth your sympathy, your help, to the prosecution of the war.
>
> With the money which you have loaned, or are going to loan them, they will make bullets not only for the Germans, but also for the Workers Soviets of Russia. Workers in the ammunition factories, you are producing bullets, bayonets, cannon, to murder not only the Germans, but also your dearest, best, who are in Russia and are fighting for freedom.
>
> Workers, our reply to the barbaric intervention has to be a general strike! An open challenge only will let the Government know that not only the Russian Worker fights for freedom, but also here in America lives the spirit of revolution.

Abrams and the others were charged under the Sedition Act, which prohibited language "tending to incite, provoke and encourage resistance to the United States in said war," and "when the United States was at war with the Imperial Government . . . unlawfully and wilfully, by utterance, writing, printing and publication, to urge, incite and advocate curtailment of production of things and products, to wit, ordinance [*sic*] and ammunition, necessary and essential to the prosecution of the war."

The majority opinion of the Court, written by Justice John Clarke, upheld their conviction, saying:

> This is not an attempt to bring about a change of administration by candid discussion, for no matter what may have incited the outbreak on the part of the defendant anarchists, the mani-

fest purpose of such a publication was to create an attempt to defeat the war plans of the government of the United States, by bringing upon the country the paralysis of a general strike, thereby arresting the production of all munitions and other things essential to the conduct of the war.[17]

Holmes, in a dissent joined by Justice Brandeis, saw it differently; he thought that the statute required that the defendants actually intend to impede the war effort and said:

I do not see how anyone can find the intent required by the statute in any of the defendants' words. The second leaflet is the only one that affords even a foundation for the charge, and there, without invoking the hatred of German militarism expressed in the former one, it is evident from the beginning to the end that the only object of the paper is to help Russia and stop American intervention there against the popular government, not to impede the United States in the war that it was carrying on.[18]

The result reached by the majority, when viewed in the light of the facts of the case, seems quite at odds with the "clear and present danger" test announced in *Schenck* less than a year before. There is no suggestion in the Court's opinion that a general strike would have been illegal, to say nothing of whether the haphazard distribution of these pamphlets in New York City presented a "clear and present danger" of causing one.

Thus, the Wilson administration, during the First World War, proved to have the same instinctive desire to suppress harsh criticism of the war effort as had the Lincoln administration during the Civil War. There were differences, however. The Wilson administration relied more on laws passed by Congress than on executive fiat, and the courts were far more involved during the First World War than they had been during the Civil War. Though the courts during this period gave little relief to civil liberties claimants, the very fact that the claims were being reviewed by the judiciary was a step in the right direction for proponents of civil liberties during wartime.

There was no effort to suspend the writ of *habeas corpus* in the

First World War, because the occasion never presented itself. There were more than two thousand people prosecuted under the Espionage Act between June 30, 1917, and June 30, 1921. Of these, a little more than a thousand resulted in convictions.[19]

There were no trials of civilians before military courts or commissions, as there had been in the Civil War. There was an effort, however, to enact a law that would have authorized such trials for persons found to be "interfering with the war effort," and would have subjected them to the death penalty. Charles Warren, Assistant Attorney General, sent a draft of such a bill to the chairman of the Senate Committee on Military Affairs, and the committee proceeded to hold hearings on the bill. It heard witnesses who said that disloyalty was rampant in the country, and it also recorded testimony from Warren in a session that was closed to the public. But the bill's prospects for passage faded when first President Wilson, and then Attorney General Gregory, denounced it. Wilson, in a letter to Senator Overman of North Carolina, said he thought the measure was unnecessary, uncalled-for, and unconstitutional. Gregory wrote to an Ohio congressman saying that Warren's actions were unauthorized and contrary to the position of the Department of Justice. In the midst of this imbroglio, Warren, quite understandably, resigned. Ironically, Warren, a respected Boston lawyer, would a few years later write a highly regarded three-volume history of the Supreme Court, in which he described the *Milligan* case (which banned military trials of civilians where civil courts were open) as one of the "great bulwarks of individual liberty."

There were race riots and at least one lynching during the First World War, but, however disturbing, these were not the result of governmental action. There was also a series of arrests, interrogations, and deportations generally lumped together under the head of the "Palmer Raids" (because Attorney General A. Mitchell Palmer—who had succeeded Gregory in Wilson's Cabinet—was the moving force behind them). But these actions occurred after hostilities were over and were more in response to perceived threats from anarchists than to antiwar activities. The nation returned to "normalcy" under President Warren G. Harding and enjoyed two decades of peace.

CHAPTER 15

World War II: Japanese Internments

THE FIRST WORLD WAR was called the "war to end all wars," but the very treaty that ended it sowed the seeds of future conflict. The Versailles Treaty saddled Germany with impossible reparations payments. Ruinous inflation and massive unemployment dogged the Weimar Republic, formed in Germany after the abdication of the Kaiser in 1918. During the 1920s, Communists on the far left and Nazis on the far right attracted more and more adherents. Hitler became chancellor in 1933, and in short order turned Germany into a one-party state.

He successively remilitarized the Rhineland, took over Austria, and dismembered Czechoslovakia. Great Britain and France, fearful of Communist Russia as well as of Nazi Germany, and still mindful of the ghastly toll on their young manhood exacted by First World War trench warfare, figuratively wrung their hands but did nothing. Benito Mussolini, the Italian dictator, supported Hitler, and the two countries formed the Rome-Berlin Axis. After the fall of Czechoslovakia in 1939, Britain and France guaranteed the integrity of Poland, now threatened by Germany. In August of that year, Hitler and Joseph Stalin, the dictator of Russia, amazed the world by signing a nonaggression treaty. On September 1, 1939, Germany invaded Poland, and within days Britain and France were once again at war with Germany.

In the Far East, similar but less-noticed developments were taking place. Japan had joined the Allies in the First World War. In 1931 her troops occupied the Chinese province of Manchuria. The United States protested, but the Japanese were not deterred; in 1937, they began a full-scale military campaign against China. The militarist faction in Japan became increasingly influential; they spoke of a Greater East Asia Co-prosperity Sphere, embracing most of Southeast Asia and dominated, of course, by Japan.

The United States had refused to join the League of Nations at the end of the First World War, and subsequent events did little to induce it to abandon the isolationist position it had adopted after that war. Many European countries had borrowed money from the United States during the war; all except Finland defaulted in their repayment. Congressional investigation in the thirties tended to blame United States entry into the war on "munitions makers" and other international villains. In 1937, at the time of the Spanish Civil War, Congress enacted a Neutrality Act that forbade the shipment of arms or ammunition to belligerents.

For months after the European war broke out in 1939, all was indeed quiet on the Western front. Germany overran Poland in a matter of weeks, and Russian troops moved in from the East to absorb what remained. Very little happened during the following winter, but by spring Hitler was ready to resume the offensive. In April 1940, Germany occupied Denmark and most of Norway. The next month it invaded the Low Countries, Holland and Belgium. France had spent years building the Maginot Line, a series of commanding forts along its border with Germany. But in one of the most superbly planned and executed campaigns in military history, German armored divisions broke through the Ardennes Forest—supposedly impassable to such forces—and into northern France. French resistance wilted, and the Germans entered Paris on June 12. Ten days later, France surrendered to Germany, and Britain was left to stand alone against Hitler and his "Fortress Europa."

President Franklin Roosevelt recognized the danger to the United States from German control of the entire continent of Europe, and sought to rearm the country and to give "all aid short of war" to Britain. Sentiment was divided in America as it had been at the time of World War I; particularly in the Midwest, there was strong feeling that the United States could best protect its interests by staying out of the conflict. But at Roosevelt's urging, Congress repealed the Neutrality Act and passed a draft law. FDR also arranged for the transfer of fifty overage destroyers to Great Britain.

Developments in the Far East at the same time were also pushing towards war. In 1940, Japan had entered into an alliance with Germany, thereby further estranging itself from the United States. The U.S. threatened to embargo shipments of oil, which were necessary for any overseas expansion by Japan, and during 1941 the two countries engaged in protracted negotiations looking to a modus vivendi. Then, on December 7, 1941, Japan unleashed a startling attack on the American naval base at Pearl Harbor, Hawaii. Roosevelt, declaring that the date "would live in infamy," asked Congress for a declaration of war against Japan, which Congress immediately granted; a few days later, Germany, in one of Hitler's major blunders, declared war on the United States. Had he not done so, it seems questionable whether Congress at that point would have declared war against Germany, since there would have been a substantial segment of public opinion that would have favored concentrating United States resources in the war against Japan in the Pacific.

The United States was a belligerent in the Second World War from December 1941 until V-J Day in August 1945. Like the First World War, the Second involved overseas combat for the American military. But in contrast to the First, American troops fought not only in Europe but around the world. They invaded French North Africa in 1942, and from there, with their British allies, moved to Sicily and then mainland Italy. In 1944 came the cross-channel invasion, where British and American air, sea, and land forces disembarked troops in Normandy on the European mainland. From there the Allies freed France and the Low Countries, finally reaching the Rhine River, while Russian armies converged on Germany from the east. Hitler committed suicide at the end of April, and the remaining German forces surrendered in early May 1945.

Meanwhile, the initial war news in the Pacific was all bad for the Allies. At Pearl Harbor, two battleships were destroyed and four others damaged. More than one hundred planes were wrecked on the ground there, and on the same day most of the B-17 bombers at

Clark Field in the Philippines were also demolished. Samuel Eliot Morison described the situation on the remaining fronts in the Far East:

> In the Far East . . . the situation was calamitous. Thailand surrendered to the Japanese, who promptly landed troops at various points on the Malay Peninsula and began a relentless march on the British base at Singapore. On 10 December the Rising Sun flag was hoisted in Guam, which had been bravely but pitifully defended by a few hundred Americans and Chamorios. The same day, England met her Pearl Harbor when the Japanese Air Force sank H.M.S. *Prince of Wales* and *Repulse* off the Malay Peninsula. Other Japanese task forces occupied the Gilbert Islands, captured Hong Kong, and jumped the Borneo oil fields. On Wake Island, a lonely outpost in the Central Pacific, Commander W. S. Cunningham and a small Marine defense force beat off a Japanese attack on 11 December, only to be overwhelmed by another on the 23rd, before the Navy managed to come to their rescue. In the Philippines, on 10 December, Japanese bombers destroyed Cavite Navy Yard. During the 17 days before Christmas, the enemy made nine amphibious landings in the Philippines. General MacArthur evacuated Manila on 27 December, withdrew his army to the Bataan Peninsula, and set up headquarters on the island fortress of Corregidor.
>
> The defense of Bataan and the Rock of Corregidor, although valiant and inspiring, proved to be a melancholy confirmation of Mahan's theory of sea power. The Japanese, controlling all sea and air approaches, enveloped both Peninsula and Rock in a tight blockade, landing fresh troops behind the American lines at will. . . .[1]
>
> Singapore, on which England had lavished millions of pounds, fell on 15 February. Java surrendered on 9 May; Rangoon, capital and chief seaport of Burma, had been occupied the day before. The Japanese were now in control of East Asia. India and Australia were tremblingly aware that their turn might come next.[2]

But the United States Navy won a decisive victory over the Japanese fleet at the Battle of Midway in June 1942. In retrospect, Midway ended any realistic threat of invasion of the west coast or even of Hawaii. Beginning with Guadalcanal in 1943, and also from Australia, American naval and military forces successfully attacked and occupied a series of Pacific islands ever closer to the Japanese mainland. Finally, in the summer of 1945, President Harry S Truman, who had succeeded Roosevelt on the latter's death in April 1945, authorized the dropping of atomic bombs by B-29 superfortresses on the Japanese cities of Hiroshima and Nagasaki. Japan surrendered almost immediately afterwards.

On the home front, gasoline, food, and other commodities were rationed. The east and west coasts were blacked out at night. The ages for drafting men were lowered to eighteen and raised to forty-five, and the physical standards were steadily diminished; towards the end of the war, it was said half in jest that the only requirements for draftees were that they be able to see lightning and hear thunder. Over fourteen million American soldiers, sailors, airmen, and marines were under arms.

The entire nation was stunned by the Japanese attack on Pearl Harbor, but it seemed much closer to home on the west coast than elsewhere on the mainland. In February 1942, oil installations in the vicinity of Santa Barbara were shelled by a Japanese submarine. The military established a Western Defense Command, which consisted of the coastal portions of California, Oregon, and Washington.

Residents became fearful of ethnic Japanese among them. Japanese immigrants had begun to settle on the west coast shortly before the turn of the century but had not been assimilated into the rest of the population. Those who had emigrated from Japan were not allowed to become citizens; they were prohibited by law from owning land and were socially segregated in many ways. The first generation of Japanese immigrants—the Issei—therefore remained aliens. But their children—the Nisei—being born in the United States, were citizens from birth. Public officials, particularly in California— Governor Culbert Olson, Attorney General Earl Warren, and Los Angeles Mayor Fletcher Bowron—began to call for "relocation" of persons of Japanese ancestry in the interior of the country. There were more than one hundred thousand of these on the west coast if one counted both the Issei and the Nisei.

General John DeWitt was the commanding officer of the Western Defense Command, and he at first resisted the clamor to remove the Japanese. But state and local public officials were insistent, and they were supported by their states' congressional delegations. The chorus became more insistent when the report of the Roberts Commission was released in late January 1942.

On December 18, 1941, President Roosevelt had appointed a commission, chaired by Owen J. Roberts, an Associate Justice of the Supreme Court. The President charged it "to ascertain and report the facts relating to the attack made by Japanese armed forces upon the territory of Hawaii on December 7, 1941." The Commission met first in Washington, then went to Hawaii, where the members held extensive hearings and heard the testimony of numerous witnesses. The principal focus of the Commission report was on what, if any, dereliction there had been in the American chain of command that allowed the Japanese to take the Americans completely by surprise. But the Commission also found that there had been espionage in Hawaii:

> There were, prior to December 7, 1941, Japanese spies on the Island of Oahu. Some were Japanese consular agents and others were persons having no open relations with the Japanese foreign service. These spies collected, and through various channels transmitted, information to the Japanese Empire respecting the military and naval establishments and dispositions on the Island.[3]
>
> It was believed that the center of Japanese espionage in Hawaii was the Japanese consulate at Honolulu. It has been discovered that the Japanese consul sent to and received from Tokyo in his own and other names many messages on commercial radio circuits. This activity greatly increased towards December 7, 1941....[4]
>
> [The Japanese] knew from maps which they had obtained, the exact location of vital air fields, hangars, and other structures. They also knew accurately where certain important

naval vessels would be berthed. Their fliers had the most detailed maps, courses, and bearings, so that each could attack a given vessel or field. Each seems to have been given a specified mission.[5]

If there was to be forced evacuation, it would have to be approved by President Roosevelt. Attorney General Francis Biddle, Secretary of War Henry L. Stimson, and Assistant Secretary of War John P. McCloy were the decision-makers for the two departments concerned. None of them favored relocation at first, but eventually, in the course of often vigorous discussions among themselves and with their subordinates, Stimson and McCloy changed their minds. On February 11, 1942, McCloy asked Stimson to find out if Roosevelt would be willing to authorize the removal of the Nisei as well as the Issei from areas of the west coast. Stimson sought an appointment with the President but was advised that the latter was too busy and would have time for only a telephone call. "I took up with him the West Coast matter first," Stimson wrote in his diary, "and told him the situation and fortunately found he was very vigorous about it and told me to go ahead on the line that I had myself thought the best."[6]

In his memoirs, which were published in 1947, Stimson, referring to himself in the third person, had this to say:

At the same time, mindful of its duty to be prepared for any emergency, the War Department ordered the evacuation of more than 100,000 persons of Japanese origin from strategic areas on the west coast. This decision was widely criticized as an unconstitutional invasion of the rights of individuals many of whom were American citizens, but it was eventually approved by the Supreme Court as a legitimate exercise of the war powers of the President. What critics ignored was the situation that led to the evacuation. Japanese raids on the West Coast seemed not only possible but probable in the first months of the war, and it was quite impossible to be sure that the raiders would not receive important help from individuals of Japanese origin.[7]

Biddle, who alone among the high administration officials involved opposed the evacuation, describes the situation in these words:

> Apparently, the War Department's course of action had been tentatively charted by Mr. McCloy and Colonel Bendetson in the first 10 days of February. General DeWitt's final recommendation to evacuate was completed on February 13, and forwarded to Washington with a covering letter the next day. Mr. Stimson and Mr. McCloy did not, however, wait for this report, which contained a "finding" on which their "military necessity" argument to the President was based, but obtained their authority before the recommendation was received. On February 11 the President told the War Department to prepare a plan for wholesale evacuation, specifically including citizens. It was dictated, he concluded, by military necessity; and added, "be as reasonable as you can." After the conference the Assistant Secretary reported to Bendetson: "We have *carte blanche* to do what we want as far as the President is concerned."[8]

Biddle speculated on Roosevelt's feelings about the matter:

> I do not think he was much concerned with the gravity or implications of this step. He was never theoretical about things. What must be done to defend the country must be done. The decision was for his Secretary of War, not for the Attorney General, not even for J. Edgar Hoover, whose judgment as to the appropriateness of defense measures he greatly respected. The military might be wrong, but they were fighting the war. Public opinion was on their side, so that there was no question of any substantial opposition, which might tend toward the disunity that at all costs he must avoid. . . .

Biddle concluded with a remarkably perceptive observation: "Nor do I think that the Constitutional difficulty plagued him. The Constitution has not greatly bothered any wartime President. That was a question of law, which ultimately the Supreme Court must decide. And meanwhile—probably a long meanwhile—we must get on with the war."[9]

Executive Order 9066, authorizing the removal of ethnic Japanese from the west coast, was signed by Roosevelt on February 19. Several weeks later, Congress passed a law imposing criminal penalties for violations of the order or of whatever regulations might be issued to implement it. First, a curfew was imposed on the ethnic Japanese, then they were required to report to relocation centers, and finally they were physically moved to camps located in the interior of California and in the mountain states. There was no physical brutality, but there were certainly severe hardships—physical removal from the place where one lived, often forced sale of houses and businesses, and harsh living conditions in the spartan quarters of the internment centers. As the war progressed, some restrictions were relaxed. Nisei volunteers made up the 442nd Combat Infantry Regiment, which fought bravely in Italy against the Germans. Other internees were issued work permits that allowed them to leave the camp. Most of those who were still interned were released by the beginning of 1945, as a result of the third Supreme Court decision in which the relocation policy was challenged.

GORDON HIRABAYASHI WAS born in Seattle to Issei parents in 1918, and by 1942 was a senior at the University of Washington. In May 1942, he disobeyed the curfew requirement imposed by military authorities pursuant to the President's Executive Order, and two days later he failed to report to register for evacuation from the prescribed military area. He was indicted and convicted in a federal court in Seattle on two misdemeanor counts, and was sentenced to imprisonment for three months on each. He contended that the orders he was charged with violating were unconstitutional, but the federal judge in Seattle ruled against him.

Minoru Yasui had likewise been born in the United States to Issei parents. He had attended the University of Oregon, from which he received A.B. and LL.B. degrees, and was a member of the Oregon bar. He too violated a curfew order made applicable to Portland, Oregon, where he resided, by the military authorities. He was convicted in the federal court in Portland and was sentenced to imprisonment for one year.

Fred Korematsu, also born in the United States to Issei parents, was convicted of remaining in San Leandro, California, in violation of a military exclusion order applicable to him. The federal court in San Francisco overruled his claim that the orders in question were unconstitutional, suspended his sentence, and placed him on probation for five years.

The three cases of Hirabayashi, Yasui, and Korematsu were argued together before the Court of Appeals for the Ninth Circuit in San Francisco, which has jurisdiction over the far western part of the United States. Because of procedural variations, they reached the Supreme Court at different times. The cases of Hirabayashi and Yasui were sent directly to the Supreme Court by the Court of Appeals, and were argued in May 1943.

The Chief Justice at this time was Harlan F. Stone, who had been born in New Hampshire and practiced law in New York following his graduation from Columbia Law School, where he later served as dean. When Calvin Coolidge succeeded Harding as President upon the latter's death in 1923, he appointed Stone Attorney General, with a mandate to clean out the then scandal-ridden Department of Justice. Stone obliged and was rewarded by appointment as Associate Justice of the Supreme Court in 1925. During his sixteen years in that position he was identified as a member of the liberal wing of the Court, along with Justices Holmes, Brandeis, and Cardozo. When Charles Evans Hughes retired as Chief Justice in 1941, Roosevelt appointed Stone as his successor.

The senior Associate Justice on the Court at the time the Japanese internment cases were heard was Owen Roberts. He was a Philadelphia aristocrat who had mixed a successful private practice with occasional stints in public service. He was a special prosecutor for the United States in several of the cases that arose out of the Teapot Dome scandals of the Harding Administration. He was appointed to the Supreme Court by President Herbert Hoover in 1930.

Next in seniority was Hugo Black, who, before his appointment to the Court, had been a Senator from Alabama when that state was part of the "solid South" that always voted Democratic. During his nearly two full terms in the Senate, Black had been a faithful party wheelhorse who had supported every piece of major New Deal legislation, including Roosevelt's court-packing plan. Immediately after the defeat of that initiative, Roosevelt had the opportunity to make his first appointment to the Court, and he chose Black. There was a public outcry when it was revealed that Black had once been a member of the Ku Klux Klan. Black took to the radio to declare that his membership in the Klan had been long before, and had been a matter of political expediency when he was running for political office in Alabama in the 1920s. He would serve thirty-four years on the Court and be one of the most influential Justices of the twentieth century.

Stanley Reed was born in Maysville, Kentucky, and practiced law there from 1910 until he came to Washington in 1928 to be general counsel to the Reconstruction Finance Corporation. Roosevelt named him Solicitor General in 1935 and appointed him to the Supreme Court in 1938. Considerably less colorful than some of the other Roosevelt appointees, Reed was often the "swing" man when the Court would split 5–4 on philosophical questions.

Next in the line of Roosevelt appointees was Felix Frankfurter—born in Vienna, Austria, in 1882, and a professor at Harvard Law School for twenty-five years before being named to the Court in January 1939. Frankfurter was a well-known legal scholar and writer and had been identified with numerous liberal causes, such as the trials of Sacco and Vanzetti in the 1920s. He would serve on the Court for more than twenty years—a brightly plumaged bird who never gave up his professorial mien in his battles for judicial restraint.

In March 1939—less than three months after he had appointed Frankfurter—Roosevelt had a fourth vacancy on the Court to fill. He chose forty-year-old William O. Douglas, a Yale Law School professor and then a member of the Securities and Exchange Commission. Douglas would serve more than thirty-six years as an Associate Justice—the all-time longevity record on the Court—and establish a reputation as a bastion of its liberal wing.

Less than a year after Douglas's appointment, Roosevelt was afforded yet another opportunity, and this time he picked Frank Murphy—a former Governor of Michigan, High Commissioner to the Philippines, and briefly Attorney General of the United States before his appointment. Murphy would serve only nine years, but that was long enough to establish him as a nearly messianic champion of the underdog.

When Hughes retired as Chief Justice in June 1941, Roosevelt elevated Stone to the center chair of the Court and appointed Attorney General Robert H. Jackson to fill the vacancy thus created. Jackson came from western New York and had served as both Solicitor General and Attorney General before being elevated to the bench. He was an excellent writer, and his opinions showed it. He left his judicial duties immediately after the end of World War II to become United States prosecutor at the Nuremberg trials, and his experience there had a profound effect on his judicial philosophy.

The ninth member of the Court to hear the Japanese internment cases was Wiley B. Rutledge—also appointed by Roosevelt. He was born in Kentucky and served as a law professor and a judge of the federal court of appeals in Washington before going to the Supreme Court in 1943. He would serve only six years, and during that time would join Murphy as a less fervent, more scholarly champion of the underdog.

The Japanese-Americans were represented in the Supreme Court by four able counsel: Edward Borchard, William Draper Lewis, Brien McMahon, and Osmond K. Fraenkel. Their basic contention was that the President's Executive Order which authorized the relocation and ultimately the internment of both Japanese aliens and American citizens of Japanese descent on the west coast, was unconstitutional because it proceeded on the basis that this entire racial group was disloyal, rather than being based on any individual determinations of disloyalty. Briefs supporting these petitioners were filed by the American Civil Liberties Union, the Northern California Branch of the American Civil Liberties Union, and the Japanese-American Citizens League.

The government in its brief recited in some detail the facts that it thought justified the orders that were being challenged:

Japanese Victories. On the morning of Decembe[r] 7, 1941, the Japanese attacked the United States Naval Base at Pearl Harbor without warning. Simultaneously they struck against Malaysia, Hong Kong, the Philippines, and Wake and Midway Islands.

On the day following, the Japanese Army invaded Thailand. Shortly thereafter, the British battleships "H.M.S. Wales" and "H.M.S. Repulse" were sunk off the Malay Peninsula. The enemy's successes continued without interruption. On the 13th of December, Guam was taken, and on December 24th and 25th, respectively, the Japanese captured Wake Island and occupied Hong Kong. On January 2nd Manila fell and on February 10th Singapore, Britain's great naval base in the East, fell; on the 27th of February the battle of the Java Sea resulted in a naval defeat to the United Nations. Thirteen United Nations' warships were sunk and one damaged, whereas Japanese losses were limited to two warships sunk and five damaged.

On the 9th of March the Japanese forces established full control over the Netherlands East Indies; Rangoon and Burma were occupied. Bataan and Corregidor, which were then under attack, subsequently gave way on April 9 and May 6, respectively. The Philippines had completely fallen.

Thereafter, on June 3rd, Dutch Harbor, Alaska, was attacked by Japanese carrier-based aircraft. And on June 7th, contemporaneously with an attack on Midway the Japanese gained a foothold on Attu and Kiska Islands, from which they have not yet been dislodged. Moreover, on two occasions, once in February and once in June 1942, the coasts of California and Oregon, respectively, had been shelled. The extent of the danger can be seen from the contemporaneous attempt of the Japanese to occupy Midway Island in June. If that attack had succeeded and Midway Island had fallen, Hawaii would have again been under the immediate threat of occupation, and peril to the West Coast itself would have mounted.

The government's brief also contained this passage:

West Coast War Industries. The concentration of war facilities and installations on the West Coast made it an area of special military concern at any time and especially after the sensational Japanese successes. Important Army and Navy bases and a large proportion of this nation's vital war production facilities were located in that region.

For the period from June 1940 through December 1941 contracts equalling in value approximately one-fourth of the total value of the major aircraft contracts let by the principal procurement agencies, were to be performed in the State of California. During the same period, California ranked second, and the State of Washington ranked fifth, of the States of the Union with respect to the total value of shipbuilding contracts to be performed therein. Of the total value of supply contracts of all types let by these agencies during this period, California was again in first place with about one-tenth of the total. The relative importance of California and Washington for the entire period from June 1940 to February 1943 in the combined production of aircraft and ships is approximately the same as for the earlier period.

In view of such concentration of defense facilities in this region and in view of the course of the war at that time, it was of the highest order of military importance to take into account the extent and nature of the Japanese residents on the West Coast and their possible cooperation with the enemy.

The states of Washington, Oregon, and California, by their respective Attorneys General, filed a brief in support of the government. It contained the following passage:

> A combat zone was established by the Commanding General. . . . For the first seven months little occurred to reduce the fear of attack. On February 23, 1942, oil installations in the vicinity of Santa Barbara, California, were shelled by a Japanese submarine. On September 9, 1942, a submarine-based plane dropped incendiary bombs in the vicinity of Brookings (Mount Emily), Oregon. The radio station at Estevan, Vancouver Island, B.C., was shelled by a submarine at midnight on June 19, 1942. A few days later, an enemy submarine surfaced and shelled shore batteries at Astoria, Oregon. On June 3, 1942, Dutch Harbor, Alaska, was attacked by carrier-based

planes. On June 7, 1942, the Japanese invaded continental North America by occupying the Islands of Attu and Kiska in the Aleutian group. There was an increasing indication that the enemy had knowledge of our patrols and naval dispositions, for ships leaving West Coast ports were being intercepted and attacked regularly by enemy submarines.

Following the oral argument and conference in the Hirabayashi and Yasui cases, Chief Justice Stone assigned the task of writing the Court's opinion to himself. He first greatly narrowed the scope of the opinion by deciding that the Court need pass only on the validity of the curfew requirement, and not on the requirement that Hirabayashi report to a relocation center. Hirabayashi had been convicted of both offenses, but his sentences for each were to run "concurrently"—that is, he would serve only three months in prison even though he had been sentenced to serve three months on each of two different charges. Under established law at that time, if the conviction on one count was upheld, the Court would disregard the conviction on the second count, since it essentially made no difference in the amount of time in prison that the defendant would spend. In this case, it meant that the Court had to tackle only the easier question of whether a curfew could properly be imposed, rather than the more difficult question of whether Hirabayashi could be required to relocate in an internment camp.

Stone's task in writing the opinion was not an easy one, because several of his colleagues had insisted that there be little or no opportunity to later challenge the order, while Justices Douglas, Murphy, and Rutledge wanted to explicitly leave open that possibility. Indeed, Murphy circulated a draft of a caustic dissent that chastised the Court for approving a program that "utterly subverts" individual rights in war. Douglas circulated a concurrence—indicating his view that at some point one who was interned under the program should have an opportunity to prove his loyalty. Murphy finally turned his draft dissent into a concurrence, saying that he thought the program "goes to the very brink of constitutional power."[10] Rutledge also filed a brief concurrence.

Stone's opinion for the Court borrowed a definition of the government's "war" from the statement made by Charles Evans

Hughes—not while he was a member of the Court, but in an article in the *American Bar Association Journal*. The "war power of the national government is the power to wage war successfully."[11] And it was "not for any court to sit in review of the wisdom of the actions of the Executive or of Congress, or to substitute its judgment for theirs. If the Court could say there was a rational basis for the military decision, it would be sustained."

Stone's opinion then adduced the facts—most of which had been set forth in the government's brief—that showed the threat by the Japanese navy to the Pacific coast immediately after the bombing of Pearl Harbor. The opinion then went on to say:

> Although the results of the attack on Pearl Harbor were not fully disclosed until much later, it was known that the damage was extensive, and that the Japanese by their successes had gained a naval superiority over our forces in the Pacific which might enable them to seize Pearl Harbor, our largest naval base and the last stronghold of defense lying between Japan and the west coast. That reasonably prudent men charged with the responsibility of our national defense had ample grounds for concluding that they must face the danger of invasion, take measures against it, and in making the choice of measures consider our internal situation, cannot be doubted.[12] . . .
>
> Whatever views we may entertain regarding the loyalty to this country of the citizens of Japanese ancestry, we cannot reject as unfounded the judgment of the military authorities and of Congress that there were disloyal members of that population, whose number and strength could not be precisely and quickly ascertained. We cannot say that the war-making branches of the Government did not have ground for believing that in a critical hour such persons could not readily be isolated and separately dealt with, and constituted a menace to the national defense and safety, which demanded that prompt and adequate measures be taken to guard against it.[13]

The Court, of course, had to respond to the charge that distinctions based on race alone were not permitted under the Constitution. The Court said:

Distinctions between citizens solely because of their ancestry are by their very nature odious to a free people whose institutions are founded upon the doctrine of equality. . . . We may assume that these considerations would be controlling here were it not for the fact that the danger of espionage and sabotage, in time of war and of threatened invasion, calls upon the military authorities to scrutinize every relevant fact bearing on the loyalty of populations in the danger areas. . . .

We have stated in detail facts and circumstances with respect to the American citizens of Japanese ancestry residing on the Pacific Coast which support the judgment of the war-waging branches of the Government that some restrictive measure was urgent. We cannot say that these facts and circumstances, considered in the particular war setting, could afford no ground for differentiating citizens of Japanese ancestry from other groups in the United States. The fact alone that the attack on our shores was threatened by Japan rather than another enemy power set these citizens apart from others who have no particular associations with Japan.[14]

Stone's opinion upholding the curfew was joined by five of his colleagues. Douglas, Murphy, and Rutledge, while voting to uphold the curfew, wrote separately.

Korematsu's case came on for argument in October 1944. Here, the Court was required to confront not merely the curfew, which it had upheld in its earlier *Hirabayashi* decision, but the far more draconian relocation requirement. But the Court also upheld this requirement, in an opinion by Justice Black, basing its reasoning largely on the earlier decision. This time, however, there were separate dissents by Justices Roberts, Murphy, and Jackson.

The flavor of Black's opinion is caught in its concluding passage:

To cast this case into outlines of racial prejudice, without reference to the real military dangers which were presented, merely confuses the issue. Korematsu was not excluded from the Military Area because of hostility to him or his race. He *was* excluded because we are at war with the Japanese Empire, because the properly constituted military authorities feared an invasion of our West Coast and felt constrained to take proper security measures, because they decided that the military urgency of the situation demanded that all citizens of Japanese ancestry be segregated from the West Coast temporarily. . . . There was evidence of disloyalty on the part of some, the military authorities considered that the need for action was great, and time was short. We cannot—by availing ourselves of the calm perspective of hindsight—now say that at that time these actions were unjustified.[15]

Murphy criticized the military for lumping together with a disloyal few of Japanese ancestry all of the others against whom there had been no such showing. Jackson said that the Court was simply in no position to evaluate the government's claim of military necessity:

In the very nature of things, military decisions are not susceptible of intelligent judicial appraisal. They do not pretend to rest on evidence, but are made on information that often would not be admissible and on assumptions that could not be proved. . . . Hence courts can never have any real alternative to accepting the mere declaration of the authorities that issued the order that it was reasonably necessary from a military viewpoint.[16]

In the case of *Endo*, argued and decided at the same time as *Korematsu*, the Court reached quite a different result. Mitsuye Endo had submitted to an evacuation order and was removed to the Tule Lake Relocation Center in the Cascade Mountains just south of the California-Oregon border, and then to another relocation center in Utah. She sued out a writ of *habeas corpus*, claiming that she was a loyal citizen against whom no charge had been made and that she was therefore entitled to her relief. The government agreed that she was a loyal citizen, and not charged with any offense. The Court decided that under these circumstances Endo was entitled to be released from confinement. The presidential order and the Act of Congress confirming it spoke of evacuation from a military zone but said nothing of detention after the evacuation. While the initial evacuation had been justified in terms of the defense facilities on the west coast, the detention of a loyal person of Japanese ancestry after the evacuation had taken place was not reasonably necessary to prevent sabotage or espionage. Two members of the Court wrote separately, but all agreed with the result.

Although the Court based its reasoning in *Endo* on the provisions of the Act of Congress and the Executive Order, and therefore Congress and the President would have been free to change those to provide for detention, the Court's opinion strongly hinted at constitutional difficulties if that were to be done. And, it should be noted, the United States' military position was much more favorable in the fall of 1944 than it had been in the spring of 1942. In Europe, the Allies had successfully conducted a cross-Channel invasion the preceding summer and were rapidly moving eastward toward the Rhine River. In the Pacific, the Battle of Leyte Gulf had been fought and won by the United States Navy on October 23–26, 1944, and American forces were moving steadily closer to the Japanese homeland. There was neither a military need nor a public demand for further restrictions on Americans of Japanese descent, and the entire program was promptly terminated after the decision in the *Endo* case.

There is a certain disingenuousness in this sequence of three opinions—*Hirabayashi*, *Korematsu*, and *Endo*. There was no reason to think that Gordon Hirabayashi and Fred Korematsu were any less loyal to the United States than was Mitsuye Endo. Presumably they would have been entitled to relief from detention upon the same showing as that made by Endo. But even had Hirabayashi tried to raise that question in his case, he would not have been successful. The Court confined itself to the issue of the curfew, not the requirement to report to the relocation center. It also appears that a majority of the Court at the time of the *Hirabayashi* decision in June 1943 was unwilling to say that one detained in a relocation center would be entitled to release upon a finding of loyalty. It was not until a year and a half later that the Court came around to this view in *Endo*, when the United States' fortunes of war were vastly improved. The traditional unwillingness of courts to decide constitutional questions unnecessarily also illustrates in a rough way the Latin maxim *Inter arma silent leges:* In time of war the laws are silent.

CHAPTER 16

Postwar Criticism

THE JUDGMENT OF postwar public opinion was that the forced relocation and detention of people of Japanese ancestry was a grave injustice to the great majority who were loyal to the United States. Eugene Rostow, then a professor at Yale Law School and later its dean, writing in 1945, declared the program "a disaster." He criticized it as representing an abandonment of our traditional subordination of military to civil authority, and as sanctioning racially based discrimination against those of Japanese ancestry. Edward Ennis, who as a lawyer in the Justice Department had opposed the adoption of the program, reappeared nearly forty years later on behalf of the American Civil Liberties Union to testify before the congressionally created commission investigating this wartime episode. He characterized the program as "the worst blow to civil liberty in our history."

In the view of the present author, some of this criticism is well justified, and some not; its principal fault is that it lumps together the cases of the Issei—immigrants from Japan—and the Nisei—children of those immigrants who were born in the United States and citizens of the United States by reason of that fact.

The cases before the Supreme Court—*Hirabayashi*, *Korematsu*, and *Endo*—all involved Nisei. The basis on which the Court upheld the plan was military representations as to the necessity for evacuation. These representations were undoubtedly exaggerated, and they were based in part on the view that not only the Issei but the Nisei were different from other residents of the west coast.

In defense of the military, it should be pointed out that these officials were not entrusted with the protection of anyone's civil liberties; their task instead was to make sure that vital areas were as secure as possible from espionage or sabotage. The role of General DeWitt, the commander of the west coast military department, was not one to encourage a nice calculation of the costs in civil liberties as opposed to the benefits to national security. Contributing to this attitude would have been the news that General Walter Short, the army commander in Hawaii, and Admiral Husband E. Kimmel, the navy commander there, were both summarily removed from their commands ten days after Pearl Harbor because of their failure to anticipate the Japanese surprise attack. DeWitt was surely going to err on the side of caution in making his calculations.

DeWitt and his associates did not at first recommend evacuation of the Issei and Nisei. The principal proponents of that idea in its early stages were three California officials—the state's Governor and Attorney General, and the Mayor of Los Angeles—and the congressional delegations of the three west coast states. Public opinion should not be the determining factor in making a military appraisal, but it is bound to occur to those engaged in that task that their names will very likely be "Mudd" if they reject a widely popular security measure that in retrospect will prove to have been necessary.

The United States prides itself on a system in which the civilian heads of the service departments are supreme over the military chiefs, so one might expect that Henry Stimson and John McCloy would have made a more careful evaluation of the evacuation proposal than they appear to have done. Far from the west coast, they would be expected to have a more detached view than the commander on the scene. But here too there seems to have been a tendency to feel that concern for civil liberties was not their responsibility. There is even more of this feeling in Roosevelt's perfunctory approval of the plan in response to a telephone call from Stimson. Biddle's protests proved to be futile even at the highest levels of government, in part because no significant element of public opinion opposed the relocation. The American Civil Liberties Union, for example, which filed briefs in the Supreme Court supporting both *Hirabayashi* and *Korematsu* when those cases were argued, was noticeably silent at the time that the program was put into operation.

Once the relocation plan was in place, it could only be challenged in the courts. Was the Supreme Court at fault in upholding first the curfew, in *Hirabayashi*, and then the relocation in *Korematsu?* In *Hirabayashi*, the first case, the Court could have decided the validity of both the relocation requirement and the curfew requirement. The "concurrent sentence" doctrine under which the Court declined to do so is not mandatory but discretionary. But counseling against any broader decision was the well-established rule that the Court should avoid deciding constitutional questions if it is possible to do so. Both the curfew and the relocation program were challenged on constitutional grounds, but the latter was a much more serious infringement of civil liberty than the former. The *Hirabayashi* decision, upholding only the curfew, left the more difficult question of the relocation program for another day.

When that day came—as it did in *Korematsu*—a majority of the Court upheld the relocation program. Justice Black's opinion for the Court in *Korematsu* followed the same line of reasoning as had Chief Justice Stone's in *Hirabayashi*. But this time there were three dissenters; they had voted to uphold the curfew but voted to strike down the relocation program.

Several criticisms of the Court's opinions in these cases have been made. The most general is of its extremely deferential treatment of the government's argument that the curfew and relocation were necessitated by military considerations. Here one can only echo Justice Jackson's observation in his dissenting opinion that "in the very nature of things, military decisions are not susceptible of intelligent judicial appraisal." But it surely does not follow from this that a court must therefore invalidate measures based on military judgments. Eugene Rostow suggests the possibility of a judicial inquiry into the entire question of military necessity, but this seems an extraordinarily dubious proposition. Judicial inquiry, with its restrictive rules of evidence, orientation towards resolution of factual disputes in individual cases, and long delays, is ill-suited to determine an issue such as "military necessity." The necessity for prompt action was cogently stated by the Court in its *Hirabayashi* opinion:

Although the results of the attack on Pearl Harbor were not fully disclosed until much later, it was known that the damage was extensive, and that the Japanese by their successes had gained a naval superiority over our forces in the Pacific which might enable them to seize Pearl Harbor, our largest naval base and the last stronghold of defense lying between Japan and the West Coast. That reasonably prudent men charged with the responsibility of our national defense had ample ground for concluding that they must face the danger of invasion, take measures against it, and in making the choice of measures consider our internal situation, cannot be doubted.[1]

A second criticism is that the decisions in these cases upheld a program that, at bottom, was based on racial distinctions. There are several levels at which this criticism can be made. The broadest is that the Nisei were relocated simply because the Caucasian majority on the west coast (and in the country as a whole) disliked them and wished to remove them as neighbors or as business competitors. The Court's answer to this broad attack seems satisfactory—those of Japanese descent were displaced because of fear that disloyal elements among them would aid Japan in the war. Though there were undoubtedly nativists in California who welcomed a chance to see the Issei and the Nisei removed, it does not follow that this point of view was attributable to the military decision-makers. They, after all, did not at first propose relocation.

But a narrower criticism along the same line has more force to it: the Nisei were evacuated notwithstanding the fact that they were American citizens, and they were treated differently from other Americans. Even in wartime, citizens may not be rounded up and required to prove their loyalty. They may be excluded from sensitive military areas in the absence of a security clearance and may otherwise be denied access to any classified information. But it pushes these propositions to an extreme to say that a sizable geographical area, including the residences of many citizens, may be declared off-limits and the residents required to move. It pushes it to an even greater extreme to say that such persons may be required not only to leave their homes but also to report to and remain in a distant relocation center.

The Supreme Court in its *Hirabayashi* opinion pointed to several facts thought to justify this treatment of the Nisei. Both federal and state restrictions on the rights of Japanese emigrants had prevented their assimilation into the Caucasian population and had intensified their insularity and solidarity. Japanese parents sent their children to Japanese-language schools outside of regular school hours, and there was some evidence that the language schools were a source of Japanese nationalistic propaganda. As many as ten thousand American-born children of Japanese parentage went to Japan for all or part of their education. And even though children born in the United States of Japanese alien parents were U.S. citizens, they were under Japanese law also viewed as citizens of Japan. The Court therefore concluded:

> Whatever views we may entertain regarding the loyalty to this country of the citizens of Japanese ancestry, we cannot reject as unfounded the judgment of the military authorities and of Congress that there were disloyal members of that population, whose number and strength could not be precisely and quickly ascertained. We cannot say that the war-making branches of the Government did not have ground for believing that in a critical hour such persons could not readily be isolated and separately dealt with, and constituted a menace to the national defense and safety, which demanded that prompt and adequate measures be taken to guard against it.[2]

There is considerable irony, of course, in relying on previously existing laws discriminating against Japanese immigrants to conclude that still further disabilities should be imposed upon them because they had not been assimilated into the Caucasian majority. But in time of war a nation may be required to respond to a condition without making a careful inquiry as to how that condition came about.

Was the condition or conditions described by the Court sufficient to justify treatment of the Nisei differently from all other citizens on the west coast? Under today's constitutional law, quite certainly not: any sort of "racial" classification by government is viewed as "suspect," and an extraordinarily strong reason is required to justify it.

But the law was by no means so clear in 1943 and 1944, when these cases were decided. The Fifth Amendment to the Constitution, adopted as part of the Bill of Rights in 1791, prohibited the federal government from depriving any person of "life, liberty or property" without "due process of law." This amendment *did not* apply to the states. The Fourteenth Amendment, adopted in 1868, *did* apply to the states. It repeated the language of the Due Process Clause of the Fifth Amendment but went on to also prohibit any state from denying to any person the "equal protection of the laws." From this sequence of events it was logical to infer that, at least in 1868, the Due Process Clause alone was not thought to prohibit the sort of discrimination at which the Equal Protection Clause of the Fourteenth Amendment was aimed. The Court's opinion in *Hirabayashi* says that distinctions based on race are "odious to a free people," but the cases it cites deal only with actions of state or territorial governments.

A decade later, the Court decided the watershed case of *Brown v. Board of Education*, holding that the Kansas legislature had violated the Equal Protection Clause of the Fourteenth Amendment by requiring public schools to segregate students by race. But with *Brown* there was argued a companion case, *Bolling v. Sharpe*, challenging a similarly imposed requirement of segregation in public schools in the District of Columbia.[3] This requirement, however, had not been imposed by a state government but by Congress. It was therefore subject to the Fifth Amendment, but not to the Fourteenth. The Court in *Bolling*, in a brief opinion not notable for clarity of reasoning, held that the Due Process Clause of the Fifth Amendment imposes on the federal government a limitation similar to that imposed on the states by the Equal Protection Clause of the Fourteenth Amendment. Had this doctrine been the law ten years earlier, the Supreme Court might have found it easier to reach a different result in *Hirabayashi* and *Korematsu*.

The discrimination against the Nisei lay in the fact that any other citizen could remain in his home unless actually tried and convicted of espionage or sabotage, while the Nisei were removed from their homes without any individualized findings at all. The proffered justification was that attack on or invasion of the west coast by Japan was reasonably feared, and that first-generation American citizens of Japanese descent were more likely than the citizenry as a whole to include potential spies or saboteurs who would assist the enemy.

This view was not totally without support. A "Magic intercept," resulting from the Americans having broken the Japanese code, dated

May 1941, contained a message from the Japanese consulate in Los Angeles that "we also have connections with our second-generations working in airplane plants for intelligence purposes." Such information might well have justified exclusion of Nisei, as opposed to other citizens, from work in aircraft factories without strict security clearance, but it falls considerably short of justifying the dislodging of thousands of citizens from their homes on the basis of ancestry. The submissions by the military showed no particular factual inquiry into the likelihood of espionage or sabotage by Nisei, only generalized conclusions that they were "different" from other Americans. But the military has no special expertise in this field, and it should have taken far more substantial findings to justify this sort of discrimination, even in wartime.

The Issei, however, who were not citizens, were both by tradition and by law in a quite different category. The legal difference dates back to the Alien Law enacted in 1798, during the administration of President John Adams. Often bracketed together with the Sedition Act passed at the same time, there is a tendency to think that both were repealed as soon as Thomas Jefferson and his Jeffersonian Republicans came to power in 1801. But while the Sedition Act expired under its own terms, the Alien Act, with minor amendments, remained on the books at the time of World War II. It provided:

> Whenever there is a declared war between the United States and any foreign nation or government . . . all natives, citizens, denizens, or subjects of the hostile nation or government, being of the age of fourteen years and upward, who shall be within the United States and not actually naturalized, shall be liable to be apprehended, restrained, secured, and removed as alien enemies. The President is authorized, in any such event, by his proclamation thereof . . . to direct the conduct to be observed, on the part of the United States, toward the aliens who become so liable; the manner and degree of the restraint to which they shall be subjected and in what cases, and upon what security their residence shall be permitted, and to provide for the removal of those who, not being permitted to reside within the United States, refuse or neglect to depart therefrom.[4]

In a case decided shortly after the end of World War II, the Supreme Court, referring to the Alien Law, said:

> Executive power over enemy aliens, undelayed and unhampered by litigation, has been deemed, throughout our history, essential to war-time security. This is in keeping with the practice of the most enlightened of nations and has resulted in treatment of alien enemies more considerate than that which has prevailed among any of our enemies and some of our allies. This statute was enacted or suffered to continue by men who helped found the Republic and formulate the Bill of Rights, and although it obviously denies enemy aliens the constitutional immunities of citizens, it seems not then to have been supposed that a nation's obligations to its foes could ever be put on a parity with those of its defenders.
>
> The resident enemy alien is constitutionally subject to summary arrest, internment and deportation whenever a "declared war" exists.[5]

Thus, distinctions that might not be permissible between classes of citizens must be viewed otherwise when drawn between classes of aliens.

The most frequently made charge on behalf of the Issei is that the government treated Japanese enemy aliens differently from enemy aliens of German or Italian citizenship, when we were at war with all three countries. It appears that there was some removal of Italian enemy aliens along the west coast for a brief period of time.[6] But there seems little doubt that the west coast Issei were treated quite differently from the majority of German or Italian nationals residing in this country. It should be pointed out, however, that there do not appear to have been the same concentrations of German or Italian nationals along the west coast in areas near major defense plants. Japanese emigration to the United States had occurred entirely within the preceding half-century, and the emigrants resided almost entirely on the west coast; Italian emigration had taken place over a considerably longer period of time, and German emigration had gone on since colonial days. People of German and Italian ancestry were far more spread out in the population in general than were the

Issei. While there were areas of German or Italian concentration on the eastern seaboard, the danger feared there was not attacks from German bombers or invasion of German troops, but the sinking of Allied merchant ships by German submarines.

On the west coast, on the other hand, there was the very real fear of attack by Japanese bombers flying from aircraft carriers, if not actual invasion by Japanese ground forces. As noted before, these fears were all but groundless after the Battle of Midway in June 1942, but the relocation program was established and put into effect before that decisive encounter. And as Chief Justice Stone pointed out in *Hirabayashi*, United States aircraft production was highly concentrated on the west coast. The capacity of those plants might have been greatly reduced by a successful air raid, and there is some evidence that residents of Japanese ancestry, loyal to Japan, had been placed in the aircraft plants.

These distinctions seem insufficient to justify such a sharp difference of treatment between Japanese and German and Italian aliens in peacetime. But they do seem legally adequate to support the difference in treatment between the two classes of enemy aliens in time of war.

CHAPTER 17

Hawaii
Under Martial Law

THE LIVES OF Hawaii's citizens had been interwoven with the United States Navy long before Pearl Harbor was bombed. Several months before that date, the territorial Governor, Joseph Poindexter, called the legislature into special session to enact a law that would grant him extraordinary powers in the event of war. Lieutenant General Walter Short, the commanding general of the Military Department of Hawaii, appeared before the legislature to urge enactment of such a law. The legislature responded affirmatively, and in early October 1941, the Hawaii Defense Act was signed into law.

A few hours after the attack on Pearl Harbor, Poindexter issued a proclamation placing the territory under martial law and suspending the writ of *habeas corpus*. He relied on the authority conferred upon him by the Hawaii Organic Act—the charter of the territory enacted by Congress in 1900—which provided that "The Governor . . . may in case of rebellion or invasion or imminent danger thereof, when the public safety requires it, suspend the writ of habeas corpus or place the territory or any part thereof under martial law until communication may be had with the President and his decision thereon made known."[1] Roosevelt was advised by cable of this action, and on December 9 he approved the Governor's action.

Poindexter went further than simply proclaiming martial law. He requested Short to exercise all the powers normally exercised by the

Governor and by the territorial judges. Short simultaneously issued his own proclamation, in which he announced that he had "assumed the position of military governor of Hawaii, and taken charge of the government of the territory." He further stated that he would shortly publish ordinances regulating, among other things, blackouts, meetings, censorship, possession of arms, and sale of intoxicating liquors. Offenders against these ordinances, he said, would either be severely punished by military tribunal or held in custody until such time as the civil courts would be able to function.

As noted by J. Garner Anthony in *Hawaii Under Army Rule*,[2] Short's proclamation seemed to contemplate a military regime that would be of short duration unless there was a land invasion of Hawaii by the Japanese. Short's executive officer promptly set up a new system for administering the criminal law throughout the territory. Civilians would be tried in provost courts manned by army officers, who could impose penalties without regard to what the applicable federal statutes or territorial ordinances provided. On Monday, December 8, Short sent the following order to Samuel Kemp, Chief Justice of the Territorial Supreme Court, who duly signed it: "Under the direction of the Commanding General, Hawaiian Department, all courts of the Territory of Hawaii will be closed until further notice. Without prejudice to the generality of the foregoing, all time for performing any act under the process of the Territory will be enlarged until after the courts are authorized to resume their normal functions."[3]

The "ordinances" of the military governor were issued in the form of general orders which were required to be published by the daily press at its own expense. General Order No. 1 appointed a committee of prominent citizens to advise the military government; that committee was never asked for its advice and did not even meet. General Order No. 2 closed all saloons, but by February 1942, a permit system for operation of bars had been established. The first military commission for the trial of offenses consisted of a former Chief Justice of the Supreme Court of Hawaii, a former circuit judge, the acting United States Attorney, and four army officers. This commission met only once; a portion of its deliberations on this occasion is described by J. Garner Anthony, who was present at the meeting:

Two of the civilian members (Steadman and Coke) at once inquired as to the kind of commission that would issue to them as military judges; who was to sign it? What oath would they take? Where did General Short get his authority to appoint judges to try civilians? The inquiries were in no sense hostile, they were simply an attempt on the part of two former judges to get at the foundation of whatever judicial power they were supposed to exercise.

The author volunteered to draft a radiogram to the Attorney General (Biddle), which would set forth the facts and ask his opinion. Messrs. Steadman and Coke thought this would be a good idea, but it found no favor with Colonel Green or his subordinates; a Major present at the conference said with finality, "we have the order of General Short, that's enough." "But what if General Short is wrong," asked Mr. Steadman. The Major replied, "a commanding general is never wrong." The conference ended on this note. . . .[4]

The order appointing this commission was revoked four days later. A later order allowed the civilian courts in the islands to reopen, but on a limited basis; no criminal cases could be tried, no juries could be summoned, and no action could be brought against any member of the armed forces or agents of the military governor. One of the resident federal judges in Hawaii, Ingram Stainback, simply closed the doors of his court and was duly appointed "legal adviser" to the military governor. By a general order issued in September 1942, civilian courts were able to resume normal business, but with the proviso that they might not issue writs of *habeas corpus*.

Military rule in Hawaii was no short-run thing. It lasted for nearly three years, until it was revoked in October 1944, by a proclamation from Roosevelt. During this time, a highly publicized feud arose between Delbert Metzger, a resident federal district judge, and Lieutenant General Robert Richardson, then commander of the Military Department of Hawaii. It arose out of two petitions for *habeas corpus* filed by naturalized Germans named Glockner and Seifert.

These two petitioners said that they were United States citizens held in custody by military authority and confined in an internment camp on the island of Oahu. They said that no charges had been brought against them and that they had violated neither any laws of the United States nor any executive or military order. They asked that an order be issued to General Richardson requiring him to show cause why they were detained.

The government moved to dismiss the petition, but Judge Metzger denied the motion. Under the proclamation issued by the Governor in early 1943, the privilege of *habeas corpus* had been restored; there was no showing that Hawaii was in imminent danger of invasion in August 1943, when this case came before the District Court. He therefore issued an order to show cause to be served on Richardson, whose office was across the street from the federal courthouse.

But Richardson successfully evaded service of the order by the United States marshal. The marshal was at one point physically confined by a military policeman at one end of the verandah of Richardson's headquarters, while Richardson and two other officers scurried down the steps and drove off in a car. The U.S. Attorney, a few days later, advised the District Court that the prisoners would not be produced. The next day, Metzger found Richardson in "open and notorious defiance of the mandate of the court," held him in contempt, and fined him $5,000. The same day Richardson issued General Order No. 31; this order prohibited the District Court from issuing process in *habeas corpus* actions, and the court was directed to discontinue all pending *habeas* proceedings. Metzger was specifically ordered to refrain from proceeding further in the Glockner and Seifert cases, and anyone who violated the order was subject upon conviction in a provost court to five years' imprisonment or a $5,000 fine. The order consisted of six sections of sixteen paragraphs, and its final section provided that it "shall be liberally construed."

This unseemly contretemps caught the attention of the Secretaries of War and Interior and of the Attorney General in Washington. Representatives of these departments journeyed to Honolulu to bring about some sort of settlement. This occurred in October 1943, when Richardson set Glockner and Seifert free, rescinded General Order No. 31, and in turn had the fine imposed upon him by Judge Metzger reduced from $5,000 to $100.

Thus were the courts spared further sparring between these officials. But two other cases arising out of the administration of martial law in Hawaii ultimately reached the Supreme Court in 1946. Harry

E. White was a stockbroker in Honolulu, and in August 1942, he was arrested by military police and charged with embezzling stock belonging to another civilian in violation of Hawaii law. Ten days later, he was brought before a military provost court which orally informed him of the charge; he objected to the court's jurisdiction and demanded a trial by jury. These objections were overruled, and White's attorney then asked for additional time to prepare the case. This too was refused, and on August 25, White was tried, convicted, and sentenced to five years in prison.

Lloyd C. Duncan was employed as a civilian shipfitter in the Honolulu Navy Yard. In February 1944, he brawled with two armed marine sentries at the yard. He was arrested by the military and charged with violation of a general order that prohibited assault on military or naval personnel. He was tried over his objection by a military court, found guilty, and sentenced to six months in prison.

Both Duncan and White sought writs of *habeas corpus* from Judge Metzger and he granted the writs, concluding that there was no military necessity for the trial of either of these defendants by military courts, and therefore they could be tried only in civilian courts.

The Court of Appeals for the Ninth Circuit, which sits in San Francisco and had jurisdiction over most of the western states and of Hawaii as well, reversed the decision of the district court, and White and Duncan took their case to the U.S. Supreme Court. In *Duncan v. Kahanamoku*, that Court sided with Duncan and White. Their case, ironically enough, was argued before that Court on December 7, 1945, exactly four years after the bombing of Pearl Harbor. The Supreme Court, in an opinion by Justice Black, decided that the Organic Act of Hawaii, in authorizing martial law, did not intend the military regime to supersede the civilian regime any more than the necessities of war might require. The Court pointed out that at the time the offenses in question were committed, the dangers apprehended by the military were not sufficiently imminent to cause them to require civilians to evacuate the area or even to evacuate any of the buildings necessary to carry on the business of the courts. The Court also pointed out that the offenses in question had no peculiar relationship to the military.

Justice Frank Murphy filed a concurring opinion, which tracked much more closely the doctrine of *Milligan* with its prohibition against trial of civilians by military courts where the civil courts were able to function. Chief Justice Stone filed a separate opinion agreeing with the result reached by the Court, but not necessarily with its reasoning. In the course of that opinion, he observed: "The full record in this case shows the conditions prevailing in Hawaii throughout 1942 and 1943. It demonstrates from February, 1942 on, the civil courts were capable of functioning, and that trials of petitioners in the civil courts no more endangered the public safety than the gathering of the populace in saloons and places of amusement, which was authorized by military order."[5] Two members of the Court—Justices Frankfurter and Harold Burton—dissented, accusing the majority of using the hindsight of 1946 to view the situation in Hawaii at the times that Duncan and White were actually tried.

But even without the benefit of hindsight, the government's position in *Duncan* was difficult to defend. *Hirabayashi* and *Korematsu* had been victories for the government, but they had been decided while hostilities were still continuing. They both involved governmental action claimed to be based on a threat to national security. But an embezzling stockbroker and a brawling shipyard worker in Hawaii could not possibly be dressed up as threats to national security. Edwin Stanton at his most autocratic during the Civil War never suggested that military commissions try garden-variety civilian offenses against state law or military orders. The post–World War II court surely reached the right result in *Duncan*.

CHAPTER 18

Inter Arma Silent Leges

T HE UNITED STATES has been engaged in several armed conflicts since the end of World War II, but in none of them has Congress declared war on another nation. Recent presidents have been eager to establish their authority to engage United States troops in foreign military operations without such a declaration, and Congress has never declared war without having been requested to do so by the President. When North Korea invaded South Korea in 1950, President Truman relied on a United Nations resolution to commit U.S. troops to fight in Korea. When the war in Vietnam escalated during the mid-1960s, President Lyndon Johnson similarly relied on the Gulf of Tonkin Resolution, enacted by Congress in 1964, for similar authority. Before the Gulf War in 1991, President Bush received approval to use armed force against Iraq from both houses of Congress. In each case, Congress has appropriated the necessary funds for the military effort, but in none was there a declaration of war.

Without question the government's authority to engage in conduct that infringes civil liberty is greatest in time of declared war—the *Schenck* and *Hirabayashi* opinions make this clear. This book is therefore limited to cases of declared war, together with the Civil War (where there was, of course, no declaration of war by the Union, because it did not recognize the Confederacy as a separate nation). But in the *Prize Cases*,[1] decided in 1863, the Supreme Court held that an insurrection could be treated by the government as the equivalent of a declared war.

There are marked differences between the government's conduct during the Civil War, during World War I, and during World War II. One of the main differences is that in the Civil War, the Lincoln administration relied on presidential authority or on the orders of military commanders to curtail civil liberties, while in the twentieth-century wars, the executive branch resorted much more to laws passed by Congress. Neither Lincoln's original suspension of the writ of *habeas corpus*, nor Stanton's order for the trial of civilians by military commissions, was authorized by Congress. The same was true of Postmaster General Montgomery Blair's suspension of the mailing privileges of New York newspapers. Those privileges were suspended during World War I by Postmaster General Albert Burleson, but he acted under a provision of the Espionage Act passed by Congress. President Roosevelt authorized the internment of west coast Japanese during World War II, but Congress immediately ratified his action.

It may fairly be asked by those whose civil liberty is curtailed, whether they are any better off because Congress as well as the Executive has approved the measure. As a practical matter, the answer may be no, but from the point of view of governmental authority under the Constitution, it is clear that the President may do many things in carrying out a congressional directive that he may not be able to do on his own. Justice Robert Jackson, in his now authoritative concurring opinion in the *Steel Seizure* cases decided during the Korean War, observed:

> When the President acts pursuant to an expressed or implied authorization of Congress, his authority is at its maximum, for it includes all that he possesses in his own right plus all that Congress can delegate. In these circumstances, and in these only, may he be said (for what it may be worth), to personify the federal sovereignty. If his act is held unconstitutional under these circumstances, it usually means that the Federal Government as an undivided whole lacks power.[2]

It should be added that Congress may not always grant the President all of the authority for which he asks. It refused, for example, President Wilson's request for censorship authority during World War I.

The second notable difference in the treatment of civil liberty is the increasing resort to the courts since the Civil War. This is partly because of the very limited jurisdiction of the lower federal courts in the 1860s. They could issue writs of *habeas corpus*, and a defendant might raise a constitutional claim as a defense. But for someone who had neither been detained nor sued but wished to challenge an action taken by the government, the only practical remedy was to sue in the state courts. Not until 1875 did Congress grant lower federal courts authority to hear cases where the plaintiff based his lawsuit on a violation of the federal Constitution. Thus, the publishers who were denied mailing privileges by Blair would have found it difficult, if not impossible, to assert any constitutional claim in a federal court. By the time of World War II, Hirabayashi, Korematsu, and Endo were all able to initiate claims of constitutional violation as plaintiffs in federal court.

There were no similar limitations on state courts, but many of these courts were neither experienced in, nor hospitable to, claims arising under the United States Constitution. Shortly before the Civil War, the Supreme Court of the United States had slapped down the Supreme Court of Wisconsin when it had sought to free a prisoner held in the custody of a federal marshal.[3] State courts at this time were not a promising forum for a suit claiming denial of civil liberty.

But an even more important reason for court involvement was increasing reliance by the government on prosecution in the federal courts for acts which had been made criminal by congressional legislation. In the Civil War, Clement Vallandigham was tried before a military commission, not for an offense against a law passed by Congress, but for violation of an order issued by the commanding general of a military department. During World War I, there were no such prosecutions; those who violated the Espionage Act were tried in civil courts by juries. In these prosecutions, the defendant was able to urge constitutional claims before judges who, if not particularly sympathetic, were far more neutral and detached than the members of a military commission. The result of these trials and appeals from them was the development by the Supreme Court of a body of case law interpreting the First Amendment.

A third great difference between the Civil War and the later conflicts was the extent to which the government sought to suppress public criticism of the administration's war effort. During the Civil War, the government used a heavy-handed, blunderbuss approach; local agents in the field would seize newspapers and confiscate the presses of those who opposed its policy. There was simply no federal challenge to these gross violations of the First Amendment. During World War I, Burleson successfully suppressed radical criticism of the administration, but at least his actions were subject to review by the courts. During World War II, there was no overt effort by the government to suppress public criticism of government war policy. Some of this change may have been due to the fact that the United States' entry into World War II was a defensive reaction to the Japanese bombing of Pearl Harbor and the German declaration of war. There was much less opposition to that war than to either the Civil War or World War I. But part of the change also resulted from the fact that the First Amendment had come into its own.

Despite this generally ameliorative trend, however, there remains a sense that there is some truth to the maxim *Inter arma silent leges*, at least in the purely descriptive sense. *Quirin*, decided during the darkest days of World War II, actually cut back on some of the extravagant dicta favorable to civil liberty in *Milligan*. Of the three Japanese internment cases, only *Endo*, decided near the end of World War II, represented even a minor victory for civil liberty. And as for *Duncan*, the good news for the people of Hawaii was that the court held that martial law there during World War II had been unlawful; the bad news was that the decision came after the war was over, and a year and a half after martial law had been ended by presidential order. Again, part of the delay in such decisions is endemic to the legal process; given a hierarchical system of courts, a decision by the Supreme Court usually occurs months, if not years, after the lawsuit was begun. But there is also the reluctance of courts to decide a case against the government on an issue of national security during a war.

Is this reluctance a necessary evil—necessary because judges, like other citizens, do not wish to hinder a nation's "war effort"—or is it actually a desirable phenomenon? Judicial reluctance can manifest itself in more ways than one. A court may simply avoid deciding an important constitutional question in the midst of a war; the Supreme Court did this when it limited itself to the curfew issue in *Hirabaya-*

shi. A court may also decide an issue in favor of the government during a war, when it would not have done so had the decision come after the war was over. Would, for example, *Duncan* have come out the same way in 1943 as it actually did in 1946?

Viewed as a matter of legal or constitutional principle, the law governing a particular set of facts—in *Duncan*, for example, whether a stockbroker could be tried for fraud by a military court in Hawaii in 1943—should not be different in 1946 than three years earlier. But one need not wholly accept Justice Holmes's aphorism that "the life of the law has not been logic, it has been experience" to recognize the human factor that inevitably enters into even the most careful judicial decision. If, in fact, courts are more prone to uphold wartime claims of civil liberties after the war is over, may it not actually be desirable to avoid decision on such claims during the war?

Lambdin Milligan, imprisoned after his trial before a military commission, surely would answer no to this question. While the body of case law might benefit from such abstention, those who are actually deprived of their civil liberties would not. But a decision in favor of civil liberty will stand as a precedent to regulate future actions of Congress and the Executive branch in future wars. We must also ask whether in every case a ruling in favor of a claimed civil liberty is more desirable, more "just," than a contrary result.

The answer to this question will depend, in turn, on just what is meant by civil liberty. It is not simply "liberty" but *civil* liberty of which we speak. The word "civil," in turn, is derived from the Latin word *civis*, which means "citizen." A citizen is a person owing allegiance to some organized government, and not a person in an idealized "state of nature" free from any governmental restraint. Judge Learned Hand, in remarks entitled "The Spirit of Liberty," delivered during World War II, put it this way: "A society in which men recognize no check upon their freedom soon becomes a society where freedom is the possession of only a savage few. . . ."[4]

In any civilized society the most important task is achieving a proper balance between freedom and order. In wartime, reason and history both suggest that this balance shifts to some degree in favor of order—in favor of the government's ability to deal with conditions that threaten the national well-being. It simply cannot be said, therefore, that in every conflict between individual liberty and governmental authority the former should prevail. And if we feel free to criticize court decisions that curtail civil liberty, we must also feel free to look critically at decisions favorable to civil liberty.

Was the dictum in the *Milligan* case, for example—saying that Congress could not authorize trials of civilians by military tribunals where civil courts were functioning and there was no invasion by hostile forces—a wise exercise of judicial power? The reasoning of the majority in that case would rule out not merely trials of civilians by military commissions but trials of civilians by a duly appointed federal judge without a jury. One may fully agree with the rather disparaging but nonetheless insightful argument of Jeremiah Black in the *Milligan* case—soldiers are no more occupationally trained to conduct trials than are sailors or sheep drovers—and yet believe that Congress should be able to provide for trial of defendants by a judge without a jury in a carefully limited class of cases dealing with national security in wartime.

The foregoing discussion deals with the judicial treatment of civil liberty claims. But this is only one part of the story during wartime. The previously quoted statement of Francis Biddle about Franklin Roosevelt's support for the internment of Issei and Nisei during World War II bears repeating here: "Nor do I think that the Constitutional difficulty plagued him. The Constitution has not greatly bothered any wartime President. That was a question of law, which ultimately the Supreme Court must decide. And meanwhile—probably a long meanwhile—we must get on with the war."[5]

Some Executive actions in time of war will be reviewed by the courts only after the fact, if at all. Lincoln believed that the very survival of the Union could depend on getting troops from the northeast to Washington in April 1861. He also believed that the suspension of the writ of *habeas corpus* was necessary to guard against further destruction of the railroad route through Baltimore used to transport these troops. Should he have carefully weighed the pros and cons as to whether he was authorized by the Constitution to do this before acting? Should he, to paraphrase his own words, have risked losing the Union that gave life to the Constitution because that charter denied him the necessary authority to preserve the Union? Cast in these terms, it is difficult to quarrel with his decision.

But the same degree of necessity surely did not obtain in the suppression of the New York newspapers, or the trial of the Indianapolis defendants by a military commission. It is all too easy to slide from a case of genuine military necessity, where the power sought to be exercised is at least debatable, to one where the threat is not critical and the power either dubious or nonexistent.

One would think it likely, of course, that a Roman legal maxim which originated two millennia ago in a legal system with no written constitution, would have only the most general application to America. But the fact that the phrase *Inter arma silent leges* is quoted by modern writers suggests that it has validity at least in a descriptive way. As such, it may have several different levels of meaning. It speaks first simply as a truism: in time of war the government's authority to restrict civil liberty is greater than in peacetime. As noted above, the *Schenck* and *Hirabayashi* cases validate this aspect of the maxim. But at another level, the maxim speaks to the attitude of wartime presidents such as Lincoln, Wilson, and Franklin Roosevelt, so well captured in Biddle's phrase "the Constitution has not greatly bothered any wartime President." Quite apart from the added authority that the law itself may give the President in time of war, presidents may act in ways that push their legal authority to its outer limits, if not beyond. Finally, the maxim speaks to the timing of a judicial decision on a question of civil liberty in wartime. If the decision is made after hostilities have ceased, it is more likely to favor civil liberty than if made while hostilities continue. The contrast between the *Quirin* and the Japanese internment decisions on the one hand and the *Milligan* and *Duncan* decisions on the other show that this, too, is a historically accurate observation about the American system.

An entirely separate and important philosophical question is whether occasional presidential excesses and judicial restraint in wartime are desirable or undesirable. In one sense, this question is very largely academic. There is no reason to think that future wartime presidents will act differently from Lincoln, Wilson, or Roosevelt, or that future Justices of the Supreme Court will decide questions differently from their predecessors. But even though this be so, there is every reason to think that the historic trend against the least justified of the curtailments of civil liberty in wartime will continue in the future. It is neither desirable nor is it remotely likely that civil liberty will occupy as favored a position in wartime as it does in peacetime. But it is both desirable and likely that more careful attention will be paid by the courts to the basis for the government's claims of necessity as a basis for curtailing civil liberty. The laws will thus not be silent in time of war, but they will speak with a somewhat different voice.

NOTES

Chapter 1

1. Sandburg, Carl. *Abraham Lincoln, The Prairie Years and The War Years,* 1-vol. edition, vol. 3, New York: Harcourt, Brace & World, 1954, p. 195.
2. Ibid., pp. 195–96.
3. Sandburg, Carl. *Abraham Lincoln, The War Years,* Vol. 3, New York: Harcourt Brace & World, 1939, p. 53.
4. Ibid., p. 59.
5. Leech, Margaret. *Reveille in Washington, 1860–1865.* New York: Harper Brothers Publishers, 1941, p. 26.

Chapter 2

1. Nicolay, John G., and Hay, John. *Abraham Lincoln, A History,* Vol. 6, New York: Century Co., 1917, pp. 80–84.
2. Sandburg, p. 215.
3. Leech, pp. 55–56.
4. Nicolay and Hay, Vol. 4, pp. 152–53.
5. Seward Papers: Carpenter, F. B. *A Day with Governor Seward at Auburn,* July 1870; No. 6634, p. 55.

Chapter 3

1. Swisher, Carl B. *History of the Supreme Court of the United States,* vol. 5, *The Taney Period, 1836–64,* New York: Macmillan, 1974, p. 17.
2. Richardson, James D. *A Compilation of the Messages and Papers of the Presidents, 1789–1897,* vol. 431.
3. *Complete Works of Abraham Lincoln,* vol. 2, Lincoln Memorial University, 1894, p. 401.
4. Ibid., pp. 465–66.

5. Swisher, p. 647.

6. Abraham Lincoln. *Speeches and Letters*, pp. 171–72 (M. Roe, editor, 1894).

7. Swisher, p. 846.

8. *Baltimore American*, May 29, 1861.

9. Ibid.

10. George William Brown. *Baltimore on the 19th of April 1861*, p. 90.

11. Lewis, Walker. *Without Fear or Favor: A Biography of Chief Justice Roger Brooke Taney*, Boston: Houghton Mifflin, 1965, p. 453.

Chapter 4

1. Cain, Marvin. *Lincoln's Attorney General: Edward Bates of Missouri*, Columbia, Mo.: University of Missouri Press, 1965, p. 1.

2. *The War of the Rebellion: A Compilation of the Official Records of the Union and Confederate Armies*. Prepared under the direction of the Secretary of War by Robert N. Scott. Washington, GPO, 1880–1900. [Gettysburg, National Historical Society, c. 1971–72] 69 v. in 127. 23 cm. p. 298. (Hereafter *The War of the Rebellion*).

3. Neeley, Mark E. *The Fate of Liberty: Abraham Lincoln and Civil Liberties*, New York: Oxford University Press, 1991, p. 14.

4. *The War of the Rebellion*, Series II, p. 1021.

5. Sangston, Lawrence. *Personal Journal of a Prisoner of State* (Baltimore, 1863), quoted in Sprague, Dean, *Freedom Under Lincoln*, Boston: Houghton Mifflin, 1965, pp. 289–90.

6. Thomas, Benjamin P. *Stanton: The Life and Times of Lincoln's Secretary of War*, New York: Alfred A. Knopf, 1962, p. 78.

Chapter 5

1. *The War of the Rebellion*, vol. 2, Series II, pp. 221–23.

2. Ibid., vol. 4, Series II, pp. 358–59.

3. Klement, Frank L. *Wisconsin and the Civil War*, Madison, Wisconsin: State Historical Society of Wisconsin, 1963.

4. *In Re Kemp*, 16 Wis. 382, 394.

5. *The War of the Rebellion*, Series I, p. 23, Part 2, p. 147.

6. *Dayton Daily Empire*, May 1, 1863, quoted in Klement, Frank L., *The Limits of Dissent*, Lexington: University Press of Kentucky, 1970, p. 152.

7. *Ex Parte Vallandigham*, 1 Wallace 243, Feb. 1864.

8. Quoted in Remini, Robert V. *Andrew Jackson and the Course of American Empire*, *1767–1821*, New York: Harper & Row, 1977.

9. *Luther v. Borden*, 7 How. 1, 45–6 (1846).

10. 7 How. at 62, Woodbury, J., dissenting.

Chapter 6

1. Horace Greeley to Abraham Lincoln July 7, 1864, Lincoln MSS, LC, quoted in Hale, William Harlan, *Horace Greeley: Voice of the People*, New York: Harper & Brothers, 1950, pp. 280–81.

2. Horace Greeley to Abraham Lincoln, August 22, 1864, Lincoln MSS, LC, quoted in Donald, David Herbert, *Lincoln*, New York: Simon & Schuster, 1995, p. 529.

3. *Complete Works of Abraham Lincoln*, vol. 7, p. 515.

4. 7 Cr. 32 (1812).

5. 1 Winthrop, Military Law 534–535 (1886).

Chapter 7

1. Klement, Frank L. *The Copperheads in the Middle West*, Chicago: University of Chicago Press, 1960; reprint, University of Chicago Press, 1972, p. 260.

2. Ibid., p. 275.

3. Ibid., pp. 282–84.

4. Carson, Hampton L. *The Law of Criminal Conspiracies and Agreements*, Philadelphia, 1887.

5. Klement, pp. 38–39.

Chapter 8

1. *Philadelphia Inquirer*, Feb. 22, 1861, quoted in King, Willard L., *Lincoln's Manager David Davis*, Cambridge, Massachusetts: Harvard University Press, 1960.

2. Cong. Globe, 37 Cong., 2d Sess., p. 28 (1861).

3. Davis' Papers, quoted in King, Willard L., *Lincoln's Manager David Davis*, p. 193.

4. Ibid., p. 191.

5. Swisher, p. 55.

6. Swisher, p. 64.

7. Swisher, pp. 232–33.
8. Swisher, p. 247.
9. 2 Warren 401.
10. Fairman, Charles. *Reconstruction and Reunion 1864–68, Part 1.* The Oliver Wendell Holmes Devise History of the Supreme Court of the United States, Vol. 6, New York: Macmillan, 1987, p. 199.

Chapter 9

1. Swisher, p. 717.
2. Ibid., p. 718.
3. Fairman, p. 201.
4. *Dictionary of American Biography*, edited by Allen Johnson, vol. 3, New York: Charles Scribner's Sons, 1929, p. 357.
5. Fairman, p. 204.

Chapter 10

1. *Ex Parte Milligan*, 4 Wall. 2 (1866).
2. 4 Wall. 2, 120–21.
3. Warren, Charles. *The Supreme Court in United States History*, 2nd ed., vol. 2, Boston: Little, Brown, pp. 427–28.
4. John Jay to Salmon P. Chase, January 5, 1867, quoted in Warren, op. cit., p. 428.
5. *New York Times*, January 3, 1867, quoted in Warren, ibid., p. 429.
6. *New York Herald*, January 2, 8, 1867, quoted in Warren, ibid., p. 432.
7. *Springfield Republican*, January 5, 1867, quoted in Warren, ibid., p. 437.
8. *New York World*, January 12, 1867; *Baltimore Sun*, December 22, 1866, quoted in Warren, ibid., p. 438.
9. *American Law Review* (April 1867, I, 572, quoted in Warren, ibid., pp. 441–42).
10. 317 U.S. 1 (1942).
11. 317 U.S. 45–46 (1942).

Chapter 12

1. Pitman, Benn. *The Assassination of President Lincoln and the Trial of the Conspirators*, New York: Moore, Wilstach & Baldwin, 1865, p. 24.
2. Ibid., p. 25.
3. Ibid., pp. 26–27.
4. Ibid., p. 28.

5. Ibid., p. 29.
6. Turner, Thomas Reed. *Beware the People Weeping, Public Opinion and the Assassination of Abraham Lincoln,* Baton Rouge: Louisiana State University Press, 1981.
7. Pitman, p. 38.
8. Ibid., p. 43.

Chapter 13

1. *Ferguson v. Georgia,* 365 U.S. 570 (1961), 577.
2. Pitman, p. 86.
3. Ibid., p. 97.
4. Ibid., p. 103.
5. Ibid., p. 236.
6. *San Francisco Alta Californian,* July 20, 1865, p. 2, quoted in Turner, *Beware the People Weeping,* p. 163.
7. Wallace, Lew. *Lew Wallace: An Autobiography,* New York: Harper Brothers, 1906, II, 848.
8. *Ex Parte Mudd,* 17 F. Cas. 954 (S. D. Fla. 1868) (No. 9,899).

Chapter 14

1. *The Selective Draft Law Cases,* 245 U.S. 366 (1918).
2. 65 Stat. 219.
3. 65 Stat. 230.
4. 54 Cong. Rec. (64th Cong., 1st Sess.), pp. 95–100.
5. Wilson letter to Representative Webb, *New York Times,* May 23, 1917.
6. 249 U.S. 47, 52 (1919).
7. Heckscher, August. *Woodrow Wilson,* New York: Charles Scribner's Sons, 1991, p. 452.
8. 244 Fed. 540 (1917).
9. 244 Fed. 541.
10. 246 Fed. 36–37.
11. *Hustler v. Falwell,* 485 U.S. 46 (1987).
12. *United States v. Burleson,* 255 U.S. 407 (1921).
13. Villard, Oswald. *Fighting Years: Memoirs of a Liberal Editor,* New York: Harcourt Brace, 1939, p. 35.
14. 158 U.S. 564 (1895).
15. 252 U.S. 206 (1920).
16. 250 U.S. at 616, 620–21 (1919).
17. 250 U.S. 622 (1919).

18. 250 U.S. 628–29.

19. *Reports of the Attorney General, 1918–1921,* quoted in Scribner, Harry N., *The Wilson Administration and Civil Liberties, 1917–1921,* Ithaca, New York: Cornell University Press, 1960, pp. 61–63.

Chapter 15

1. Morison, Samuel Eliot. *The Oxford History of the American People,* New York: Oxford University Press, 1965, p. 1003.
2. Ibid., p. 1004.
3. "Attack upon Pearl Harbor by Japanese Armed Forces," Senate Doc. No. 159, 77th Cong., 2d Sess. (1942), p. 12.
4. Ibid., p. 14.
5. Ibid.
6. Bird, Kai. *John J. McCloy,* New York: Simon & Schuster, 1992, p. 152.
7. Stimson, op. cit., p. 406.
8. Biddle, Francis. *In Brief Authority,* New York: Doubleday, 1962, p. 218.
9. Ibid., p. 219.
10. 320 U.S., at 390.
11. 320 U.S., at 93.
12. 320 U.S., at 94.
13. 320 U.S., at 99.
14. 320 U.S. 100–01.
15. 323 U.S. 223–24.
16. 323 U.S. 245.

Chapter 16

1. 320 U.S., at 94.
2. 320 U.S., at 99.
3. 347 U.S. 497 (1954).
4. Act of July 6, 1798, 1 Stat. 577.
5. *Johnson* v. *Eisentrager,* 339 U.S. 763 (1950).

Chapter 17

1. 31 Stat. 153 (1900).
2. Anthony, J. Garner. *Hawaii Under Army Rule,* Stanford, Calif.: Stanford University Press, 1955.
3. Ibid., p. 10.

4. Ibid., p. 12.

5. 327 U.S., at 337.

Chapter 18

1. 67 U.S. 635.

2. *Youngstown Sheet and Tool Company v. Sawyer*, 343 U.S. 579, 635–36.

3. *Ableman v. Booth*, 21 How. 506 (1859).

4. Hand, Learned. *The Spirit of Liberty*, New York: Alfred A. Knopf, 1952, p. 191.

5. Biddle, *In Brief Authority*, p. 219.

BIBLIOGRAPHY

Allen, Mary Bernard. *Joseph Holt, Judge Advocate General 1862–75.* Chicago: University of Chicago Press, 1927.

Anthony, J. Garner. *Hawaii Under Army Rule.* Stanford, Calif.: Stanford University Press, 1955.

Baltimore Sun, November 7, 1860.

Baltimore 200th Anniversary 1729–1929. Baltimore: Baltimore Municipal Journal, 1929.

Basler, Roy P., ed. *The Collected Works of Abraham Lincoln.* New Brunswick, N.J.: Rutgers University Press, 1953.

Belknap, Michael. *American Political Trials.* Westport, Conn.: Greenwood Press, 1994.

Biddle, Francis. *In Brief Authority.* New York: Doubleday, 1962.

Bird, Kai. *John J. McCloy: The Making of the American Establishment: The Chairman.* New York: Simon & Schuster, 1992.

Bryan, George. *The Great American Myth.* Chicago: American House, 1990.

Calhoun, Frederick S. *The Lawmen: United States Marshals and Their Deputies, 1789–1989.* Washington, D.C.: Smithsonian Institution Press, 1989.

Campbell, Helen Jones. *The Case for Mrs. Surratt.* New York: G. P. Putnam & Sons, 1943.

Chafee, Zechariah, Jr. *Free Speech in the United States.* Cambridge: Harvard University Press, 1942.

Coben, Stanley. *A. Mitchell Palmer: Politician.* New York: Columbia University Press, 1963.

Complete Works of Abraham Lincoln. Vol. 6. Lincoln Memorial University, 1894.

Daily Baltimore Republican, May 28, 1861.

Department of Justice. *Official Opinions of the Attorneys General of the United States, Advising the President and Heads of Departments in Relation to Their Official Duties*, vol. 8. Washington, D.C.: GPO, 1856–57.

Dewitt, David Miller. *The Judicial Murder of Mary E. Surratt*. Baltimore: John Murphy & Co., 1895.

Dictionary of American Biography, edited by Allen Johnson. Vol. 3. New York: Charles Scribner's Sons, 1929.

Dodge, David. *Death and Taxes*. New York: Macmillan, 1941.

Donald, David Herbert. *Lincoln*. New York: Simon & Schuster, 1995.

Dunn, Robert W. *The Palmer Raids*. New York: International Publishers, 1948.

Fairman, Charles. *Reconstruction and Reunion 1864–68, Part I*. Vol. 6, The Oliver Wendell Holmes Devise History of the Supreme Court of the United States. New York: Macmillan, 1971.

Foulke, William Dudley. *Life of Oliver P. Morton*. 2 vols. Indianapolis: Bowen-Merrill Company, 1899.

Freund, Paul A., ed. *History of the Supreme Court of the United States*. Vol. 5, *The Taney Period 1836–64*, by Carl B. Swisher. New York: Macmillan, 1974.

Gradzins, Morton. *Americans Betrayed: Politics and the Japanese Evacuation*. Chicago: University of Chicago Press, 1949.

Gray, Wood. *The Hidden Civil War: The Story of the Copperheads*. New York: Viking Press, 1942.

Hale, William Harlan. *Horace Greeley: Voice of the People*. New York: Harper & Brothers, 1950.

Halsbury's Statutes of England and Wales. 4th ed. Vol. 9. London: Butterworths, 1929.

Hanchett, William. *The Lincoln Murder Conspiracies*. Urbana and Chicago, Ill.: University of Illinois Press, 1983.

Hay, John. *Lincoln and the Civil War in the Diaries and Letters of John Hay*. New York: Dodd, Mead & Company, 1939.

Heckscher, August. *Woodrow Wilson*. New York: Macmillan, 1991.

Holdsworth, Sir William. *A History of English Law*. London: Methuen & Co., 1941.

Irons, Peter. *Justice at War*. New York: Oxford University Press, 1983.

Jensen, Joan M. *Army Surveillance in America, 1775–1980*. New Haven: Yale University Press, 1991.

Jones, John Paul. *Dr. Mudd and the Lincoln Assassination: The Case Reopened*. Conshohocken, Pa.: Combined Books, 1995.

King, Willard L. *Lincoln's Manager David Davis*. Cambridge: Harvard University Press, 1960.

Klaus, Samuel. *The Milligan Case*. New York: Da Capo Press, 1929.

———. *American Trials Ex Parte: In the Matter of Lambdin P. Milligan*. New York: Alfred A. Knopf, 1929.

Klement, Frank L. *Wisconsin and the Civil War*. Madison: State Historical Society of Wisconsin, 1963.

———. *The Limits of Dissent*. Lexington: University Press of Kentucky, 1970.

———. *The Copperheads in the Middle West*. Chicago: University of Chicago Press, 1960. Reprint, Chicago: University of Chicago Press, 1972.

———. *Dark Lanterns: Secret Political Societies, Conspiracies, and Treason Trials in the Civil War*. Baton Rouge: Louisiana State University Press, 1984.

The Law Reports. The Public General Statutes, Passed in the Fourth and Fifth Years of the Reign of His Majesty King George the Fifth, vol. 52. London: Eyre and Spottiswoode, 1914.

Leech, Margaret. *Reveille in Washington, 1860–1865*. New York: Harper and Brothers Publishers, 1941.

Lewis, Walker. *Without Fear or Favor: A Biography of Chief Justice Roger Brooke Taney*. Boston: Houghton Mifflin, 1965.

Madison, James H. *The Indiana Way*. Bloomington: Indiana University Press, 1986.

Meador, Daniel J. A Conference at the White Burkett Miller Center of Public Affairs; University of Virginia: January 4–5, 1980. *The President, The Attorney General, and The Department of Justice*. 1980.

Neely, Mark E. *The Fate of Liberty: Abraham Lincoln and Civil Liberties*. New York: Oxford University Press, 1991.

Nicolay, John G., and John Hay. *Abraham Lincoln: A History.* 10 vols. New York: Century Co., 1886–90.

Niven, John. *Salmon P. Chase, A Biography.* New York: Oxford University Press, 1995.

150th Anniversary of the Founding of the City of Baltimore. Baltimore: C.W. Schneidereith, 1880.

O'Toole, G. J. A. *Honorable Treachery: A History of U.S. Intelligence, Espionage, and Covert Action from the American Revolution to the CIA.* New York: Atlantic Monthly Press, 1991.

Parker, Joel. *Habeas Corpus and Martial Law: A Review of the Opinion of Chief Justice Taney, In the Case of John Merryman,* 2d ed. Philadelphia: John Campbell, 1862.

Pitman, Benn, ed. *The Trials for Treason at Indianapolis, Disclosing the Plans for Establishing a North-Western Confederacy.* Salem, Ind.: The News Publishing Company, 1892.

———, ed. *The Assassination of President Lincoln and the Trial of the Conspirators.* Cincinnati: Moore, Wilstach & Baldwin, 1865.

Presidential Elections 1789–1992. Washington, D.C.: Congressional Quarterly Inc., 1995.

Randall, J. G. *Lincoln the President: Springfield to Gettysburg.* Vol. 1. New York: Vail-Ballou Press, 1946.

———. *Constitutional Problems Under Lincoln.* Urbana, Ill.: University of Illinois Press, 1951.

Rankin, Robert S. *When Civil Law Fails: Martial Law and Its Legal Basis in the United States.* Durham, N.C.: Duke University Press, 1939.

Report of the Commission on Wartime Relocation and Internment of Civilians. *Personal Justice Denied.* Washington, D.C.: US GPO, 1982.

Revised Statutes of the United States, 1873–74; Title LXX, pp. 1040–41. Washington, D.C.: GPO, 1875.

Richardson, James D. *A Compilation of the Messages and Papers of the Presidents 1789–1897.* Vol. 6. Authority of Congress, 1897.

Sprague, Dean. *Freedom Under Lincoln.* Boston: Riverside Press Cambridge, 1965.

Swisher, Carl B. *Stephen J. Field, Craftsman of the Law.* Washington, D.C.: Brookings Institution, 1930. Reprint.

———. *History of the Supreme Court of the United States.* Vol. 5, *The Taney Period, 1836–64.* New York: Macmillan, 1974.

Taylor, John M. *William Henry Seward: Lincoln's Right Hand.* New York: Harper- Collins, 1991.

Thomas, Benjamin P., and Harold M. Hyman. *Stanton: The Life and Times of Lincoln's Secretary of War.* New York: Alfred A. Knopf, 1962.

Tidwell, William A. *Confederate Covert Action in the American Civil War: April '65.* Kent, Ohio: Kent State University Press, 1995.

Tidwell, William A., James O. Hall, and David Winfred Gaddy. *Come Retribution: The Confederate Secret Service and the Assassination of Lincoln.* Jackson, Miss.: University Press of Mississippi, 1988.

Turner, Thomas Reed. *Beware the People Weeping: Public Opinion and the Assassination of Abraham Lincoln.* Baton Rouge: Louisiana State University Press, 1982.

U.S. Congress. *House Documents. 55th Congress, 3rd Session. No. 66.* Washington, D.C.: GPO, 1897.

U.S. Reports, 71.

Van Deusen, Glyndon. *Horace Greeley: Nineteenth-Century Crusader.* Philadelphia: University of Pennsylvania Press, 1953.

———. *William Henry Seward.* New York: Oxford University Press, 1967.

The War of the Rebellion: A Compilation of the Official Records of the Union and Confederate Armies. Series II, Vol. 1. Washington, D.C.: GPO, 1894.

Warren, Charles. *The Supreme Court in United States History.* Vol. 2, 2d ed. Boston: Little, Brown & Company, 1926.

Works Projects Administration in the State of Maryland. *Maryland: A Guide to the Old Line State.* New York: Works Projects Administration, 1940.

Wright, R. S. *The Law of Criminal Conspiracies and Agreements.* Philadelphia: Blackstone Publishing Company, 1887.

INDEX

A Note About the Author

William H. Rehnquist is Chief Justice of the United States. He was an Associate Justice of the Supreme Court of the United States from 1972 to 1986.

A NOTE ON THE TYPE

This book was set in Janson, a typeface long thought to have been made by the Dutchman Anton Janson, who was a practicing typefounder in Leipzig during the years 1668–1687. However, it has been conclusively demonstrated that these types are actually the work of Nicholas Kis (1650–1702), a Hungarian, who most probably learned his trade from the master Dutch typefounder Dirk Voskens. The type is an excellent example of the influential and sturdy Dutch types that prevailed in England up to the time William Caslon (1692–1766) developed his own incomparable designs from them.

Composed by ComCom,
an R. R. Donnelley & Sons Company,
Allentown, Pennsylvania
Printed and bound by Quebecor Printing,
Martinsburg, West Virginia
Designed by Virginia Tan